A Diagnosis for Eternity . . .

Be sure to check out Dr. Viehman's website for additional information, companion study guide, updates on his next book, speaking and book signing engagements, ordering personalized signed copies and contact info: www.goddiagnosis.com

Here is what respected reviewers are saying about the book . . .

"The God Diagnosis" is an intriguing look at a personal journey to discover meaning in life. Dr. Viehman shares the story of how a life that had everything the American dream could offer – education, money, position, popularity, and a loving wife and family – left him profoundly empty and angry. With a great distaste for empty religion and its hypocritical proponents, he shares what would turn out to be his greatest medical discovery. The examinations are thorough, the tests complex, and the diagnosis unmistakable—he was dead. As you read these pages, you will not only find the concrete proof for his diagnosis, but you will also discover the cure. This book is a must read for everyone who truly wants to find meaning in life.
Alan T. E. Benson, BA, MM, MDiv.

This is the most profound and compelling personal testimony of a man seeking answers for eternity that I've ever read. Dr. Viehman vividly articulates his passage through all the stages of this journey with such clarity and realism the reader relives it with him. His chronicled blend of personal reflections and accounts, scrutiny of scripture pro and con, and historical information is both riveting and soundly convincing of the veracity of his final diagnosis. This is the remarkable adventure of a medical doctor who in his mid-thirties made a discovery that permanently changed his life and eternity, and Dr. Viehman's diagnosis may change yours too.
Mike Hockett, Retired Colonel USAF

A must-read! Strap yourself in for a journey into the unseen. See through the eyes of a keen observer and the mind of a trained medical doctor following the evidence wherever it leads. Bring along both your head and your heart to see clues assembled like a crime-scene investigation. But it's not a crime scene we are investigating . . .
Bill Dunn, MSAE

In his quest for *truth* and *proof*, Dr. Viehman's meticulous, scientific approach to finding answers to questions of the heart will resound with all men and women . . . "The God Diagnosis" will lead readers to examine the evidence and embrace a conclusion that will impact the heart and soul for eternity.
Lynne Fortunis, Administrator

A captivating journey of a successful, family-oriented surgeon who by the world's standards had everything to make him happy, however, he soon discovered that fame and fortune only left him empty without peace or meaning in his life. In "The God Diagnosis" Dr. Viehman uses his training as a researcher and physician to make the most critical diagnosis of his life.
S. Duane Tester, RPh, MBA

Diagnosis? God? Really? A diagnosis requires real evidence that you can analyze. Isn't faith a belief in something that you cannot prove? The doctor is Greg Viehman, and his diagnosis will challenge what you believe, make you think about why you believe, and motivate you to live what you believe.
Rick E. Graves, JD

Dr. Viehman is a physician in his lab coat, stethoscope around his neck with the results of a total examination in hand informing us of the diagnosis for the human race. He concludes we are not spiritually healthy, not just sick, not even terminal. We are already dead – flat-lined. The examination concluded we can't get better on our own no matter our goodness or resources.

The diagnosis and treatment come from a noted physician who had to recognize the paradox of misery brought on by success. A must read for all who are searching!
Thomas C. Womble Jr, MDiv, DD

This is the account of a man searching for truth in a world filled with facades. As a pastor, I receive many books through various sources to read and review. Honestly, most of them warrant a chapter or two, and then they end up on my shelf. Greg's book was different in that it was honest, straight-forward, humorous, refreshing, and well-written. I was captivated by Greg's story, his experiences, the emotions he felt, and his honest assessment of his life. I would recommend this book to anyone.
Clay Ritter, Senior Pastor Calvary Chapel Wilmington

Unsettled by the mysteries of purpose and destiny, Dr. Viehman takes the reader on an emotionally palpable and transforming journey through cynicism, skepticism, and discovery. "The God Diagnosis" is a detailed and compelling testimony of a successful and skilled surgeon who himself undergoes "a heart transplant." It is a provocative and challenging book for anyone questioning the existence of God.
William J. Vanarthos, MD

Dr. Viehman's book is an amazingly candid journey through his systematic and logical exploration of the foundations of Christianity in order to disprove and dismiss it. Through his research he encounters the life-giving breath of God and finds what his heart has been crying out for- true living Love. This work is an incredible resource for those who are searching for abundant life.
Kerri Andrews, RN

Is there more to life than this? The question has plagued many people throughout history. Dr. Greg Viehman embarks on a fascinating voyage to find the real answer to this question and after close examination of the facts provides his diagnosis. "The God Diagnosis" is a must read for anyone who has ever sought to get the answers to life's most important questions.
Johnny Rivera, Pastor, Calvary Chapel Cary

. . . If you have questions or searching for answers, or perhaps there's something missing in your life, this book is for you.
Pastor Rodney Finch, Senior Pastor, Calvary Chapel Cary NC

Dr. Viehman has been on an amazing journey. In "The God Diagnosis," he combines a lucid writing style with his knowledge and skill as a physician to provide a very candid account of his search for eternity. His writing is refreshing, informative, encouraging and honest. It is "fast-paced," thoughtful and thorough.
He provides a wealth of instruction based upon his own careful research and experiences. This book is an outstanding read for anyone having doubts about the veracity of Scripture and the restoration of man to the life mankind was originally designed to enjoy.
David S. Braden, B.S.C.E., M. Div.

. . . "The God Diagnosis" reveals the condition and provides the answer . . .
Carol Casale

ACKNOWLEDGEMENTS

I am very grateful to many people who helped me complete this book. Their contributions, time, and insights have been invaluable. My wife Ruth has given me the time, encouragement, and strength to spend the countless hours needed over the last seven years. Bill Dunn was a mentor, friend, and editor whose input provided direction and perspective. Dr. Bill Vanarthos assisted with editing and design concepts. Greg McElveen's role as an editor and creative writing coach immensely enhanced this project and brought the story to life. Leslie and DeeAnn Williamson were stellar editors for content, punctuation, and grammar.

Also, many people contributed their comments and ideas before the final version was written. I thank them for their time, interest, and contributions. Finally I thank the LORD who is the true author of my life and the inspiration behind this book. God has enabled me to do something not possible without Him

Greg E. Viehman, M.D.

THE
G+D
DIAGNOSIS

A Physician's Shocking Journey to Life After Death

Greg E. Viehman, M.D.

Big Mac Publishers
Sylacauga, Alabama, 35151

Author: Greg E. Viehman, M.D.
Editor: Greg McElveen
Reviewers   DeeAnn Williamson / Leslie Williamson
Cover Illustration, design © 2010   Marketing Ministries
Cover Photo © 2010   Chris Davis
Interior photos © 2010   Greg Viehman

Scripture quotations marked "NKJV™" are taken from the New King James Version®. Copyright © 1982 by Thomas Nelson, Inc. Used by permission. All rights reserved.
Scripture quotations marked "NIV" Holy Bible, New International Version®, NIV®. Copyright © 1973, 1978, 1984 by Biblica, Inc.™. Used by permission of Zondervan. All rights reserved worldwide. www.zondervan.com
Scripture quotations marked "NLT" are taken from the Holy Bible, New Living Translation, Copyright 1996 and 2004. Used by permission of Tyndale House Publishers, Inc., Wheaton, Illinois 60189. All rights reserved.
Scripture quotations taken from the "NASB," New American Standard Bible®, Copyright © 1960, 1962, 1963, 1968, 1971, 1972, 1973, 1975, 1977, 1995 by The Lockman Foundation. Used by permission. (www.Lockman.org)
Scripture quotations marked "TLB" or "The Living Bible" are taken from The Living Bible, Kenneth N. Taylor. Tyndale House, Copyright © 1997, 1971 by Tyndale House Publishers, Inc. Used by permission. All rights reserved.
Excerpts taken from "The Case for Christ" by Lee Strobel. Copyright © 1998 by Lee Strobel. Used by permission of Zondervan, www.zondervan.com.
Excerpts from "The New Evidence That Demands A Verdict" by Josh McDowell. Copyright © 1999 by Josh McDowell. Reprinted by permission of Thomas Nelson.

Library of Congress Control Number: 2010933798

1. REL006080 RELIGION / Biblical Criticism & Interpretation / General
2. SEL032000 SELF-HELP / Spiritual
3. PHI008000 PHILOSOPHY / Good & Evil
4. REL067030 RELIGION / Christian Theology / Apologetics

BISAC / BASIC Classification Suggestions:

1. Bible -- Evidences, authority, etc.
2. Jesus Christ -- Historicity
3. Jesus Christ -- Divinity.
4. Apologetics
5. Christianity -- Controversial literature

ISBN-13: 978-0-9823554-7-3   ISBN-10: 0-9823554-7-5   V 1.0
Big Mac Publishers Book Titles may be purchased in bulk at great discounts by retail vendors, or for educational, business, fund-raising, spiritual or sales promotional. Contact info @ Big Mac Publisher's website.www.bigmacpublishers.com.

Published by Big Mac Publishers
www.bigmacpublishers.com / Sylacauga, Alabama, 35151
Printed and bound in the United States of America

Table of Contents

Introduction

While I was in college I saw a play that deeply affected my life and perception of everyday reality. Our Town by Thornton Wilder features Emily Gibbs, a young woman who dies while giving birth and is then allowed to come back and observe her life for one day. Emily discovers the horror of wasted memories and a world without eternity as her life is now viewed from a new perspective. She realizes for the first time that everyone is so busy running around, working, and doing small chores that they aren't even looking at each other or enjoying each other's company. She desperately wants to see her family stop for just a second to embrace and enjoy the little things in life, but they never do.

Emily sees how the meaning and essence of life are lost moment by moment in a sea of distractions. Precious moments are not truly treasured. They are unappreciated and forever lost in time without anyone seeming to notice. Emily concludes that humans don't even know they are alive until they are dead. They take life for granted until life is taken away.

The stinging truth of this play goes right to the heart of everyone who sees or reads it. When I first saw it at age nineteen I realized that I had lived in Our Town my entire life and never knew it. My heart told me it was true. Something resonated deep within my soul that something was wrong with the world I was living in, but I quickly forgot it all in the midst of college life. You see, I returned to Our Town, the very place I didn't want to go.

The best characterization of my life is that I just lived. I never considered my own existence or what it meant. Life, health, and family were daily assumptions as time raced by, and I was unaware of it. I was caught up in a cycle of chasing one goal after the next. I lived day by day with my eyes on the future while the present disappeared.

This became much more profound and heart wrenching when I was blessed with a wife and children. I found our Great Vacations and best memories always ended so quickly. I realized that life was passing me by faster than I could comprehend. Photographs and the best home videos couldn't recreate or capture my reality, but somehow they reminded my heart of how quickly time passes and how it yearns to stop or relive it. The attempts to capture time backfired by paradoxically revealing to me there is never enough time to spend with the people you really love. My life was going so quickly, and there was nothing I could do about it.

I intrinsically knew that I never wanted my family and relationships to end. My heart yearned for eternity, but a world of relative truth and evolution made each beat seem even more meaningless. Pressure, stress, and frustration were being buried deep within my heart, a heart that was crying out for an answer in a world that says there is no answer. This is where Our Town hid me from the pain of no answer one distraction at a time. Our family spent a lot of time together in Our Town hiding from the fact that we couldn't capture the love we never wanted to end. It was easier to become Emily Gibbs and let the daily distractions of life protect our hearts and minds. Living in Our Town is comfortable as long as you don't know where you are. I lived there in a state of deception my entire life.

Somehow I knew my searching heart was crying out for eternity, a place where love never dies or ends, and this led me to The Cure. I thought I knew everything, but now I understand that I didn't know anything. The world told me I had everything, but I had nothing. It is difficult to fathom that God was right beside me, all around me, and only a breath away my entire life, even though almost everything in the world I had ever seen and heard taught me that I couldn't know him. How could the world's reality be so out of sync with what my entire life had shown me? Everything from my paradigm of existence to the meaning of life instantly became a lie when I made The God Diagnosis.

Greg E. Viehman, M.D.

Chapter One

The American Dream or Nightmare?

By age thirty-six I had everything I wanted in life. I had reached the pinnacle. I was a doctor who had graduated number one in his class, had graduated from the finest schools, was working in a successful practice, had married a beautiful wife, had two sons, drove a hot car, wore nice clothes, owned a cute dog, and lived in a gorgeous home in a great city. I had reached heaven on earth on my own—The American Dream. I had done it! I had solved the maze of life.

Brick by brick I had built my own ivory tower from the plans that the world provided me. I was taught to depend upon myself and make a name for myself, to build my own empire so I could have a nice life and provide security for our family. I was a warrior filled with selfish ambition, fighting to get ahead by letting self-discipline and self-determination provide self-accomplishment. The world kept patting me on the back for a job well done. My view of life was well cemented by worldly success and a comfortable lifestyle. I was bricked in with the mortar of pride and had no idea.

Here is our family in 2002. Isn't it picturesque and wonderful? Doesn't it exemplify what America is all about? How did it feel living The American Dream?

I was lonely, frustrated, unfulfilled, empty, bitter, disenchanted, and confused. Something was still missing in my life. None of my achievements, possessions, or experiences ever brought me what I thought they would. I had tried to fill my heart with *hobbies*: running, triathlons, wine, and mountain biking; *possessions*: sports cars, large home, jewelry, clothing, watches, and stereo equipment; *entertainment*: movies, vacations, and fine restaurants; *people*: parties, cultural status, and many friends. Each of these satisfied temporarily, but their allure and attraction always faded quickly, sometimes almost overnight or even during the experience. I spent many years running from one thing to the next in the "dating game" of my heart.

Depression began to set in when my heart realized there wasn't much left to try. I was hungry but couldn't be filled. I was thirsty but never quenched. The more my heart ate and drank, the worse it got! I reached a point where I dreaded the next "thing" because I already knew it wasn't going to give me what I was hoping it would.

One day I understood: *I have been living like this my entire life and never realized it.* Ever since I could remember, even back into child-hood, the toys and presents I received never kept their appeal. I quickly got bored and tired of them.

"Greg? Why aren't you playing with your new pinball machine? You wanted one all year long," Mom asked when I was eight years old. "You have only had it a week."

I didn't answer. I was sitting on the floor next to it, biting my nails in frustration. Inside I was simply bored of it. The anticipation of get-ting it was more exciting than actually playing with it. It had gotten old so quickly!

For this reason, I constantly looked forward to the *next* toy. Since I was a child in a wealthy family, it was always around the corner, which kept my heart going. The intermittent void and boredom never lasted long enough to do much damage. Matchbox to Mercedes, Legos to brick houses, superhero watch to Rolex, and printed T-shirts to Armani. I was now living the adult version of something that had started a long time ago.

Inside I felt like a sterile, cold, and damp white-walled room filled with empty space and echoes of my heart yearning for peace and satis-faction. The void was a bottomless pit that consumed anything and eve-rything with no mercy or pity for me. It felt like being continually dumped by a girlfriend. One minute I was excited and enamored with the latest purchase, hobby, or experience, but the next moment it left me in the dust without a goodbye or care in the world. I could be at the most exciting event and still feel absolutely disenchanted inside. Many times I was surrounded by family and friends but still felt alone!

I continued analyzing my past in search of answers and remem-bered something interesting from our family vacations. Every year around Christmas time we took trips to the Caribbean to places like

Aruba, St. Thomas, and the Bahamas. What always struck me as a child was that most of the people there were miserable and grouchy. Here they were on vacation in a beautiful resort with nothing to do but relax, eat, sleep, and have fun, and yet almost all of them were not having a good time. I always thought their misery was an outward manifestation of an internal frustration. Now I wondered if once they got there, their hearts quickly realized, *This isn't going to fill me either*. I was about to find out for myself.

THE GREAT VACATION

In the summer of 2000, when our kids were two and three, we planned our first family Great Vacation to the Outer Banks of North Carolina. The kids were finally old enough to go to the beach and play without being a nightmare. For six months I planned the trip in my mind and anticipated the wonderful family moments we would share. Whenever I felt down or empty, I reminded myself about our upcoming Great Vacation. The hope and expectation always lifted me up.

"Okay, guys, it's finally here! We are leaving for the beach today. It's our first family vacation!" I spouted off in joy like a geyser that had waited to burst. Scurrying, packing, and loading the car brought a rush of happiness to my heart.

"Look what I got, Daddy," my two-year-old son said. He had a grin from ear to ear as he held up his new bright blue bucket and shovel and waddled towards the car. It was a six-hour ride to get there, but it flew by in no time. I couldn't wait!

This is it! I thought. I have a family, a good job, a beautiful wife, and we are living The American Dream. This vacation is going to be the answer to my emptiness and frustration with life. I just haven't quite gotten there yet, but I am about to!

When we finally arrived we drove to the very end of a cul-de-sac street to the rental beach house. It was a gorgeous ocean front cottage with a shake roof. I rolled down the window and could hear the waves crashing and thundering in the background. A cool rush of ocean air filled the car. *Yes, this is it. We made it!* I thought. Then I exclaimed, "This is the house! We are here, everyone!" The boys were so eager to get out, they were bucking in their car seats like bulls in a rodeo. They were elated.

We rushed into the house and unpacked. Everyone quickly got on their bathing suits and headed out to the beach. I had to make two trips to carry in all of our paraphernalia: toy bulldozers, buckets, nets, umbrellas, water, snacks, towels, chairs, and reading material. The beach was breathtaking and very private. Our first day was a dream come true. Sand castles, walks on the beach, boogie boarding, and shell finding filled our day. *What more can I ask for?*

Day two was even better! We slept in, went out for breakfast, and did it all over again. After a long day at the beach the kids took naps, and my wife and I relaxed on the porch watching the waves.

On day three my heart started to sink and I had no idea why. I was now a little irritable and grouchy. *What is wrong with me?* I wondered. The ocean wasn't as alluring, the sand wasn't as comforting, and the relaxation wasn't as peaceful. My restlessness was building. "I know! Let's go play miniature golf and get ice cream tonight!" I said to everyone. This idea quickly quieted my aching heart. I was looking forward to a new adventure and didn't realize I had fallen into the same old trap of distractions.

On day four I woke up depressed. *The trip is going so quickly! It's almost over. Time goes so fast!* I thought. The first three days made a week seem like eternity, but now the end was in sight and closing in on me. Many thoughts filled my mind. I was watching our sons play at the beach. They were building a large mound of sand into a toddler style castle. Their cute little voices were mimicking the sounds of real tractors. "Urrrr. Mmmmmm…" I stared at them with both joy and sadness in my heart. *What a precious moment! Where do these memories go? Will my sons and their memories simply cease to exist one day? Will they be lost in the earth as recycled matter? In one hundred years will someone else be moving around the dirt that used to be my family?*

Their mound was now complete. It was misshapen and barely recognizable as a castle. A few tiny twigs were scattered along its surface for flags. They looked at it for a moment and then got out their bulldozers from the beach bag. "Rrrrrrrrr. Rrrrrrr. Kkkuhhh! Kuhhhhh!" were their new sounds as they knocked it over. In about two minutes their achievement was leveled back into the rest of the beach. It was gone and assimilated into the mass of sand. I couldn't help but realize that life on earth seemed to be uncannily similar. *Why isn't this trip what I thought it would be, even though it's the greatest family moment of my lifetime? How can this be?* I wondered.

Each day got worse and worse until we left. I despised day six. I didn't want to do anything and couldn't wait to get out of there and back home. I realized that not only was my life unfulfilled despite having everything, but in a world of evolution, it was also slowly dy-

ing back into recycled matter. There wasn't much more that I could hope to achieve or experience, and all that I had, including my wife and children, was meaningless without eternity, without permanence. They would disappear one day along with all of our memories. During the drive home I was deep in thought.

How and why am I feeling this way on the best vacation of my life?! It was an inescapable paradox. *I can't tell anyone because it's embarrassing*, I lamented to myself. In the past it was the anticipation and process of buying or experiencing new things that often maintained the false and temporary feeling of satisfaction. Once I had actually purchased or experienced what I was seeking, it was suddenly empty and depressing. The only solution was to keep it going with newer, bigger, and better—until now.

If I can only make it through medical school. If I can only make it through residency. If I can only have my own practice. If I can only move into a big house. If I can only take a Great Vacation. These thoughts summarized my life. Now I was out of "if onlys" and I felt like the "only one." The last grains of sand had fallen through the hole in the hourglass of my heart—another unexpected leak. My empty heart had run out of sand, and I couldn't patch the holes anymore. I felt betrayed by my paradigm of life after delaying gratification for many years only to find it wasn't gratifying but horrifying. What else was there to look forward to? Where else could I go for an answer?

The fact that I couldn't tell anyone due to shame and embarrassment added another dimension to the void that can't be easily described in words. The seeds of hopelessness were sprouting. Cynicism, bitterness, impatience, irritability, and callousness were all growing in the fertile soil of emptiness, loneliness, and finite time. I was depressed, confused, and even in silent despair. I enjoyed wine because it gave me a sense of peace and serenity that I craved and enjoyed. Somehow I knew it was artificial because it still fell short of what I was looking for.

I also felt very spoiled and bratty for not being content living The American Dream. In theory and appearance my life was a story book of success, but in my heart it was shockingly an empty abyss. *I worked my entire life to get to this point. What is happening? What am I looking for? What is wrong with me?* I cried inside.

DIGITAL ETERNITY

When I got home from The Great Vacation, I tried to capture and stop the merciless march of time by taking home videos and pictures of all our family events. I recorded everything. I also purchased an Apple computer and learned how to burn the movies into DVDs. I felt as if I was stopping the bulldozers from knocking over my castle. I now had digital memories of our family that could be passed down so we wouldn't be forgotten. I hoped that I would be able to relive these moments anytime I wanted to. *They weren't gone anymore! I had them trapped on my computer! Yes! This is it! I have beaten time! I have captured it!*

The satisfaction of capturing precious memories gave me comfort for about two years, until I began to play them back.

"Honey, tonight we are going to look at our home movies," I said with excitement to my wife, Ruth.

"Okay. Great. I'll get the kids," she replied.

Everyone gathered in front of the television. I popped in a DVD. I was so eager to watch that I sat on the floor right in front of the screen like when I was a kid.

As it began to play my heart started to sink. The kids have grown up so much, I thought. I forgot how small they used to be. Time goes so fast. Where does it go? It seems like only yesterday, but it has been two years!

Within five minutes I couldn't take it anymore. I was shocked and horrified to discover that my entire project had backfired on me. For some reason the photo album and movies only reminded me more of how quickly time passes. The inability to stop or capture time was more evident and devastating than before. It was now apparent that my heart wanted more than a digital re-creation of our memories. It wanted eternity, but eternity didn't exist. Depression came like a tidal wave. I left the room and went into the basement to grab a glass of wine to ease the pain. From that day forward I stopped making movies and taking pictures. It was easier to not look back.

I sat alone on the family room couch sipping the wine. On the walls were family portraits that were several years old. I stared deeply at them. I realized I couldn't escape the truth. My life is fleeing away from me, and there is nothing I can do about it. It could already be almost half over. Tears welled up in my eyes as I stared at our family portraits on the wall. *What will happen to us? Where do our memories go? Something is really wrong*, I thought. *I never expected things to turn out this way. This isn't the way it's supposed to be! How did I get here? What is wrong with me?* I lamented inside.

The buzz from the first glass began to set in, and I started to reminisce about the past, searching for answers. The God Diagnosis was about to begin. I found myself remembering a strange incident from high school that I had not thought about since it happened. From there I went back as far as I could remember.

Chapter Two

The Journey

THE SKI TRIP KOOKS

In my senior year of high school I went on The Ski Trip with a friend. It was with a Christian group, but I didn't know it. I simply thought I was going skiing. Everything seemed normal until the first night when we got to the ski lodge after a long day on the slopes. We were staying in a cozy log cabin in the mountains. Snow was covering the ground and trees.

I was exhausted and couldn't wait to relax. A fire in a large stone hearth was beckoning me. I headed over to it and slouched in a comfortable chair. I took off my gloves and boots. My cold hands were tingling as if pricked by pins and needles. I began to defrost them and my feet in front of the warm, crackling fire. Suddenly five people, each carrying black leather books, approached and surrounded me. As soon as I saw them coming I knew something was wrong. I was filled with dread and fear, but why? Then it came to me. I used to have this same feeling whenever I had done something wrong and was about to get caught and confronted with it. My mind flashed back to my dad yelling at me, "Greg! Greg Edwin Viehman, come down here!"

"Why, Dad? I'm busy," I hesitantly replied, trying to avoid the inevitable.

"Get down here now!" he sternly retorted, causing a heaviness to fall over my body. My ears began to quietly ring. *He knows*, I thought in disgust.

The five-second flashback ended abruptly when I realized the group was already standing over me. My heart was racing from an adrenaline surge. I felt the same pressure when my dad used to summon me. *Why was I feeling like I was about to be busted?* I thought. *I haven't done anything wrong, and I don't know these people.*

"What's up?" I asked while I squirmed in my seat trying to hide what I was feeling.

"Do you believe in God?" asked one of the guys as the others stared at me. Before I could answer, the girl next to him asked, "Do you believe in Jesus Christ?"

I was completely blindsided by the topic and by their approach. I immediately sat up and was on the defensive as a rush of tension overcame my body. Instantaneously, I felt an uncontrollable combination of anger and fear. This feeling was also familiar, but in a strangely related way. I felt as if I was in a fist fight! A flash from childhood came to me. "Come on, you sissy, aren't you going to hit me back?"

"Why do you ask?" I sneered sarcastically, looking away from their gaze. I noticed they all had a weird gleam in their eyes that made me uncomfortable. My heart was pounding. I didn't want to look at them. I wanted to get out of there and escape, but I was trapped.

"We want to explain to you how the first people created by God, Adam and Eve, sinned. Their sin separated them from God and caused death to enter the world. It has affected everyone that came after them, including you and me. Jesus Christ came to pay for your sins and end the separation."

Before she could get another word in, I immediately interjected, "What in the world are you guys talking about? Man has evolved over billions of years! Are you kidding?!" Raw tension was evident in my voice. I had never heard about Adam and Eve, and these born-again Christians believed it was literal history?!

"Jesus loves you," one of them remarked out of nowhere. For some reason this set me off. I stood up in rage. My veins were bulging and my skin felt hot and sweaty. "Do you really expect me to believe that man was created by God?! I have lived for eighteen years and never heard about this anywhere from anybody! I have written a term paper on evolution: 'Lucy, the Missing Link Between Man and Ape,'" I yelled, waving my hands in the air.

I kicked the nearest chair into some other empty chairs, causing a loud crash. I stormed away from them. "Greg, what's wrong?" a friend from high school asked. He was sitting on the other side of the room near the exit door I was headed for. I stopped and looked at him. "Shut up! Just shut up!" I screamed and kicked open the door to get outside and away from those freaks.

Later that night they timidly approached me, and tried to show me how these "facts" were written in the Bible, but I wouldn't look. I ignored them the rest of the trip but remained troubled in my heart for many days afterward. I could not admit even to myself that my paradigm of life could be a lie. I kept telling myself they were crazy religious fanatics. *If man had been created and not evolved, then surely I would have been taught this in school. When we studied evolution in school no one ever mentioned creation. There is nothing wrong with me,* I reassured myself. I continued to find comfort in the fact that I had never heard about this during my life.

Something was still wrong, though. *Why was I so upset over this? Why was I feeling like I had done something wrong?* I asked myself repeatedly on the bus ride home. I stared out the window and wanted to get away from those people. My trip had been ruined.

When I got home to my parents I was still upset and felt very unsettled. My hands were jittery and slightly sweating as I told them what had happened. They told me not worry about it. "We are fine, son. Some Christians can be fanatical. Forget about them. You're okay." By the next day it was over, and I forgot about God for a long time. It wasn't hard since I had rarely even heard about him in my entire life.

I was still on the couch daydreaming. From here my memories went back all the way to the beginning. I found myself reviewing my entire life and focusing on the few times anything about God was involved.

CHILDHOOD

I was born in Wilmington, Delaware, in 1967. I was an only child in a nice family, but God was not a part of our lives in any way. My parents had religious backgrounds, but they chose to let me decide for myself what to believe later in life. Hypocritical aspects of religion had turned them off. I grew up not even thinking about or hearing of God or a god. We did not attend church, discuss the Bible, or talk about God. God was abstract, distant, unknowable, and irrelevant to our everyday lives. The world around me testified to this in every way.

My maternal grandmother was the only occasional experience with God I had, but it was extraneous and without real meaning to me. She would pray before holiday meals to a "Heavenly Father," but who was that? A Bible was in her house and a few times I paged through it, but I didn't know what it was about. She talked occasionally about "the Lord," but I did not understand. When I was bad she told me, "The good Lord will punish you." I cannot recall ever going to church. In fact I considered it normal not to go, since this was all I knew. She went all of the time, but we stayed at home on Sunday mornings.

By age eleven the world had shaped my heart. Here is what I wrote for an autobiography assignment at school when I was eleven:

I hope to have a nice house with lots of trees around. I plan to get married and have a wife and kids. I plan to have lots of money. If I have a great deal of money then I will donate some of it to charity, to the poor. I am planning to have a successful life, for things to turn out well. When I retire I will go to Florida and live there until death. I want to travel around the world a bit to see how other people live and earn a living. I hope to die of old age, not by some disease. I don't want to suffer. I think life will turn out somewhat like I expect it. I think it will be nice and pleasing, a happy life.

I had a great childhood, many friends, a nice house, great parents, and lived The American Dream. Except for my grandmother and few random incidents, from my perspective God was not evident in the things I heard, saw, or learned from the world. Christmas was about Santa Claus and presents. Easter was a time to get candy and find eggs.

HIGH SCHOOL

I graduated high school in 1985 at the age of eighteen. My best friends were Jewish, and we did not discuss religion. I don't think religion or God ever came up in my school years, except for The Ski Trip. We were all too busy studying, having fun, and living our lives. In school, God was clearly considered to be inconsequential, since he was never part of the teachings or conversations we had.

I knew people who went to church, but they didn't talk about Jesus Christ or the Bible. I never saw a single person in school ever reading or holding a Bible. If Jesus was a part of their lives then he was never mentioned or discussed in any public situations. It was all about "going" to church, and this included kids who went to Christian schools. As far as I could see, there was no difference in their lives compared to the rest of us. The connection between church and daily life was never manifested. The things that they did and said behind closed doors never extended to showing me the type of behavior even I would have expected from someone claiming to believe in a moral God, whoever he was.

During summer vacations, I frequently went to a supposedly "Christian" summer camp, but there was no religion or discussion of God there either. The Bible and Jesus Christ were never talked about. On Sunday there was a generic worship service that the campers suffered through. Bad language, drinking, smoking, and secret sexual encounters abounded.

COLLEGE

I went off to college at Penn State University, but after one semester I transferred to the University of Delaware to be closer to home after what felt like a "heart attack." For reasons I did not understand then, and only really understood a few years ago, I suffered from a bad case of separation anxiety. It manifested when I first went off to college. Out of the blue I had anxiety, fear, and sudden bouts of impending doom. My heart and nerves were a wreck, and I didn't know why.

Cellular Molecular Biology

Things got better closer to home. I was a biology major planning on medical school. God was still not someone who entered my mind even during this very difficult time in my life.

In my third year of college there was one specific event when I did think about God. I was taking cellular molecular biology and studying a primitive form of DNA gene regulation in bacteria.

As I watched the professor explain the system I was struck with an uncomfortable thought: *The intricate design and regulation pathways seem to be intelligently engineered!* I analyzed what I was seeing more closely and was startled with another realization: *There are multiple interdependent parts that have no function without the others. If even one is missing the entire system fails. How could this be if life evolved?* Evolution teaches that slowly, over millions of years, mutations cause new changes that are selected by nature because they are useful. This was an entire integrated system, however, that could not evolve sequentially.

I also realized that DNA contains information. How could information be encoded in our genes by chance over time? *If I see a book then I know someone wrote it. If I find a watch then I know someone made it*, I reasoned. These thoughts kept nagging me. My heart was suggesting "intelligent design," but that would mean everything I had learned was wrong! My mind fought back with *that just can't be!*

I digested this further and came up with the idea that maybe God was someone who existed somewhere in an abstract way. He might have started life and then let evolution take over under his guidance. The Ski Trip kooks came to mind, but I had decided God couldn't be knowable, personal, or active in our world today or someone other than religious fanatics would have told me about him. My teachers, parents, the news, or somebody would have said something. I was feeling apprehensive and internally frustrated, but I was able to bury these conflicting ideas because of fear of their implications.

Church

Later in college, I attended church one time with a girlfriend and her family. I felt very out of place. I wanted to get out of there, like on The Ski Trip. I didn't know how everyone knew what to chant or say at the same time. I simply went to be with my girlfriend, and I got through the service. It was the proper thing to do, and I had great respect for her father and family. I noticed many other kids were distracted. As I looked around I saw them staring at the ceiling, fidgeting, sleeping, chewing gum in secret, with total disinterest in the pastor. I felt better.

The Man with the Cross

One day, in the middle of the main mall on campus, a disheveled man was standing in a walkway to a class. His beard was long and brown-gray with dirt and knots in it. A large wooden cross was over his shoulder. He was jerking his head back and forth and glaring at the mass of students scurrying to class. He was yelling and screaming passionately at the students, "Repent! Let Jesus save you from your sins and hell! Your college education is worth nothing without Jesus Christ. You are deceived! It's not about this world! Repent!" No one listened. He was a kook. I think campus police took him away.

Our Town

In my senior year of college I took some drama classes. I had a theater minor, which I greatly enjoyed. I had to see a play for class and went alone. *Our Town* by Thornton Wilder features Emily Gibbs, a young woman who dies while giving birth and is then allowed to come back and observe her life for one day. Emily discovers the horror of wasted memories and a world without eternity as her life is now viewed from a new perspective. She realizes for the first time that everyone is so busy running around, working, and doing small chores that they aren't even looking at each other or enjoying each other's company. She desperately wants to see her family stop for just a second to embrace and enjoy the little things in life, but they never do.

Emily laments how the meaning and essence of life are lost moment by moment in a sea of distractions. She realizes precious moments are not truly treasured. Emily concludes that humans don't know they are alive until they are dead. They take life for granted until life is taken away.

I was deeply moved by this play. It stung my heart because I realized I had lived in Our Town an entire life and never knew it. My eyes began to well up uncontrollably with *Tears?! Are you kidding me? You wimp! Knock it off!* I thought pulling myself together. *Is there more to life than I know? Is Emily Gibbs right about life?* Something resonated deep within my soul that something was wrong with the world I was living in, but I quickly forgot it all in the midst of college life.

College Life

Two of my roommates in college went to church regularly, but we did not discuss the details of their faith. They were sincere and reverent, but I simply blocked them out. God was important to them, but I did not understand this. They never pressured me either, which I liked. I didn't really think about their church attendance. Most people were recovering from hangovers on Sunday. I was still busy living my life, having a great time, and preparing for medical school.

I took Philosophies of Religion one semester. We studied many different famous philosophers and their books on religion, but not Jesus or the Bible. We were taught that man made up many theories about God to deal with the painful realities of our world. The concept of "God" was a response by man to hide from his heart the pain of death, disease, and tragedies. I was taught there was not a correct answer about God and to respect all religions for what they were.

My summers during college were spent at the beach. I was a lifeguard and disc jockey. I was partying, drinking, chasing women, and working. It was all about me. I did very well in college and graduated Magna Cum Laude. I entered medical school in 1989.

MEDICAL SCHOOL

The first three years of medical school didn't leave much time for the wild lifestyle I had been enjoying. I was in books twenty-four hours a day, seven days a week. I excelled in medical school. I had a good memory and was able to read quickly. I graduated first in my class.

I was learning about the human body and how it functioned. It was awesome and absolutely amazing, but it did not trigger thoughts about God since I believed in evolution. Medical studies are all about the human body, but there was no mention of God or creation in anything I was taught or had read. If God had any role in the human body then he was left out of the one place I might have expected him to be recognized. Years of silence about any divine influence in life were creating engravings on my heart with a magnitude and impact I didn't realize.

I remember dissecting a human brain. I picked it up for the first time with awe and wonder. I couldn't help but think, I am holding in my hand a brain that had a life, family, and many memories. Where do these go? Are they gone? How can this white gelatinous mass have love, feeling, and emotions? I realized that this same type of matter was inside of me. My brain was just like this! It became personal. Where do my memories go? Are they nothing more than nerve synapses and chemicals? I was horrified. All these thoughts raced through my mind, but there were no answers. When I die someday, will the love for my wife and children get lost in decaying matter? Is that what I am headed toward? Something didn't make sense. My heart sank and my stomach knotted up every time I had this class. I was glad when it was over.

My life was consumed by school. I was lonely but constantly distracted by the never-ending work load. I lost my college girlfriend and felt even more alone. God was the last person on my mind, however. There was nothing I had seen or experienced in my twenty-four years that made me think he was necessary or desirable.

I took another sip of wine and continued the trip down memory lane. I had never played my life back from this perspective before.

MARRIAGE

I met Ruth, my wife to be, in my third year of medical school, and we married a little over one year later in 1993. And, yes, we got married in a church. We met with the pastor twice for "marriage lessons." The pastor was a very nice man. To me, church was nothing more than a place to learn some lessons about life. The pastor was not concerned about my relationship with God or lack thereof, which reinforced the idea to me that God was not important in the real issues of life. I didn't tell my fiancé, but I kept waiting for the pastor to corner me about Jesus. He didn't! I was thrilled! If Jesus was alive, knowable, and of critical importance like The Ski Trip kooks claimed, then why didn't a pastor tell me, when it was obvious by my responses during the lessons that I didn't believe? He silently reinforced my worldview.

I began a one-year internship in internal medicine at the Hospital of the University of Pennsylvania. I was basically annihilated for one solid year with nothing but work, work, work. Even though we were constantly around people who were dying, no thought or discussion of God or an afterlife ever took place among doctors or nurses that I witnessed. In the hospital dead was dead.

So far most of my experiences related to God had been negative, and even a pastor had failed to discuss God with me. I was doing well and on my way to a successful career. I had a great wife and family. My parents were proud of me, and life was wonderful! Society certainly did not embrace God or send the message that he was real and alive. College had taught me that there is no absolute truth; truth is relative to your belief system.

In 1994 I became a resident in dermatology at Duke University Medical Center. I worked very hard for three years, fully consumed by learning dermatology and being married. My wife was busy with a pharmaceutical job. Everything was going as planned. The modern paradigm of life was to be successful and do as well as we could. That is exactly what we were doing.

During my residency, in 1995, we moved to Apex, North Carolina, and bought a house. Ruth had been raised "Christian," but she had not been going to church since we met. She tried to get me to go a few times at Christmas and Easter, but I refused. She did not seem interested in God, per se, but rather in the occasional attendance of church on special occasions. It seemed clear to me that churchgoers were just being religious. It served no purpose for me. I could do something much more useful on my Sundays like sleep in, recover from a hangover, go for a run, or mountain bike.

One day a new acquaintance invited Ruth to church and she went. I stayed at home. The next week she got a call from a woman she had met there. The woman wanted to visit with her. They went for a walk in the woods, and the woman cornered Ruth about her belief in Jesus Christ. Ruth felt very uncomfortable and left as soon as possible. "I told you they are a bunch of kooks," I said. This turned her off as well.

I graduated from Duke in 1997 and joined the faculty as a skin cancer surgeon and fellow. One year later I opened a private practice with my mentor in Cary, North Carolina. This project involved a tremendous amount of work that kept me happily distracted. I was now a full-fledged citizen of Our Town. That same year we had our first son.

MARCO ISLAND

When our first child was about one year old we took a trip to visit Ruth's parents in Marco Island, Florida. Her parents were Christians and wanted the baby baptized.

"Honey, what does baptizing a baby do?" I asked.

"I'm not sure. I think if a baby isn't baptized and dies early it may not go to heaven." she replied, her voice wavering with uncertainty.

I exploded. "That's absurd! I want to meet with your parents' pastor and discuss this nonsense!" I clenched my jaw and knew I was getting angry. "No one will tell me anything about our baby son!" I shouted.

I wanted to meet with him pronto. I was anxious and anticipated a good debate. I already didn't like him. He was irritating me before I even met him. Surprisingly, I felt some of the same sensations I had experienced during The Ski Trip. Anger, fear, uncertainty, helplessness, and a lack of control were gripping my heart. I wondered, W*hy do I feel anxious and unsettled every time Christianity comes up?*

We arrived in Florida and met with the minister of her parents' church the next day. I was short-fused all morning before the meeting. He was sitting at the back of a small café at a round table, sipping casually on a cup of freshly brewed coffee. To my shock, he was very pleasant and had a glowing smile and peaceful demeanor.

"We want to know about baptizing our child," I asked curtly. To my surprise he explained to us that it wasn't necessary and that baptism did not "save" a child anyway. He said this idea of salvation from baptism is completely unbiblical but a common misconception. He explained that it could be used as an outward sign of a commitment to raise the child Christian. He recommended we not baptize the child if we were not committed Christians. I was now relieved and more comfortable. I wasn't expecting this answer from him at all.

I wanted to ask him some questions that had been nagging at me. He was quietly sipping on his coffee across the table from me.

"What about the millions of people in the world who do not believe in Jesus Christ?" I asked with a slightly sarcastic tone. I continued, "Do you believe that they are wrong and you are right? Are they headed to hell?" I paused for effect and then added confidently, "I am convinced that no 'loving God' would condemn these people. I think everyone is right, but in different ways. This is what society has taught me. Aren't we living in the age of tolerance?" I leaned back in my chair; I was sure I had him stumped.

He looked at me with warm eyes, grabbed his bushy white beard, and said, "Jesus is the only way to heaven, because he is God and only God can die and pay for man's sins. Other religions don't have a savior or an answer for sin. What you don't realize or hear about are the thousands of missionaries in every country. God is saving multitudes of people every day all over the world through Jesus." He then turned the tables on me when he added, "Why are you upset about there being only one way instead of rejoicing that at least there is one guaranteed way to heaven and that heaven actually exists?"

I was speechless and confused. I hadn't thought about it that way. As most people are, I was afraid to die, and evolution was not comforting when it came to death.

"Okay. Thank you, sir, for your time," I hastily said to end the conversation and get out of there. I wanted to get away from him but didn't know why. I had feelings of anxiety, irritation, and panic that I couldn't explain, but it was eerily familiar. "Greg Edwin Viehman, get downstairs right now!" my dad was yelling again in my head. I only knew that if I left, it would go away. Out we went and gone it was. Whew! Little did I know my wife's father was plotting round two.

Later that evening my father-in-law told me that two members from his church were coming over to talk with us. *Uh-oh,* I thought. About an hour later I heard a knock at the door. I peeked around the corner and saw the door open. A man and his wife, both in their sixties, made their way in. Suddenly, uncontrollably, I sensed an importance to this meeting and felt a presence. It was as if someone invisible came in with them. *Why am I feeling this way? What is going on?* I wondered. *Why do I feel a peace in the room?! I should be angry and frustrated.*

I had never experienced peace except when drinking alcohol. I was confused but intrigued. This all happened in a matter of seconds, and absolutely no one could sense what I was thinking and feeling. We sat down together on the white Florida style couch. "We want to tell you about Jesus Christ," they politely said.

"Go ahead," Ruth replied. I felt like giving her the elbow to the ribs, but they would have seen me.

They explained what they called "the Gospel," the story of God's plan to save mankind from their sins. It took them about fifteen minutes, and I listened very carefully. In a nutshell, Jesus died for my sins. They said he took my place and punishment on the cross. If I trusted in Jesus and turned from my sins then God would forgive me and provide me eternal life. It seemed too easy. I was shocked that it made sense and was even attractive, but it seemed very farfetched and too good to be true. They implied that I was in trouble without Jesus but did not specifically mention hell. As they talked I wondered, *Why had I never heard this before in thirty years except on The Ski Trip? Wouldn't people be talking about it if it were true? I seem okay in everyday life. How could something be wrong with me?*

My mind was racing from thought to thought. My heart was beating so hard I could practically hear it, and that uncomfortable and irritated feeling was coming over me again. This time it was similar to the initial climb of a big roller coaster, when you are just waiting for the first car to go over the hump and drop. I listened and said nothing more. We thanked them and they left. I think they could sense I wasn't interested in asking questions. I was terrified of that roller coaster plunging down and crashing at the bottom. I didn't know what was over that hump and didn't want to.

After they left I was still sensing a presence, a state of peace, and kept thinking about what they had told me. It was bothering me that I didn't know what the presence was and couldn't make it go away. *I can't tell Ruth or she will think I am crazy*, I thought. I could not get their message out of my mind. I was feeling drawn to study the Bible when I thought I didn't want to! My heart seemed to be changing, even softening. *What in the world is this? I can't read the Bible. People will laugh at me*. This was so out of character for me.

Three days later we drove home. I thought about it all the way. *If they are right then everything I know and think about life is a lie.* I kept thinking, *It's just too weird.* When we got in bed that night I asked Ruth, "Do you think we should read the Bible?" Inside I was thinking, *I can't believe you just said that.*

I was pleasantly surprised when she replied, "Yes, I'll get one tomorrow. Let's read it together before bed each night."

The next day Ruth came home with a new Bible. I was relieved, since I didn't want to buy one myself. That would have been too embarrassing for me.

Our reading started off strong three nights in a row. We read one chapter each night. On day three we read about Adam and Eve and the so-called "fall of man" where they sinned against God. The story was too much for me. I said, "Ruth, this is stupid. I am a scientist and a physician. I have studied the human body for eleven years. There is no way two people were created from nothing. Maybe this is just a parable to teach us about life, but it's not literal history." She agreed and we stopped reading. I was angry and upset again but didn't know why. It bothered me that I was mad, which made me even madder!

The next night when I went to bed Ruth was asleep. I ducked in under the covers with my head pecking out, and there was the Bible sitting on the night stand. This may sound crazy, but I felt as if it was staring at me. I couldn't get those dumb stories out of my mind. The next thing I knew I was picking it up and reading again. *Why am I feeling drawn to read this stupid religious book with fairy tales in it?* I thought, anger brewing again. I was even more irritated to find that Adam and Eve were clearly portrayed as literal people. They had kids and their genealogies were listed. A few passages later, I read that people were living for hundreds of years! I chuckled aloud to myself "Yeah, suuuuure they did—and donkeys fly."

This pattern continued for the next three nights. The story of Noah's Ark was the last straw. "That's it. I am done with this ___," I mumbled under my breath. Disgustedly, I threw the Bible down on the floor and it made a loud thud.

My wife was out cold, but this startled her wide awake. "What's happening?" she murmured as she sat up.

"It's that ___ Bible. It's filled with stories that can't be true. They were invented by simple people thousands of years ago who were ignorant and didn't know any better!" I railed.

"Okay, but why are you so angry? Calm down and go to sleep," she said reasonably.

"I don't want to sleep!" I retorted and pounded my fist on the bed.

My heart once again was quickly back in a fist fight and headed down the stairs to face up to Dad for what I was guilty of! I glared at my wife and said vehemently, "The intelligent man of 1998 knows for certain that these stories are impossible. I have proof and they have nothing. No proof at all. Fools! I have science on my side and they have nothing but blind faith!"

Ruth clearly didn't want to engage me. She shook her head and said wearily, "Just go to sleep and forget about it. I'm tired." With that, she rolled over and fell right back to sleep. Not me! I needed to stew for another thirty minutes.

CHURCH

The next Saturday our neighbor prodded me to go to church. "Church is good for you. You get to meet people and make business contacts," he said.

"I don't think so. It's not my thing," I replied. Later that day Ruth informed me that we were going to try a church her friend recommended. It was the same denomination she grew up in. I agreed to go. I felt it couldn't hurt anything.

On the way there I was pensive and didn't talk much. My attitude was very callous and prideful as I walked in. What a bunch of weaklings needing a crutch, I thought. Look at the men. They are sissies. Their wives look like Holly Hobby. I am sick and tired of their stupid smiles and robotic sense of joy.

When we walked into the service it had already started. Inside there were three sections of cushioned chairs about fifteen rows deep facing a central stage. Everyone was standing up singing. I hated singing even outside of church. I looked around and many people were holding their hands up in the air with their eyes closed. "More weirdoes," I whispered to my wife. We suffered through the service and bolted out of there. Everything religious ended right then and there. No more Bible reading, church, or thinking about foolish fairy tales. I felt relieved as we both agreed we were done with religion.

I was certain I had made the right decision. I had found more weirdoes, foolish fairy tales about miracles, and people acting like they knew and were experiencing God. I was done! I knew I was right! I was a doctor, number one in my class, a scientist, a scholar, and I knew better than these fools. I wouldn't sit in church to appear good or follow society's definition of righteousness. I refused to do it just to meet people or make business contacts even though *many* people encouraged me for this exact reason. I didn't need their honest, off-the-record side benefits of church. I knew these guys on the weekends. They were saying and doing the same things I was.

After all, my wife and I were successful and making good money, and we had a nice house, a son, and great jobs. We had no need for church or religion, especially since all of our experiences with them had been weird. We had tested religion, and it failed for us. I had always gotten angry and shook up. It didn't make sense to continue with something that made me miserable.

We did have some friends who had found a more "normal" church that delivered a low-key message, but we were not interested in any of it. We were good people in a nice neighborhood, and I was very busy starting a new private practice and raising a new baby boy. It was over. *What a relief!* I thought. I was excited to finally be done with it.

THE NEW NEIGHBORHOOD

In 1999 we moved into a much larger house. Money was not an issue for us, and life was without stress, except for our kids. We had another son, and our life was busy managing two young children. The goal was to work hard and save as much as I could for retirement and our family. I believed that money could buy security and some degree of control over life. I had achieved what our society taught was the primary goal of living: The American Dream.

The neighborhood we moved into was different, though. In the old neighborhood everyone was friendly. They were always outside, talking, and interacting like one big family. That was not the case here. Many neighbors ignored us or barely gave an acknowledging "hello."

One time I was chatting with a new neighbor in her driveway when a woman I had never met walked up. She started talking to the woman I was talking to and ignored me as if I wasn't there. *Is this woman really going to pretend I am not here? What's up with this?!* I thought. I waited a few minutes until it became awkward and I left. While walking home I was fuming, since I had been dealing with this new neighborhood thing for a few weeks.

"I can't believe this neighborhood! What is wrong with these people? Why is everyone so strange?" I shouted as I walked into my house and met Ruth in the kitchen.

I explained what happened and she said, "You know, I have heard that street is filled with born-again Christians."

"Yeah, well, it isn't doing them any good. Our old neighborhood was normal," I exclaimed. I smirked and gleefully added, "I was warned the more expensive the neighborhood the weirder it gets. And when you add in those Christian freaks it is a real zoo!"

At least things were normal at work. Jesus wasn't brought up there either, but for one interesting exception. A woman who worked in the lab was always reading her Bible and talking about "the Lord" and his work in her life. The Bible Woman, Tammy, obviously didn't respect our freedom of religion in this country.

"Hey, what's up with her?" I asked the lab director.

"She's just real religious," he replied.

"Why is she reading the Bible all the time?" I asked.

"Yeah, it's kinda silly, isn't it?" he jested in reply. We both snickered.

She was very pleasant and warm and had a peace about her. Her religious stuff was weird to me, but it was obviously real to her in a way I had never seen before. *How could she be talking about the Lord doing things in her life? What Lord? Did she mean God was personally working in her life?* I asked myself. *How can someone be so religious that she actually believes God is speaking to her?* I wondered. I carefully watched her for a few weeks and decided whatever she had, it worked for her.

I liked to joke around a lot in the lab at work. When a hurricane would make landfall in North Carolina, I would say, "I am going to build an ark!"

Tammy always replied, "No, God is not going to do that again. He said so." The crazy thing is, that's all she said! *How did she know? Did she really believe in Noah's ark? How silly!*

One time there was a big hurricane coming. It was pouring buckets outside. You could hear the pounding of the rain through the roof in the lab. I decided to needle Tammy again. "I am going running tonight," I exclaimed with pride.

"You shouldn't go out in this weather" she cautioned.

"Even God himself can't get me out there!" I jeered in reply.

She flinched, and I quickly realized she was uncomfortable by what I had said. Her gaze startled me since she looked at me with a tangible alarm, her eyebrows slightly raised with a subtly disapproving connotation. The Ski Trip feelings were now starting to trickle in again. *What did I say? Why is she looking at me like that? Did she think God was going to zap me for being irreverent?*

RUTH'S FIRST BIBLE STUDY

In the spring of 2003 Ruth shocked me when she said, "I think I am going to start going to a Bible study."

"What?! Why in the world are you going to do that?!" I asked disdainfully.

"I was invited, and I think I want to go," she plainly stated.

"Okay. You go ahead and go to your Biiiible study," I condescendingly replied. I was irritated, but I shook it off in disgust. "Just don't become a religious weirdo on me," I added and then dropped the topic.

What I didn't know but learned later was that something had happened to Ruth a few weeks earlier. She was in a fabric store when a woman came up to her and handed her a small slip of paper and walked away. It said "How do you know you are going to heaven?" She tossed the paper onto the passenger seat and began driving home. The little piece of paper, just sitting there wadded up, started bugging her. The first thing she did when she got home was to check the mail. Coincidentally, in the mailbox was an invitation to a Bible study. This freaked her out. She wondered if God was trying to get her attention. She decided to go to the Bible study just in case. She was raised Christian, after all.

She attended the Bible study for a few months, and then one day out of the blue she blurted out, "Jesus is coming back and you are headed to hell." Ruth was always blunt and to the point, but this was crazy.

I kept on walking right past her up the stairs and said, "Yeah, suuuuure he is," in a mocking tone with a chuckle in my voice. I thought maybe these women were drinking or smoking something at the "Bible study." In fact, I thought it was so ridiculous that it didn't worry me or cause tension in our marriage. I felt it was a laughable and harmless phase Ruth was going through. The rest of the time she seemed normal and left me alone.

Well, not completely alone; she bought me a book, *The New Evidence That Demands a Verdict* by Josh McDowell. It was a big book. She looked at me calmly but stated firmly, "I want you to read this book. This guy didn't believe in Jesus. He set out to prove it wasn't true but became a believer. It's very intellectual."

I took it, rolled my eyes, and then placed it on my night stand. "Oh, brother," I mumbled under my breath.

BACK TO REALITY

My long walk down memory lane ended as Ruth snapped me out of my reverie by yelling at me from upstairs, "Greg! Greg? Where are you? Are you down there? We are supposed to be watching the home videos as a family. What are you doing?"

Startling me back to reality, I realized that I had lost all track of time while I'd been sipping my wine and contemplating my life. I quickly yelled back, "I'll be right up!" I chugged the rest of the glass and left it downstairs on the bar. I trudged up the stairs knowing Ruth was going to be mad.

"What were you doing down there? You just left us," she said with an edge to her voice.

"I just needed to be alone. It's been a long week at work. I am glad the weekend is here."

"You look sad. Is everything okay?"

"Yeah. I'm all right. Have you ever noticed how old pictures and home videos make you realize how short life is?"

"Yes, but why are you getting all sappy tonight?"

"I don't know. It's been bugging me for a while. Never mind. I just want to go to bed. I'm exhausted."

THE LAST STRAW

The next day the neighborhood issues got worse and came to a climax. "Dad, the kids down the street don't want to play with us. They ignore us," our five- and six-year-old sons sobbed as they came stomping through the garage door.

"What do you mean?" I asked angrily.

"I don't think the other boys in the neighborhood want to play with us," one son stuttered between sobs.

"Every time we go out to play they pretend like we are not there. They never ask us to play," our other son chimed in. "And, Daddy, one girl just told another girl that she was not a *real Christian*," he added.

I was livid! Now this street of Christians had their kids pulling this crap! "That's it! I have had enough of this ___!" I yelled right in front of the kids. "I am sick of feeling excluded, alienated, and unwelcome!" I turned to my wife and said, "I am buying a Bible. I am going to prove these Christian hypocrites are a bunch of fakes!" I slammed the porch door so hard it rattled the frame and glass.

The next day at work I told the lab staff what had been going on in the neighborhood. Tammy, The Bible Woman, from the lab, raised her eyebrows but made no comment. "If my children and I are going to be judged, then I want to know on what basis. I am going to the Christian bookstore to buy a Bible." Tammy looked me right in the face with a twinkle in her eyes. I thought I even caught her suppressing a smile.

She still said nothing. *Why isn't she worried I will debunk her faith? In fact, she seems almost happy about the whole incident!*

After work I drove to the Christian bookstore and bought another Bible. Our first Bible was nowhere to be found in the house. As I pulled up to the store my heart raced and I felt apprehensive. I didn't want to be seen in a Christian bookstore, especially buying a Bible. I parked the car three stores down so it wouldn't be seen right in front. I put on a baseball hat and sunglasses as a disguise. I surveyed the area for a moment to make sure I didn't see anybody I knew, and then I went in. I felt like an alien. I got in and out as quickly as I could. When I got home I quickly realized something. A Bible looks like a Bible! I didn't consider this when I bought it. *I can't be seen reading the Bible.* I now had to go back and go through the whole routine again!

I used the same stealth precautions as before at the Christian bookstore. This time, though, I bought a computer study version of the Bible for my laptop computer, because I was embarrassed to be seen with a printed Bible. I mainly used the computer Bible so no one would know what I was doing. Patients always brought reading material with them to the office and almost no one was ever reading a Bible. If they were reading anything but the Bible then I certainly wasn't going to be seen reading one.

I decided to start with the New Testament since my experience with the Old Testament had been a failure. I had no idea what I would read except that Jesus, Mary, and the wise men would be in there. I went in with a clean slate and no preconceived ideas about the content. I was on a personal mission. I was in search of ammunition with no interest in Christianity itself. I wanted to read the legal document to find clauses that would support my case. I began to read. I had no idea what was about to happen to me. The God Diagnosis was beginning.

Chapter Three

The Investigation Phase I:

The New Testament

THE FOUR GOSPELS
Matthew and Mark

I started by reading the first two books of the New Testament, Matthew and Mark, in four days. I turned on my old medical school brain. It had been inactive for a while. In medical school one reads all of the time. Luckily, my capacity to assimilate a lot of new information kicked back in with full force.

Matthew and Mark were pretty similar in their stories. I didn't get it. Why tell the same story twice? The first four books of the New Testament were called the Gospels and described the life of Jesus. I had thought gospel was a type of music. I did a little digging in the study Bible and discovered that the word gospel literally means "good news."

Jesus was raised in a small town in northern Israel called Nazareth. His parents were common, ordinary people. His life seemed to have been plain and uneventful until he turned thirty years of age and began his teachings. There was very little mention of his early life, but he was noted to have been a carpenter.

Jesus was unlike anyone I had ever read about. He was portrayed as having authority over nature, disease, creation, sin, life, and death. I realized no one but a God could have dominion over every aspect of life. The Bible claimed that Jesus knew what people were thinking, that he forgave their sins, and that he healed a Roman centurion's servant without even seeing the man he healed. If so, this would mean Jesus was in control of that servant's body and disease even though the servant was miles away. Could anyone but a real God do this? The physician within me was very curious about the claimed medical healings of Jesus, even though I didn't believe them.

My medical brain was baffled by the healing of the paralytic man, as depicted in Matthew chapter nine. Jesus simply told this man to get up and walk, and he did! I am a doctor. I know that paralysis is a complicated problem that involves both nerves and muscles. His leg muscles would have atrophied terribly over the years from non-use, leaving them weak, wasted, and stiff. In order for the man to walk so suddenly, both his nerves *and* muscles would have to be instantaneously restored. This would require brand new muscle and nerve tissue to appear in a split second. No one but a God, if one existed, could perform such a feat.

The Gospels claimed that Jesus was God, and Jesus also portrayed himself as God. In fact, this was the primary reason religious people wanted to kill him, because it was blasphemy for anyone to call themselves God in that era. The following passage illustrates these points:

> *The high priest said to him, "I charge you under oath by the living God: Tell us if you are the Christ, the Son of God."*
>
> *"Yes, it is as you say," Jesus replied. "But I say to all of you: In the future you will see the Son of Man sitting at the right hand of the Mighty One and coming on the clouds of heaven."*
>
> *Then the high priest tore his clothes and said, "He has spoken blasphemy! Why do we need any more witnesses? Look, now you have heard the blasphemy. What do you think?"*
>
> *"He is worthy of death, they answered." (Matthew 26:63-66 NIV)*

I was captivated by the notion that Jesus claimed to be God. From the Gospel accounts, he appeared to be like everyone else. No one noted anything visually unique about him. How could he be a human and God at the same time? I didn't believe him, but he sure got my attention. It was a fascinating claim. I wasn't aware of anyone significant in any religious system ever making such an outlandish assertion. I kept wondering, *Could this be true?*

I was intrigued by many of the parables that Jesus taught. A parable is simply a short story or illustration designed to teach a truth or moral lesson. They were deep. I had to slow down and really think about their meaning. Jesus seemed to have an unusual level of understanding of human nature. Something resonated within me that his teachings might actually be true, but I didn't know why. I kept on reading in secret. Even though I had announced my intentions to my wife and kids and to the lab staff at work, I still didn't want anyone to know I was actually reading the Bible.

Luke

Luke is the third book in the New Testament. The same basic story was being told again! *S*everal things caught my eye this time. Luke, the author of the book, was a physician like me and was said to have been an excellent historian. Consequently, I did extra research about him.

I learned that Luke was very precise in the naming of cities, countries, and rulers in his writings. In fact, modern archaeology and geography have verified the historical accuracy of Luke's writings.[1-6] I was impressed by the amount of material available to confirm this. Luke's writings were applauded by modern historians for their precision and easily rivaled the most renowned works of other ancient writers. Sir William M. Ramsay, a famous historian and archaeologist, wrote:

Luke is a historian of the first rank; not merely are his statements of fact trustworthy, he is possessed of the true historic sense...in short, this author should be placed along with the greatest of historians.[7]

Consider Luke's strong statement at the beginning of chapter one:

Many have undertaken to draw up an account of the things that have been fulfilled among us, just as they were handed down to us by those who from the first were eyewitnesses and servants of the word. Therefore, since I myself have carefully investigated everything from the beginning, it seemed good also to me to write an orderly account for you, most excellent Theophilus, so that you may know the certainty of the things you have been taught. (Luke 1:1-4 NIV)

Luke claimed to have researched the eyewitness accounts of Jesus. Jesus drew huge crowds due to his teachings and the miracles he performed. He was under intense scrutiny by religious rulers who wanted to discredit him. Luke either carefully interviewed those who saw these things firsthand or checked out their stories while visiting Israel. Physicians even in his day were highly trained in taking a good history. He applied these skills in his research into the story of Jesus. This really raised my curiosity, and my doubting heart began to waver just a bit. I felt that I could trust a fellow doctor and colleague.

Many of the miracles Luke described involved the healing of medical conditions. For me, there could be no better investigator than a physician. I was very intrigued, because physicians usually emphatically discount miracles! Any doctor would ask pointed questions and be very qualified to ascertain the validity of eyewitness accounts. Luke would have been able to interview, examine, and test the people who were healed or who saw the miracles. Luke was attesting that he personally investigated each and every miracle that he recorded in his Gospel and found them to be genuine. *Wow!* I thought. This gave the account more credibility to my scientific mind. I began to focus and read more intently.

When I read about Jesus raising a little girl from the dead, I was awestruck. Her father, Jairus, had come to Jesus in a panic because his little girl was dying. Jesus, however, was delayed by another incident, and the young girl died. Here is Luke's account:

> When he arrived at the house of Jairus, he did not let anyone go in with him except Peter, John and James, and the child's father and mother. Meanwhile, all the people were wailing and mourning for her. "Stop wailing," Jesus said. "She is not dead but asleep."
> They laughed at him, knowing that she was dead. But he took her by the hand and said, "My child, get up!" Her spirit returned, and at once she stood up. Then Jesus told them to give her something to eat. Her parents were astonished, but he ordered them not to tell anyone what had happened. (Luke 8:51-56 NIV)

This story gripped me and wrenched my heart in a way that I had never experienced before. I identified with the father because I had two young children of my own. *Did this really happen?* I asked myself over and over. I realized that Luke may have interviewed this girl when writing his account. Although I didn't know if she was still alive at the time it was written, it could have been an amazing interview for him. A doctor would investigate a claim of this type thoroughly. A miracle of healing is one thing, but being raised from the dead is quite another. Even though I still didn't believe it, something inside of me wanted it to be true. *Maybe it's because I have children and I am afraid to die, afraid for them to die,* I thought. I realized if this resurrection was true, then it would explain many things.

I had always fretted about something happening to my family because I was taught via evolution that we are nothing more than highly evolved organic soup. My heart never wanted this to be true, especially now that I had a family of my own. I wanted there to be an answer to death. The story of Jairus's daughter gave my heart hope, even though the story seemed farfetched. My heart began to process that if this were true, then eternal life was a possibility. I finally realized that eternal life was what my heart had been yearning for. The cries of my heart for eternal life had been garbled by evolution that made living forever impossible. I couldn't understand what my heart was saying because my paradigm of life made the words of eternity unintelligible. If eternal life was a reality, it would answer my uncertainty about the future of my family and my memories. If my memories were to have any meaning, they had to be rooted in eternity. They had to be permanent and last forever, since there is never enough time with the people you love. I was fascinated.

By this time, I had forgotten about my Christian neighbors. I wasn't even thinking about finding evidence to demonstrate their hypocrisy. I was fully engaged in researching Jesus. If I came across a reference that was interesting, I purchased the book from Amazon. All of my free time was consumed reading and researching anything and everything I could find.

John

The fourth book in the New Testament is John, written by the apostle John who lived with Jesus for three years. An apostle was a close follower of Jesus who witnessed his miracles and physically saw him after he was resurrected. Apostles were specifically chosen and commissioned by God to preach the message of salvation. I was immediately drawn into the meaning of the text. I began to focus more intently on the actual words Jesus spoke.

The concept of Jesus being God in human form was fascinating. John clearly stated that Jesus was God visiting his creation called earth. I was thinking, *Whoa! If this really happened, it would be the most remarkable event in human history.* Jesus also made some profound statements that kept me thinking for days. An example follows:

Philip said, "Lord, show us the Father and that will be enough for us."

Jesus answered: "Don't you know me, Philip, even after I have been among you such a long time? Anyone who has seen me has seen the Father. How can you say, 'Show us the Father'? Don't you believe that I am in the Father, and that the Father is in me? The words I say to you are not just my own. Rather, it is the Father, living in me, who is doing his work. Believe me when I say that I am in the Father and the Father is in me; or at least believe on the evidence of the miracles themselves. (John 14:8-11 NIV)

Jesus was telling the disciples they were looking at God face to face. Jesus was claiming to be the express representation of God in the flesh. I learned that this is referred to as "God incarnate." This blew my mind, but I wasn't yet fully convinced. These verses made me ponder:

Jesus said to her, "I am the resurrection and the life. He who believes in me will live, even though he dies; and whoever lives and believes in me will never die. Do you believe this?" (John 11:25-26 NIV)

Jesus was clearly saying he possessed eternal life. I did not understand a lot about religion, but I knew of no other religion that ever claimed God himself had come to earth professing to have the power of eternal life. The promise of life after death flooded my mind and pumped hope into my heart. I wasn't going to cave in yet, but it was an awesome concept to reflect upon.

I began to notice a difference in my attitude and motives as I continued to investigate Jesus. I started off angry and seeking evidence against Christian hypocrisy, but now that was all gone. I was searching for answers to questions in my heart that I didn't know were there until I started reading the Bible. The words seemed to reveal and expose some of my deepest yearnings and questions about life. The stories made me think about things I had never considered before.

As I continued to read, the words seemed alive. My heart was racing and goose bumps were appearing on my arms along with a tingling sensation. *What is happening to me?* I wondered. *This book is moving me, and I don't understand why. It seems to be talking to me directly.* It felt crazy to have those thoughts, but my gut instinct knew the words were speaking to me personally. I couldn't stopping reading the study Bible on the computer.

The next day, while on a plane trip to New Orleans, I continued reading the book of John. By now I was so caught up in these new ideas, I didn't even care if others saw me reading the Bible. In fact, as I was reading John, I unexpectedly began to tear up. I was horrified. I was in public and water was welling up in my eyes and even spilling out. *Why in the world am I crying? What is wrong with me?* I shifted in my seat to face the window in fear that the man next to me would see me. I shook my head and smacked myself on each cheek to "wake up." The guy next to me *was* staring at me. He was alarmed with a puzzled look on his face.

The words were doing something to me in the depths of my being that I could not understand. They were grabbing me and beckoning me to ponder them. *The level of comprehension of human behavior in these stories is profound!* I marveled. I kept asking myself, *What human being could come up with such words, lessons, or revelations?* I had to stop and really think about what was being said. I felt something resonating deep within my heart.

THE THREE QUESTIONS

While the crucifixion of Jesus is described in all four Gospels, I was struck by several things during my reading of this event in the book of John. I particularly wanted answers to the following questions:

1. Why couldn't Jesus just give everyone eternal life if he was God? Why couldn't God simply forgive everyone?

2. If Jesus was God, then why was he crucified? Why did he have to die to provide me eternal life? Was the death of Jesus really necessary?

3. Why didn't God create many ways to heaven instead of only one?

I mulled over these questions for a long time. For some reason, I had passed over the significance of the crucifixion as I read the first three Gospels. Before finishing the New Testament I needed to find answers. Since my computer study Bible included lengthy explanations to help explain certain verses and passages, that is where I started my search.

First, I first learned that I was considered a sinner. I thought about it for a minute and had to admit this was true. I had lied, stolen, cheated, and done a lot of bad things, but so had everyone else I had known. Okay, so I was a sinner. So what?

I also learned from the Bible that the penalty for my sin was death—eternal death. And then it sunk in. Flashbacks from The Ski Trip and Marco Island came rushing back into my mind. If God was sinless, perfect, and pure, then he could not tolerate any sin in his presence. Not even one. Eternal life with God could only be accomplished if I had no sins. If eternal life was spent with God then eternal death was spent without him. *Is this what going to hell meant?* I wondered. This would mean that death is not the end like evolution had taught me, but the start of eternity.

I began to put it together. My sins would separate me from God forever unless there was a way to completely remove them. How could I do that, though? The Bible taught me that I couldn't, but God provided a way for me through his son Jesus. I found a Bible verse that summed it up in one sentence:

God made him who had no sin to be sin for us, so that in him we might become the righteousness of God. (2 Corinthians 5:21 NIV)

This verse teaches that because of what Jesus did on the cross, God is able to give sinful man a sinless standing before him. Jesus, who was sinless, somehow became sin and bore the judgment of sin in order to pay the price for sin. *Wow! What a wild concept*, I thought. But there was a catch! It didn't happen automatically. I had to *believe* in Jesus as the son of God, *accept* his sacrifice, and *turn away* from my sins.

I had to digest that for awhile. It was beginning to make sense to me, but it was a heavy concept to grasp. My goal was to understand the Christian doctrine as best I could before I decided whether or not to reject it.

I was very intrigued about what I had just learned about the possible relationship between sin and death. I was very familiar with the concept of physical death and was also afraid of it, as most people are. I had always been taught that death was a natural part of human existence and the driving force behind evolution. In that scenario, death naturally selected out those life forms that were weaker and less able to survive in an evolving world: "survival of the fittest." Death and randomness were the "creators."

I must admit, though, that evolution and death never made sense to me. Why would we evolve simply to die? Why would human life evolve to a point of having love, memories, and families only to watch them slowly perish and decay back into nothing? Are we truly highly evolved beings if our love is nothing more than a fleeting moment of chemical reactions slowly fizzling out towards the final reaction, death? My heart had never been satisfied with this explanation of death even though it was scientific. I was very intrigued that death might have an explanation and origin. The Bible said that the origin and reason for death was sin.

I had a hard time with this concept, because even the New Testament asserts that death entered the human race through the initial sin of Adam. I felt as though I was back with The Ski Trip kooks, but I put up with it because it *did* provide an explanation for why death exists in our world. I was also very curious, because the story of Adam and Eve suggested that man was not originally created to die. Man, according to the Bible, was created to live forever. This meant that something was wrong with our current world and state of existence. Death is not "natural", just "part of life," or the means for evolutionary progress like I had been taught, but the result of a tragedy, when man first sinned against God.

This resonated with me, since eternity was written all over my heart. I didn't want to die and leave my family, and the idea of death never felt right or natural to me. *Could this be the reason?* I wondered. *Could it be that death seems so wrong and painful to me simply because it's not supposed to be this way?*

I flashed back to the death of my grandfather when I was eight years old. My mom came into the room sobbing. Her hand was over her eyes to hide the tears running down her face. "Your 'Pop Pop' has died," she whimpered.

"What do you mean?" I asked.

"He's gone. He died last night in his sleep."

The car ride to my grandmother's house was long and everyone was silent. It didn't really hit me what death meant until we got there. He was the first person close to me who had died. As we drove up it began to set in. The old white house with the picket fence seemed empty. He used to greet us at the gate, but no one was there. As we walked up I noticed his sweater wasn't on his lawn chair. His slippers were not by the door. Everything seemed cold, empty, and barren. My heart couldn't understand where he went or why he was gone.

When we walked inside, my grandmother was in the kitchen. As soon as she saw us she started crying. Pop Pop's wheelchair wasn't by the radio anymore. I didn't hear his shuffle coming to greet me. I went into the living room and began to sob. It hurt so badly. A part of me and my memories had been ripped out of me and thrown into an unknown and lost place. There were no answers or explanations. I wasn't comforted by the remarks everyone was saying. "He lived a 'good long life' and had 'passed away peacefully.' " No! Something was dreadfully wrong. I didn't know how to express myself except with tears and groans. I wanted him back! I missed his hugs! I wanted to hear his snoring one more time.

I also realized I hadn't said goodbye. I had never told him I loved him. I had taken him for granted whenever I was there. I had let him go about his old man routine without sitting down and playing with him or talking to him, and now he was gone. I had always assumed he would be there. My "Mom Mom" held me and told me he was "in a better place," but where was that? Her words seemed like nice ideas made up to make me feel better.

The next day we drove to the funeral parlor. My heart was in my stomach. Everyone was dressed up, mostly in black. We went in and sat down near the front. The casket was open and I could see Pop Pop's nose sticking up out of the coffin. A man gave a speech I didn't hear because I was staring and fixated on the coffin. When we finally walked by the coffin to "pay our respects" it was awful, scary, weird, sad, and heart wrenching at the same time. He looked pale, silent, and stiff. I kept waiting for him to sit up, but he didn't.

How could this be my Pop Pop? How could he be gone? Why? Where did he go? What did this all mean? My nice little Brady Bunch life had been torn wide open by death.

My thoughts lingered here for a while. When my thoughts returned to the present I realized I had been weeping thinking about him. It hit me harder the second time, because now I had a family. Would my children and grandkids have to go through this with me one day? Was life even worth it? I couldn't bear such questions anymore and snapped myself out of it. Where was I? I got back into my thought processes to try to forget the pain.

I had been thinking about sin as a possible reason for death, but this involved Adam and Eve. The Bible was clear that they were created. I knew it wasn't just a parable or story, because Jesus mentioned them and their son in the New Testament as real people. I also thought, *Could I really have been created?* Creation had seemed stupid and impossible when I was eighteen, but now it was actually a little attractive. There was nothing comforting, meaningful, or encouraging about being a random chance event in time that only existed for itself with nothing to look forward to but non-existence. If I was created, then God had created me, and that would imply that I have meaning and value to God. God certainly would not create junk! My heart yearned for meaning, but my mind quickly rebuffed the idea by reminding me of the consequences. If true, then as God's creation, I would also be accountable to him. I didn't want that! These were wild thoughts I was having, but if there was even a remote chance that it was all true, I wanted to know.

THE THREE QUESTIONS ANSWERED

I was now able to answer the three sets of questions. I had expected to find dumb or illogical religious answers based on fluffy, sissy faith stuff, but I was wrong. The answers actually made sense to me. I was able to understand the reasoning behind the doctrine, but I wasn't ready to accept it.

1. Why couldn't Jesus just give everyone eternal life if he was God? Why couldn't God just forgive everyone?

I read an interesting analogy which provided the answer. In a court of law if I have a fine, it has to be paid. The judge does not dismiss the fine because he is a nice guy or a loving judge. God as a righteous judge has to punish sin. He can't just dismiss everyone's case. It also occurred to me that if a person owed me money and asked me to forgive the debt and I did so, then I still paid for it. There was still a cost to me. This made sense to me and helped answer question number two.

2. If Jesus was God, then why was he crucified? Why did he have to die to provide me eternal life? Was the death of Jesus really necessary?

I learned that as a righteous judge God has to punish sin, but as a loving God he also wants to save sinners. He demands that the fine be paid, but then he paid it through Jesus and his death on the cross. If the penalty for my sin is death and separation from God, then my substitute would have to be another man dying in my place. God had to both become a man *and* die in order to perfectly and exactly take my place.

I recognized that another sinful man couldn't take my place, much less everyone who has ever lived. Only God who is sinless and perfect could be capable of dying once for the sins of the entire world, past, present, and future. If dying for someone to pay for his or her sins was possible, then only God could perform such a rescue mission.

I discovered that another reason that God had to be the sacrifice was the requirement to enter heaven. If sinful man needs God's perfect and sinless standing to be with him in heaven, then it makes sense that only God can provide this. I didn't necessarily believe any of this, but the explanations were logical and intuitively coherent.

3. Why didn't God create many ways to heaven instead of only one?

This was a topic that usually made me angry. The "only one way to heaven" idea was very irritating to me. I already understood the idea that God had to come as a man and die. The reason is that no one but God could be the perfect, sinless sacrifice and substitute for all of humankind to satisfy the death penalty for sin. If God had to become a man and die, then there is "only one way" by definition. If Jesus really was God and death was sin's penalty, then he had to be the only way. I had to admit this to myself. Again, this assumed that Jesus was God and that the reason for death was sin.

My heart was softening because I began to marvel that God, if he really existed, sacrificed his only son! I was awestruck that God subjected himself to incomprehensible sufferings and limitations by send-ing Jesus to earth for the purpose of dying on the cross for sin. If this was true, then God did everything imaginable to save mankind. The "only one way" provision for us, that previously had made me furious, was actually an incomprehensible choice of God's. If God really did this, it would be the most amazing and mind-blowing rescue mission of infinite love ever performed.

I mused that this seemed like a pretty crazy story for someone to have dreamed up or invented in their mind. Who could ever conceive of such a story? The possibility of the God-man on earth to save mankind by dying for mankind was such an incredible story that it paradoxically made it a little more believable to me. Maybe people didn't make it up. Could it really be from God?

I continued to be awed by the possibility that God died for me to save me from my sins and separation from him forever. Jesus was a savior from sin and hell. The entire Christian message began to appear more like a rescue mission sent from heaven than the phony religious rituals and Sunday charades I thought it was. The real meaning and power behind a so-called "savior" finally began to impact me. The idea of God on earth in the flesh blew my mind, but God on earth as a savior for me personally was unfathomable. I was still slightly irritated and offended by the idea of needing someone to save me, but I kept on go-ing in my reading. I was very torn, because everything I was discover-ing made sense. It was "good news" and something my heart actually wanted, but my mind just couldn't accept something so far gone from the world in which I was raised.

I continued reading the last few pages in the book of John. A real zinger came at the end when he wrote,

"Jesus did many other miraculous signs in the presence of his disciples, which are not recorded in this book. But these are written that you may believe that Jesus is the Christ, the Son of God, and that by believing you may have life in his name. This is the disciple who testifies to these things and who wrote them down. We know that his testimony is true." (John 20:30-31, 21:24 NIV)

My heart sank. John was saying, "I was there. I saw, touched, and walked with God. Eternal life really exists because of what Jesus has done. I saw him resurrected." I kept thinking about this claim. *If true, then John walked, ate, lived, and talked with God*! This was a mind-blowing possibility. I had no idea the Gospels had this information! *Why in the world didn't I know about this?* The reality that this was an actual eyewitness account impacted me greatly.

Well, the first four books of the New Testament certainly had my mind reeling. They had stories I didn't expect and explanations that surprised me, and they contained the only real message of hope that I had ever heard of. I was taken aback by the Bible. I felt weird being so "into it." I was reading it every moment I could spare. There were still a lot of books I had not yet read in the New Testament, and I wasn't about to make any hasty decisions. I kept reading.

THE APOSTLE PAUL

The next book after the Gospel of John is called Acts, and it describes events that took place after Jesus was allegedly raised from the dead. It is the fifth book in the New Testament and tells the story of how the first converts to Christianity spread the Gospel. They began meeting together and eventually started churches.

Acts includes the story of a man named Saul, a religious Jewish leader who persecuted and killed Christians. Many of the Jewish religious leaders believed that the teachings of Jesus were contrary to the religious laws they had received from God. They felt so strongly about this that they were killing and incarcerating Christians. Saul had everything going for him in life. He was highly educated, in a position of prominence and power, and very dedicated to his religious leadership. Saul's life was completely changed when he supposedly had an encounter with the resurrected Jesus.

After his encounter with Jesus, Saul's complete reversal from hating and killing Christians to a defender and evangelist for the Christian faith blew me away. For a religious Jewish leader to suddenly proclaim Jesus was God was career suicide in his day. I couldn't think of any logical reason to explain Saul's behavior. I didn't want to face the obvious reason that would easily explain his transformation. The book of Acts claimed that Jesus directly and personally revealed himself to Saul during a trip on which Saul was on a mission to kill Christians. If this was true and Saul had indeed met God, then I had a great explanation for Saul's behavioral flip-flop, but if it wasn't true, I had no reasonable explanation for his lifelong change. This really bugged me.

I kept reading and learned that Saul's name was changed to Paul a little later. He also went on to write much of the New Testament. I continued reading the New Testament and read more of Paul's writings. I was in a stupor about this man's passion for Jesus. I begrudgingly couldn't think of any logical reason for Paul's behavior, except that he actually saw the resurrected Jesus and was directly commissioned by him to spread the good news, just like the Bible said.

Later on in the New Testament, Paul further revealed his heart and dedication towards Jesus. Some of Paul's statements were very profound. For example, he wrote a letter to a church in a city called Philippi and said this:

> *For to me, living means living for Christ, and dying is even better. But if I live, I can do more fruitful work for Christ. So I really don't know which is better. I'm torn between two desires: I long to go and be with Christ, which would be far better for me. But for your sakes, it is better that I continue to live. (Philippians 1:21-24 New Living Translation)*

What could make this guy say that his existence on earth was living for Jesus? Paul was absolutely certain that he was going to heaven. He knew that if he died then he was going to be with Jesus. In his heart, he actually wanted to die because he knew how much better it would be in heaven. I had never heard of anyone with that kind of certainty about death. Something struck me.

Paul wasn't just some man who heard about a religion and decided to convert. He was an eyewitness originator and founder of Christianity who claimed to have personally met the resurrected Jesus and received direct instructions from him. Paul claimed that he received firsthand information directly from God. He claimed that God chose him as an original messenger for the Christian faith. If Paul did not really see Jesus then Paul would have knowingly built his life on a lie. Intellectual theories or even the most zealous religious beliefs don't make someone change permanently and maintain their convictions if they *know* they are making it up. Many religious people sacrifice themselves for what they believe, *but* they don't know it's a lie or false. In fact, they passionately believe in what they are doing.

If Paul, however, really did see Jesus, then Paul's behavior made all the sense in the world. His world would have been turned upside down. His paradigm of life would have been reversed. Yes, I had to agree: *I too would drop everything and follow God if this happened to me.*

A little later in the same book, Philippians, Paul wrote this:

I was circumcised when I was eight days old. I am a pure-blooded citizen of Israel and a member of the tribe of Benjamin—a real Hebrew if there ever was one! I was a member of the Pharisees, who demand the strictest obedience to the Jewish law. I was so zealous that I harshly persecuted the church. And as for righteousness, I obeyed the law without fault.

I once thought these things were valuable, but now I consider them worthless because of what Christ has done. Yes, everything else is worthless when compared with the infinite value of knowing Christ Jesus my Lord. For his sake I have discarded everything else, counting it all as garbage, so that I could gain Christ and become one with him. (Philippians 3:5-10 NLT)

I was dumbfounded by this perspective. Paul had everything going for him in life and suddenly counted it all as worthless refuse?! From killing Christians to this?! Paul wasn't even looking for Jesus or searching for answers in life before his fateful journey on which he met Jesus. Jesus intervened and got Paul's attention. The entire story of Jesus was about what God initiated to save man. Christianity seemed to be God seeking man. I marveled at this for many hours. Questions flooded my mind. If God was the initiator, had I been ignoring or rejecting his calling me in the past? Were my grandmother, The Ski Trip kooks, the college campus kook with the cross, cellular molecular biology, Marco Island, and *Our Town* his attempts to reach me? If God is real, is he still active today?

Paul also described something else that caught my attention:

For what I received I passed on to you as of first importance: that Christ died for our sins according to the Scriptures, that he was buried, that he was raised on the third day according to the Scriptures, and that he appeared to Peter, and then to the Twelve. After that, he appeared to more than five hundred of the brothers at the same time, most of whom are still living, though some have fallen asleep. Then he appeared to James, then to all the apostles, and last of all he appeared to me also, as to one abnormally born. (1 Corinthians 15:3-8 NIV)

Paul claimed that over five hundred people saw the risen Jesus at one time. This greatly surprised me. After having read the first four books of the New Testament that described the life of Jesus, I thought that the alleged sightings of the resurrected Jesus were only witnessed by a few people at a time. Five hundred people at once was quite a bold claim.

Furthermore, this was written at a time when Paul's claim could have and most assuredly would have been disputed or refuted, but it never was. I knew such a statement would never hold up under the scrutiny and persecution of the times in which Paul lived unless it was true. You just couldn't manufacture such a story and get away with it. Why would he even make such a statement if it were not true? Why risk it? What would Paul have to gain by lying? He had already ruined his career and entire life as a prominent Jewish religious leader. Why be made a laughingstock and be called a liar? He became neither. That was compelling.

His boldness, passion, and motives for such a complete transformation perplexed me. He was always getting beaten, thrown in jail, and persecuted for his message about Jesus, for claiming adamantly that Jesus was the answer. This wasn't an attractive religion to join or make up, and yet Paul gave up everything for it only to face adversity. Why? His committed message and consistent life continued to bother me.

THE DILEMMA AND STRUGGLE

I kept reading and finished the entire New Testament. I was now faced with a dilemma. Jesus was portrayed as the one and only true God, who not only created me but also came and died for me to save me from sin because he loved me. I was very uncomfortable about outright rejecting Jesus without further thought or investigation. What if it *was* true? I asked myself, *Was there anything negative about this message?* From what I had discovered so far, I had to admit the answer was no. It was all positive, but something was still holding me back. My heart said "yes," but my mind said "no way."

I couldn't even fall back on a popular belief I had read about on the Internet, that Jesus was nothing more than a great moral teacher or wise man. This line of thinking stated that Jesus didn't perform real miracles, of course, nor was he really the son of God. He was just a good man, a religious prophet. After having objectively read and studied the entire New Testament, however, I knew for certain that these ideas were completely false. It was absolutely clear to me that Jesus was claiming to be God in the flesh. And if he was only a great moral teacher, then why would he blatantly lie about who he was? What kind of great moral teacher would that be? Would his disciples passionately live for an obvious liar—after he had died? Are doctors who lie to their patients about their diagnoses to make them feel better good doctors?

I was very confused because I was finding answers that intuitively made sense to me, answered many baffling questions, and explained a lot of what I was feeling and had experienced in life. The conflict was raging because the answers seemed too radical, very outrageous, and too good to be true. If something is too good to be true then it's usually not. I knew that the things I was reading and learning were not mainstream ideas. My mind couldn't tolerate such thoughts, even though my heart wanted answers. I had to keep going. It was all or nothing now.

Chapter Four

The Investigation Phase II:

The Resurrection of Jesus

If eternal life existed, then I wanted it. I recall saying to myself, *This will be the most important question I have ever tried to answer*. If Jesus really arose from the dead, then the resurrection was the final proof that Jesus was God. The resurrection would validate that Jesus accomplished his mission of dying for the sins of the world, and this event would prove that eternal life really existed. Jesus would be the only way because as God he died for the sins of mankind. The only question was, could I *really* believe it? Everything now hinged on the resurrection of Jesus. Did it *really* happen? I decided to examine the resurrection in detail. If everything hinged upon Jesus being God, then this was *the test*.

I remembered the book my wife had given me. I rushed upstairs. There it was, still on the night stand where I had left it months ago. It had been quietly irking me for months because of its title, *The New Evidence That Demands a Verdict* by Josh McDowell.[8] Subconsciously, the word "demands" had been nagging at me. *Oh, yeah? Demand this!* I had thought in the past, when I left it sitting there without even touching it. *You can't make me read you!* I would smirk, but now, ironically, I wanted to.

I walked over to the table and stood over it. I hesitated, but then picked it up with both hands and read the title again. *What evidence?* I wondered. I was surprised at its size now that I was actually holding it. It reminded me of medical school textbooks. As I skimmed through it, I saw that it was a textbook that assimilated and compiled facts and opinions from a plethora of sources. There was an entire section on the resurrection of Jesus, and it was loaded with references.

I checked out Josh McDowell on the internet and discovered he was a well-known Christian who defended the Christian faith. I was immediately concerned about bias, but I still wanted to read what was in this book. I also purchased other books and references that were mentioned.[9-11] I wasn't too worried since I could make my own decisions from reading the four Gospels myself.

I began my intensive investigation into the evidence for the resurrection of Jesus by looking for historical facts. What facts could I find about the resurrection story of Jesus? I wanted to start with easy and noncontroversial facts. Being a doctor, I started with the medical aspects of crucifixion.

THE DEATH

Did Jesus really die? I read about an explanation called the "swoon theory."[12] This proposed that Jesus didn't really die on the cross. Instead, he remained alive and was able to escape from the tomb. This would explain his appearances, to some extent. This immediately seemed farfetched, but I wanted to examine all the possibilities for myself.

After a few hours of study, it was clear to me that this was not a plausible theory. Jesus was beaten beyond recognition, crucified, and stabbed in the side with a spear. He would have suffered heavy internal bleeding, a collapsed lung, severe dehydration, a possible punctured heart, and shock from blood loss, just to a name a few of the complications. The Roman guards didn't break his legs because he was dead, according to John's Gospel (John 19:32-33). It was very clear that the Roman guards and the ever-present Jewish religious leaders wanted him dead and would have made sure of it.

I was surprised to find a modern article on the crucifixion of Jesus in *The Journal of the American Medical Association*.[13] By using a modern medical analysis of the facts, my doctor colleagues had confirmed that Jesus could not have survived the crucifixion. I was now satisfied, along with my peers, that Jesus had died on the cross. This was my first fact.

THE BURIAL

All four Gospels, which were biographies of Jesus, by Matthew, Mark, Luke, and John, stated that Jesus was buried in a tomb that belonged to Joseph of Arimathea. Joseph was a prominent Jewish religious leader and a member of the Sanhedrin. The Sanhedrin was the religious ruling council that had condemned Jesus during their trial of him. According to Luke, this Joseph was a secret disciple of Jesus and had not consented to the Sanhedrin's decision, even though he was a member. Joseph went to Pontius Pilate and asked for the body of Jesus so he could bury it. Nicodemus, who was also a Jewish religious leader, helped Joseph by wrapping Jesus' body in burial clothing and ointments. Why spend the time, effort, and money to wrap the body if it wasn't going to be buried? This placed two unlikely witnesses at the burial site for Jesus, and they could confirm he was actually dead and buried.

It seemed obvious to me that this was not a story early Christians would have made up if it were not true. Two prominent Jewish religious leaders burying Jesus would be scandalous in the volatile times surrounding the death of Jesus. This would have been refuted publically and easily proven to be a lie if it were not true.

The Bible also records that Roman guards were placed outside the tomb and a large stone was placed in front of the entrance. In those days a tomb was sealed off by rolling a large stone, usually one to three tons, in front of the entrance to the tomb. This adds at least two more witnesses to the burial site, verifying its historicity. Adding these four witnesses to the two women and two disciples who went to the tomb brings the number of witnesses to at least eight. If Jesus had not been buried, many people could have easily refuted the claim that he was, but no one ever did. I was satisfied that Jesus was actually buried in a tomb as the Bible states. This was my second fact.[14]

THE EMPTY TOMB

I next wanted to establish that the tomb of Jesus was truly found empty on the Sunday after his burial. Surprisingly, substantiating that this was true was easier than I anticipated. The evidence that the tomb was empty was a historical fact that did not appear to even be disputable.[15] If the tomb was not empty, then Christianity would have been destroyed in a few days. The religious authorities would have been eager to produce the body of Jesus and end the hoax right then and there. Furthermore, the Gospels state that the Jewish leaders paid the soldiers to claim that the body was stolen. Why would they claim that if the body was still in the tomb? I couldn't argue with this logic.

The first witnesses were women, which didn't seem to be a big deal to me, until I learned that in the Jewish patriarchal society the testimony of women was not considered trustworthy nor was it admissible in court.[16] This was another interesting twist in the events surrounding the resurrection story that an author would have no motive to make up.

If, somehow, the women and disciples had mistakenly gone to the wrong tomb, then the body of Jesus was still in the right tomb. It wouldn't have taken long for Jesus' body to have been found and paraded in the streets of Jerusalem to destroy the Christian message. I grudgingly acknowledged that the empty tomb was not in dispute and was an easy third fact.[17, 18]

THE BODY

If the tomb was empty, then the body went somewhere. It is a historical fact that the body of Jesus was never produced. Where could it have gone? There were three possibilities. First, the body could have been removed from the tomb by the disciples of Jesus. Second, the body could have been removed by Jesus' adversaries (e.g., the Romans or the Jewish religious leaders). The third possibility is that Jesus rose from the dead (i.e., was resurrected).

Did the disciples of Jesus steal his body as part of a resurrection hoax? At first thought, I really liked this hypothesis because I knew from watching the news over the years that religious people will do crazy things. Once I began to examine it in detail, however, this theory fell apart. [19]

Stealing the body would have required the disciples to somehow get past the Roman guards and move the several-ton stone from the front of the tomb without anyone realizing what had happened. The Roman guards were facing the death penalty if they failed in their orders to guard the body.[20] The disciples had no motive or presupposition to invent an idea like the resurrection. They were shocked and in mourning that Jesus was dead. Even though he had spoken to them about his return, they didn't yet understand and weren't expecting anything, so pretending that he was resurrected by stealing the body wouldn't make sense to them. I had to agree that this scenario was not believable.

The enemies of Jesus could have easily gotten the cooperation of the Roman guards and taken his body, but I had to concede they also had no motive. If the enemies of Jesus did take the body, they would have quickly produced it to display all around Jerusalem when the stories of the resurrection started surfacing. This would have killed Christianity once and for all. I agreed that this also was not a possible explanation.

The Gospels also record that the linen cloths used to wrap and embalm the body of Jesus were left in the tomb. The handkerchief that had been around Jesus' head was also folded separately by itself. If someone stole the body, why would they take the time to unravel all the linens? John records that one of the disciples saw the linen cloths and immediately believed (John 20:8). Luke reports that Peter marveled when he looked into the tomb (Luke 24:12). Why? These two men must have seen something extraordinary in the arrangement of the burial cloths and linens that could not be explained. If these cloths were simply unraveled after three days, they wouldn't be able to be restored to an orderly arrangement.

I had a wild idea. If Jesus had been resurrected, then God could have left the burial garments intact as they were originally wrapped, but without the body inside. If this was the case, how could anyone explain how the body was removed from the many layers of wrappings without disturbing them? This would be a miracle that could explain the reaction of the disciples. The Romans and the Jewish leaders surely must have examined the tomb, but they remained silent. I was fascinated. This led me to the last possibility to explain the empty tomb: the resurrection. I next examined the claims that the resurrection actually happened.

THE APPEARANCES

All four Gospels document separate occasions where multiple people actually saw and touched the resurrected Jesus. There are several independent attestations of His appearances, including documentation by the apostle Paul. For example, Paul, John, and Luke each affirm that Jesus appeared to the remaining disciples. The women who arrived first at the tomb are attested to by both John and Matthew. As previously mentioned, Paul documents in the New Testament book 1 Corinthians that Jesus appeared to over five hundred people at once. He even states that many of those people were still alive at the time that he later wrote his account. In all, fifteen different appearances of the resurrected Jesus are mentioned in the New Testament.[21]

I couldn't find any documentation where someone contested the appearances of Jesus to his followers. There was absolutely zero refutation of the resurrection by the Jews or anyone opposing Jesus.[22] Their silence was shocking. Why wasn't the resurrection adamantly contested if it was false?

I now had to account for these alleged appearances of Jesus and the rise of Christianity out of nowhere. *Could the disciples have merely convinced themselves that they saw Jesus by hallucinations or vivid imaginations?* I wondered. Medically, people on drugs or with organic brain disease can suffer from hallucinations. I quickly determined, however, that this theory was not plausible. It didn't explain what happened to the body or the behavior of the disciples; it didn't even fit with typical hallucinations or imaginations.[23] Too many people would have had to imagine or hallucinate the same thing at the same time, for instance. The disciples' behavior in no way suggested imaginations or hallucinations. The disciples had nothing to gain by inventing such a story. The Bible is clear that the disciples saw, touched, and even ate with the physical and literal resurrected Jesus. A hallucination, a spirit, or a ghost cannot eat real food or be touched.

If the resurrection was not hallucinated or imagined, then could the followers of Jesus, who wished to carry on his ministry, have intentionally made up the resurrection story? Could Jesus be a myth or a legend?

If this happened immediately after his death, then many of the same problems with the disciples stealing the body of Jesus apply, because they have to get rid of the body. There is no proof that they stole the body or that this was even possible. Why would they choose women witnesses whose testimony was not even admissible in court as the first ones to find the empty tomb? If there was a conspiracy, they would surely stack the deck in their favor rather than include such embarrassing facts as having women as their primary witnesses. What possible motive could they have had? If Jesus was dead, if he hadn't been resurrected, there would have been no power or conviction behind their ministry. In fact, quite the opposite happened.

Is it possible then that the story of Jesus and his resurrection slowly became a legend over many years? This also makes no sense, based on the biblical accounts. It doesn't explain the empty tomb or the sudden appearance of Christianity right after the crucifixion. If later followers slowly added to and made up the stories, they still would have been circulated when hostile witnesses were alive. It would have been easy to demonstrate that the resurrection was an invented legend or hoax. There were too many details recorded that the Jewish religious leaders could have easily shown to be falsified. In the books of Luke and Acts, Luke claimed to have interviewed eyewitnesses and constructed his accounts during his own lifetime.

I ran through all of these scenarios in my mind, but none of them were logical or fit the facts. Something caused this movement of Christianity to catch fire and keep burning even in the face of fierce opposition. This puzzled me and didn't make sense. Even the Jewish religious leaders expected it to fizzle out—unless it was truly from God.

A Pharisee named Gamaliel, who was an expert in religious law and respected by all the people, stood up and ordered that the men be sent outside the council chamber for a while. Then he said to his colleagues, "Men of Israel, take care what you are planning to do to these men! Some time ago there was that fellow Theudas, who pretended to be someone great. About 400 others joined him, but he was killed, and all his followers went their various ways. The whole movement came to nothing. After him, at the time of the census, there was Judas of Galilee. He got people to follow him, but he was killed, too, and all his followers were scattered. So my advice is, leave these men alone. Let them go. If they are planning and doing these things merely on their own, it will soon be overthrown. But if it is from God, you will not be able to overthrow them. You may even find yourselves fighting against God!" (Acts 5:34-39 NLT)

Something else caught my attention about the initial disciples who supposedly saw Jesus resurrected. It was very interesting that they had to be convinced that Jesus was really alive. They did not believe it at first! The disciples were devastated, afraid, and not even anticipating that Jesus would be resurrected. Their leader was dead and they were dejected. Their dreams died at the cross with Jesus.

THE WRONG EXPECTATIONS

Why weren't the disciples expecting Jesus to rise from the dead? Looking back at Jewish history, I learned that the Jewish people were expecting a military leader to appear in Israel who would deliver them from Roman oppression. They called this person the Messiah, which means savior. I discovered that some of their religious leaders did not even believe in resurrection. Those who did taught that it would only occur after the end of the world. The disciples were not expecting the Son of God to die for the sins of the world, culminating in his resurrection. Jesus did not match their idea of the Messiah, and his resurrection was outside their religious beliefs and expectations. They had even argued among themselves about their roles in the supposed "coming kingdom," which they thought was very close to happening.

RADICALLY CHANGED LIVES

After Jesus was allegedly raised from the dead, the disciples were radically changed.[24] Before the resurrection Peter denied Jesus three times when Jesus was arrested, and the rest of the disciples scattered like scared sheep. They went from depressed and scared unbelievers to very courageous and elated proclaimers of eternal life. In the book of Acts, they boldly proclaimed the resurrection of Jesus despite imprisonment, death threats, and beatings. They were ostracized from the mainstream Jewish community. Why would someone do that if they knew it was a hoax that they had dreamed up? I couldn't find a way to explain what could cause these men to suddenly change and come up with an un-Jewish, unprecedented, and unlikely story.

WILLING TO DIE

Another profound fact I discovered was that ten of the remaining apostles of Jesus, including Paul, died cruel and tortuous deaths because they believed Jesus was God and proclaimed that he rose from the dead.[25] I was haunted by the fact that if Jesus had not really risen from the grave, then these men would have died knowing it was a lie.[26] Yet not one of them ever recanted their faith, even under tremendous torture, pain, pressure, and death.[27] I couldn't imagine that one of them wouldn't have cracked if they all knew it was a lie. This was incredibly compelling to me.

Many people die for a lie, but they don't know it's a lie.[28] The disciples would have known they were dying for a lie if they had made it up. *Who would do such a thing?* I wondered. Everything they were hoping for died on the cross if Jesus was not resurrected. All of Jesus' promises about eternal life, heaven, and the forgiveness of sins were null and void if he was dead. A falsified story about a risen carpenter would be absolutely useless to them. I couldn't explain this away for all of these men.

SUMMARY

The historical facts showed that Jesus died and was buried in a tomb which was discovered empty three days later with no explanation for the whereabouts of the body. Immediately after that, multiple people began to allegedly see and interact with the resurrected Jesus, causing the sudden emergence of Christianity. This new religion was started by the Jewish disciples of Jesus, even though it went against their own previous religious beliefs and expectations for the Messiah.

The only logical explanation was the resurrection of Jesus. Based upon the facts, this was the best explanation of the evidence, *but* this involved a miracle of all miracles. My scientific mind had a problem with this, even though I had no other explanations. My heart was excited, but my mind was skeptical. My heart and mind were still at war. I was torn. I felt frustrated that there wasn't a better natural explanation. As I replayed the facts in my mind, I realized that I had overlooked a critical investigative tool, one that should have been triggered by my years of medical training.

Chapter Five

The Investigation - Phase III:

The Ancient Hebrew Scriptures "Old Testament"

I need a stat EKG and cardiac enzymes on this patient! He could be having a heart attack!" I exclaimed to the nurse.

"Okay, Doctor Viehman. I'm calling for them now. I'll get the monitor and call the team."

The secondary tests did indeed confirm the original diagnosis of a heart attack. As a doctor I rarely relied on one piece of evidence to make a diagnosis. During medical training I spent a lot of time in cardiology. When making the diagnosis of a heart attack we relied upon several tests that were independent of each other. The electrocardiogram, or EKG, and a series of blood tests were both used to determine whether or not the patient was having a heart attack. The EKG measures electrical changes in the heart, while the blood tests evaluate damage to the heart cells. When both tests are positive the diagnosis of heart attack is almost certain.

As I considered this memorable moment it occurred to me that there might be an entire line of evidence for Jesus that is completely independent of the four Gospels and eyewitnesses testimonies that I had reviewed. If this indeed turned out to be verifiable then the possibility of the resurrection being a true historical event would be catapulted to a new level of credibility.

I had to persevere to find the truth. This was potentially the most important investigation of my life. With eternity on the line, it was worth the effort. Even though I was feeling a bit worn down and lazy, I realized that in the past I had spent much more time analyzing the stock market and researching investments. With such high stakes, how could I stop now if there was a realistic way to show with absolute truth that God existed?

THE MESSIAH

The apostles of Jesus pointed to the resurrection as proof that he was the savior of the world, but this was not their only piece of evidence used to convince people. The apostles also strongly appealed to the fulfillment of prophecy from their own Hebrew Scriptures as further proof that Jesus was God. Most people did not get a chance to actually see Jesus resurrected, but everyone could be shown the Scriptures. The apostles directly quoted prophecies from their Scriptures and related them to the birth, life, crucifixion, burial, and resurrection of Jesus described in the New Testament. They claimed that Jesus fulfilled these prophecies. This was a major selling point that convinced many people, including Jews, to convert to Christianity. Why? I had to find out.

What were these prophecies from Scriptures? I wondered. I did some research and easily found out. The Hebrew Scriptures were a compilation of ancient writings written by many different authors over an approximate one thousand year period of time. The Jews believed that these writings were the word of God. In other words, God directly inspired certain men to record and write the essential message he gave them. The Scriptures were viewed as sacred. They were diligently kept for thousands of years by men whose entire lives were devoted to copying and accurately preserving them for the next generation. The Scriptures included the history of Israel, genealogies, regulations for religious practice, writings of the prophets, songs, and poems. The last collection of Old Testament Hebrew Scriptures was written around 400 B.C.

What I hadn't realized was that the Jewish people were actually waiting for a Messiah, a savior. They believed this because their ancient Scriptures contained direct prophecies that described many aspects of this Messiah. This was part of their history and would have been common knowledge among the Jews, including Jesus' apostles. They expected their Messiah to be a great person who would save them from their enemies—the Romans, in that day.

Throughout my first reading of the New Testament I saw countless references to these prophetic Scriptures, but I passed them by without giving them much attention. I recalled that King Herod consulted with all of the chief Jewish religious leaders when the wise men went to Jerusalem looking for the one "born King of the Jews." The religious leaders responded yes, the Messiah was to be born in Bethlehem, according to their Scriptures. In Matthew 2:6, they directly quoted one of these Old Testament Scriptures, from Micah 5:2, in substantiating their belief about the Christ to King Herod. The authors of the New Testament kept pointing out how Jesus supposedly fulfilled what was written about the Messiah hundreds and even a thousand years earlier in the Hebrew Scriptures.

Jesus himself also claimed that he was fulfilling the prophecies.

Do not think that I came to destroy the Law or the Prophets. I did not come to destroy but to fulfill. (Matthew 5:17 New King James Version)

He also said the ancient Hebrew Scriptures were written about him.

You search the Scriptures, for in them you think you have eternal life; and these are they which testify of Me. (John 5:39 NKJV)

Jesus even directly claimed that he was the Messiah.

The woman said to Him, "I know that Messiah is coming" (who is called Christ). "When He comes, He will tell us all things."

Jesus said to her, "I who speak to you am He." (John 4:25-26 NKJV)

I had no idea, however, that these Scriptures were basically the same as the Christian Old Testament. Today these same Jewish Scriptures form the Jewish Bible. Their Bible has the books in a different order and combines some of them, but the actual text is almost identical. This was something I didn't know but found very odd.

I didn't know a lot about religion, but it was evident to me that Christianity and Judaism were separate religions in today's world. Most Jews and rabbis do not believe in Jesus. I would thus never expect to find anything related to Jesus in the Hebrew Scriptures (Old Testament), especially because the Old Testament was finished four hundred years before Jesus was born. Neither Jesus nor any reference to him, direct or indirect, would be included in these ancient Scriptures unless he was indeed the fulfillment of the Messiah, as prophesied.

I now understood why Christianity doesn't claim to be a "new" religion but the fulfillment of ancient Judaism. In other words, Christians believe in all of the Hebrew Scriptures as the Word of God. They believe that the God of the Jews is the only true and living God. Christian faith maintains that Jesus Christ is the Messiah that the Jews were waiting for and who was prophesied about in the Bible. I was surprised to learn that early Christianity was mainly Jewish! The apostles and Paul were all Jewish. With the exception of the books of Luke and Acts, the entire New Testament was written by Jews.

It was apparent that these prophecies were potentially very powerful in making a case for or against Jesus. If the Old Testament truly contained unmistakable prophecies that Jesus fulfilled, then this would be very compelling support for Jesus being God's plan to save mankind. I knew it was impossible for someone to write about the future life of an individual in an exact and precise way, and then have it happen exactly as it was foretold, unless there was a divine connection. This would also confirm the inspiration and preservation of the Scriptures.

Looking back on prophecy, the New Testament doctrine of Jesus and salvation from sin was not a new concept. The disciples of Jesus didn't invent a new religion. They were witnesses to the revelation of their own Jewish beliefs and the fulfillment of its prophecies. It would be very difficult to believe that Jesus was only a legend or a myth if his life was actually predicted and described throughout the ancient Hebrew Scriptures, as the authors claimed.

I was immediately captivated, because I realized that the Jews who claimed to know the *only* true and living God believed they had divine revelation from God that a Messiah was coming. It seemed more than coincidental to me that someone claiming to be God came on the scene and claimed to be this Messiah. I was also confused, because I discovered that most Jewish people did not believe Jesus was this Messiah.

The real questions then were, What did the Hebrew Scriptures say about the coming Messiah? What were the prophecies, how many were there, and did Jesus fulfill some, all, or none of them? If they were truly from God and Jesus was God, then He should have fulfilled all of them. I also wanted to know why the Jews rejected Jesus as the Messiah if Jesus did fulfill their own Scriptures.

Before I could make judgments about them, I first needed to understand what a prophecy actually was. I learned that a prophecy is a direct description of a future event. These were written down and proclaimed by men called prophets. This was one of their functions, but they also had many more. Did these ancient Hebrew Scriptures, some written more than a thousand years before Jesus lived, actually contain details about his life? I wanted to find out the truth for myself.

Evidently, there were also "pictures" of Jesus throughout the Old Testament. A picture, used in this context, is an indirect enactment of a future event by an occurrence in the past, or you could say it is a series of circumstances and actions that indirectly describe a future incident in advance. Another word for this is "foreshadowing," so called because it shows a future event in a graphic way, much like a shadow is an outline of an actual physical form.

I looked at the prophecies first, since they were supposed to be direct references to the Messiah. They were present throughout the Old Testament and were written by many different writers at different periods in Israel's history. The prophecies supposedly described the Messiah's birth, life, death, and even his resurrection. My study Bible had a table of many of them. I decided to take them at face value according to Christian tradition first and then examine the other side.

THE PROPHECIES OF THE MESSIAH

I started with a prophecy that described the place of the Messiah's birth. It was written by the prophet Micah around 700 B.C.

But you, Bethlehem Ephrathah,
Though you are little among the thousands of Judah,
Yet out of you shall come forth to Me
The One to be Ruler in Israel,
Whose goings forth are from of old,
From everlasting. (Micah 5:2 NKJV)

The Messiah was to be born in Bethlehem and was everlasting or eternal (always was and always will be). Jesus was born in Bethlehem *and* claimed to be God, who is eternal. This brought to mind a verse I read from John. John describes Jesus as "the Word." He wrote:

In the beginning was the Word, and the Word was with God, and the Word was God.

And the Word became flesh and dwelt among us, and we beheld His glory, the glory as of the only begotten of the Father, full of grace and truth. (John 1:1,14 NKJV.)

John was describing Jesus as God who became a man. Jesus did match these two prophecies, but they were still a bit vague.

Around 700 B.C., a prophet named Isaiah wrote about the manner of the Messiah's birth.

Therefore the Lord himself will give you a sign: The virgin will be with child and will give birth to a son, and will call him Immanuel. (Isaiah 7:14 NIV)

This one got my attention. The Messiah was to be born of a virgin and he was to be called Immanuel, which means "God with us." I shifted in my chair and took a big swallow as I realized Jesus was supposedly born from Mary, who the Bible claimed was a virgin. If Jesus was God then he would have literally been "God with us."

This was such a remarkable prophecy that I analyzed it more closely. The ancient Scriptures were written in Hebrew, but I was reading an English translation. Does the Hebrew really say "virgin," since it was the most critical part of the prophecy? The answer is that Hebrew does not have a specific word for virgin. The Hebrew word used here could mean virgin or a young maiden. The Hebrew Scriptures, however, were translated into Greek by Jewish scholars several hundred years before Jesus. This is called the Septuagint. The Greek language does have a very specific word which can only mean virgin. I wanted to know what the Jewish translators understood the word to mean when they translated it several hundred years before Jesus. I was suspicious that the Christians just assumed it meant a virgin to fit their doctrine. The Septuagint would provide me an unbiased answer. I was shocked to discover that they chose the Greek word that could only mean virgin. There was no way to prove, however, that Jesus was really born from a virgin.

The Messiah was also to be born from the line of King David. King David was the most famous Jewish king, who lived about a thousand years before Jesus. The Jewish people knew from their Scriptures that the Messiah would come from David's lineage. I then remembered that both Luke and Matthew include the genealogies of Jesus. Matthew traces the lineage for Joseph, his father, and Luke delineates Mary's genealogy. Both of Jesus' parents were from King David's lineage. Now I understood what these authors were trying to accomplish. They were making a case for Jesus being the prophesied Messiah by showing that he was a descendant of King David.

I kept on going through the prophecies until I hit upon this one, which was written around 1000 B.C.:

They pierced My hands and My feet;
I can count all My bones.
They look and stare at Me.
They divide My garments among them,
And for My clothing they cast lots. (Psalm 22:16-18 NKJV)

I was shocked. This writer described marks identical to those from crucifixion before crucifixion was even devised as a tortuous method of putting people to death! A reference was made to the piercing of hands and feet before this was even in practice. I discovered that two other prophets mentioned the piercing of the Messiah. How could this be? I couldn't think of any other way this could have happened except by crucifixion. My mind was reeling with the awareness that these three writers had described something that didn't even exist in their day.

And this particular prophecy described that the Messiah's clothing would be divided and gambled for. I had to admit that all three of these things happened to Jesus one thousand years later. These were things that Jesus could not have manipulated or somehow magically caused to happen.

Then the soldiers, when they had crucified Jesus, took His garments and made four parts, to each soldier a part, and also the tunic. Now the tunic was without seam, woven from the top in one piece. They said therefore among themselves, "Let us not tear it, but cast lots for it, whose it shall be," that the Scripture might be fulfilled which says:

"They divided My garments among them,
And for My clothing they cast lots."
Therefore the soldiers did these things. (John 19:23-24 NKJV)

The New Testament writer directly quotes from the Hebrew Scriptures and states that these things fulfilled Scripture. I found direct quotations from the Hebrew Scriptures, like this one, throughout the New Testament. This was impressive, but I was still skeptical. I wanted more, something that would really prove to me that prophecies were real.

This next prophecy was what I was looking for. It was written by Isaiah around 700 B.C., and it blew me away.

Surely He has borne our griefs
And carried our sorrows;
Yet we esteemed Him stricken,
Smitten by God, and afflicted.
But He was wounded for our transgressions,
He was bruised for our iniquities;
The chastisement for our peace was upon Him,
And by His stripes we are healed.
All we like sheep have gone astray;
We have turned, every one, to his own way;
And the Lord has laid on Him the iniquity of us all.
And He bore the sin of many,
And made intercession for the transgressors. (Isaiah 53:4-6,12 NKJV)

The Messiah was described here as someone who would suffer as a sin substitute for others. He would be beaten by a whip receiving stripes. As I read it, I realized it sounded like a passage from the New Testament. The parallels to Jesus were so close that it seemed like an intentional fraud, but that was impossible since it was written seven hundred years before Jesus was born.

In summary, the Messiah was to be born in Bethlehem of a virgin from the line of David. He would have his hands and feet pierced, and he would be a sin substitute sacrifice for sinners. His existence was eternal in origin, and he would be called "God with us." Jesus clearly matched every one of these prophecies, according to the New Testament. I was now very curious and agitated at the same time. Could there be more?

The next prophecy I looked at came from the book of Daniel. It gave a calculation that would supposedly predict the exact day that the Messiah would arrive in Jerusalem. *Now this would be impressive*, I thought. I was in a stupor after I learned that, in fact, the exact day when Jesus rode into town on Palm Sunday presenting himself as the Messiah matched this calculation precisely.[29] The exact day! This seemed to be so specific that it had to be a hoax, but it wasn't.

Daniel also described that the Messiah would die.

"And after the sixty-two weeks
Messiah shall be cut off, but not for Himself." (Daniel 9:26 NKJV)

This was important, since I wouldn't expect a "savior" to die. I wasn't alone. The Jews didn't expect it either, but there it was, in their Scriptures. The wording also implies that the Messiah would die for others and not himself. I had a weird feeling come over me when I read this. My heart sank in awe that Daniel predicted exactly when the Messiah would come and that he would die, but not for himself. How many other men in history could match this description? I was confounded.

Every time I read a prophecy and studied it, I wanted one more. In each instance, Jesus was an exact match to the prophesied Messiah. I could explain away by coincidence many of them, but after a while the sheer number became overpowering. My mind tried to fight back by saying, "This is impossible. It's all a coincidence. There is no way these passages can refer to Jesus." My heart, however, was overwhelmed by the number of direct and indirect references to a Messiah that exactly matched Jesus in a collection of Scriptures written hundreds of years before he was born.

After a while I stopped looking. There were just too many. The Messiah had over three hundred prophecies written about him. Sixty-one of them are viewed as major ones.[30] Jesus fulfilled every one of them. The statistical probability of any man fulfilling even just eight major prophecies was off the charts of probability. I read in Josh McDowell's book that the actual number was 1 in 10^{17}, or 1 in 100,000,000,000,000,000!!![31]

> *"Now these prophecies were either given by inspiration of God or the prophets just wrote them as they thought they should be. In such a case the prophets had just one chance in 10^{17} of having them come true in any one man, but they all came true in Christ. This means that the fulfillment of these eight prophecies alone proves that God inspired the writing of those prophecies to a definiteness which lacks only one chance in 10^{17} of being absolute."[32-33]*

This was claiming that the statistical probability of one man fulfilling even eight major prophecies, when Jesus fulfilled all three hundred, was so improbable that it basically proved God inspired their writing. I didn't know what to think. I realized that only God, if he truly existed, could describe so many details about a man's life before he actually lived.

At this point I was taken aback. I didn't have an explanation for this. It just seemed too crazy to be true. There actually seemed to be *too many* of them. I quickly thought that maybe Jesus intentionally tried to fulfill the prophecies, until I realized that many of them were out of his control. I had a very hard time swallowing the astounding number and accuracy of the prophecies. It was like those times in life when you know something is true but you don't want to admit it to yourself.

I looked for other opinions on the internet and found a landslide of criticisms and rebuttals to the prophecies of the Messiah. Some claimed that they were taken out of context, while others pointed out that some of them were never intended to be prophecies in the first place. Many of the points raised were valid and convincing individually. It was amazing to see polar opposite opinions on the same prophecies.

I wasn't sure what to think at this point. I escaped from a decision by moving on in my studies to examine a few of the "pictures."

THE PICTURES OF THE MESSIAH

As mentioned previously, a picture is a foreshadowing or "pre-enactment" of future events by occurrences in the past. A future incident is indirectly described before it happens by a series of circumstances and actions that foreshadow it. Pictures are in effect prophecies themselves, because they describe and act out what will occur in the future. If the Hebrew Scriptures contain pictures of the sacrifice of Jesus in the stories of ancient Israel then this would be a strong witness that they are of a divine origin. In order to be convincing there would have to be several of them that are specific and undeniably similar to what is described in the New Testament.

The Jewish Sacrificial System

I looked first at the Jewish sacrificial system that was supposedly given to them by God. In their religious system, the death and blood of an innocent animal was used to make atonement for sin. The animal's death took the place of the sinner. I remembered the words the couple spoke to me on Marco Island: "Jesus was innocent and without sin. He died in your place. His blood has forgiven your sins if you believe in him, repent, and trust him." The idea was that all of the animal sacrifices were a portrait of and led up to Jesus as the final true sacrifice. This certainly fit with the doctrine of the New Testament. The idea of a sacrifice paying the price for sin at least had a firm basis and wasn't something new. I had no idea that the Jews were very accustomed to substitutionary death and blood paying the price for sin. *The illustration and parallels are striking between the two beliefs*, I thought.

The Passover

The Passover was another religious ceremony reported to have strong symbolism related to Jesus. The only thing I knew about this Jewish holiday was that my childhood friends couldn't eat bread for a week. They had to eat matzoh instead. I needed to learn more than this. I found the description in chapter 12 of Exodus, which is the second book of the Old Testament.

The Passover was the original and first Jewish holiday. It is still celebrated by Jews today. It was instituted when Moses led the captive people, who would later be known as Jews or Hebrews, out of Egypt towards the "Promised Land." They had been held captive as slaves in Egypt for four hundred years. God sent Moses to tell the Pharaoh, "Let my people go," but Pharaoh refused. God then sent nine plagues on the land of Egypt, but the Pharaoh still would not release the slaves. Finally, God told Moses one final plague would convince Pharaoh to let the people go free. All of the eldest sons in the land would die on this night of judgment. This evidently included anyone living in the land, including the Jews.

God, however, gave Moses detailed instructions on how the captives could be saved from this judgment. If they followed God's instructions by faith, then their sons would be spared. They were to sacrifice a perfect male lamb and apply its blood to their doorposts. They had to believe that the blood of this sacrifice would save them. If they applied the blood to their doorposts, then the angel of death that God sent would "pass over" their houses and not harm their eldest sons. This is how the holiday got its name.

I thought about this. The blood of a perfect male sacrifice could save people from the judgment of God. I couldn't mistake or ignore the direct symbolism to the basic Christian doctrine that the death and blood of Jesus, who was sinless, when applied, saves people from the judgment of God.

I then recalled John the Baptist saying, *"Behold! The Lamb of God who takes away the sin of the world!"* (John 1:29 NKJV) He was alluding to Jesus being the final sacrifice, a picture of the slain Passover lamb, who would provide payment for the sins of the world. I had to admit that Jesus was just like the Passover lamb. I was then shocked to learn that Jesus was crucified *on* the Passover. This seemed like a really weird coincidence.

Critics contend that the Passover lamb was not an atonement for sin. They add that lambs that were offered for the Passover needed to be without blemish, and point out that Jesus was badly beaten and marred when he was crucified.

I understood their points, but had to disagree. The New Testament claimed that Jesus was a perfect sinless man while alive on earth. Just as the lambs were "without blemish" so was Jesus. The method of death had nothing to do with their prior unblemished status, and I felt naysayers were reaching to claim it did. His scourging and marred body did not negate the picture in my opinion. The same was true for his death, which does according to Christians save from the judgment of God even if it's by the forgiveness of sins.

In studying this holiday, I also discovered that God gave the Jews an exact method of applying the blood to the doorposts of their homes. The blood of the lamb was to be placed in the basin at the opening of the door. The basin was a trough dug in the ground that was designed to keep the rain out. A bunch of hyssop plant was to be used like a paint brush. They were instructed to dip the hyssop in the blood in the basin, and then touch the top of the doorpost (lintel) first and then each side of the doorpost.

I almost passed out when I realized that the motion to place the blood of the lamb on the door formed a cross! They were painting crosses with the blood of a spotless male lamb whose death and blood saved them from the judgment of God! This felt surreal. *How could this symbolism be embedded in the national holiday of Jewish people and instituted over 1,000 years before Jesus was born?!* I was astonished. "How many other such symbols could there be? This is crazy!" I said aloud in my office one night.

Abraham and Isaac

The next one I found left me speechless. In Genesis chapter twenty-two a man named Abraham was told to take his only son up a mountain and sacrifice him. The son went up the hill carrying wood on his back. He was following the will of his father. The mountain was called Moriah. For three days Abraham had considered his son as good as dead. In the final moments God provided a ram to take Isaac's place.

After a little digging, I discovered that the location of this event was in the same vicinity where Jesus was crucified, a place known as Calvary today, on a hill called Golgotha. Jesus carried a wooden cross with help up to the top of Mount Moriah as the only Son of God. Jesus was following the will of his Father, God, just like Isaac followed his father Abraham. Jesus was dead for three days and was a sacrifice for others.

Another verse I had read popped into my mind.

For God so loved the world that He gave His only begotten Son, that whoever believes in Him should not perish but have everlasting life. For God did not send His Son into the world to condemn the world, but that the world through Him might be saved. (John 3:16-17 NKJV)

Over 1,400 years before Jesus was sacrificed, Abraham and Isaac were acting out a mirror image of what the New Testament said was

God's plan for salvation in the same location where it would occur! Maybe the picture isn't perfect because Isaac himself did not actually die, but the principle of substitutionary death was clearly present in that God provided a ram to take Isaac's place, a ram that did in fact die.

I have only discussed a few of them here. I was amazed to discover that there are many more throughout the Hebrew Scriptures. I tried to think of something that could explain away these incredible foreshadowing symbols, but I kept coming up empty. I was frustrated and excited at the same time. I felt as if I was being cornered and closed in.

These prophecies and pictures were not vague generalizations that could apply to anyone, but vivid, exact, and precise direct and indirect descriptions that fit exactly with the life of Jesus. There was no way for me to invoke a motive or intentional writing of these prophecies based upon religious bias either. First, they were written before the events occurred, and there are copies in existence dated well before Jesus was born. Second, the fact that many of the Jews did not believe that Jesus was the Messiah negates the idea that they might have changed or altered their Scriptures to make Jesus fit. Their unbelief was a strong testament that their Scriptures were accurately preserved.

Intentional collusion was simply impossible for the pictures. How could Abraham and Isaac act out this scene in the same location and be accused of knowing what would happen over a thousand years later? The prophecies and pictures were written before Jesus was born by many different authors over a thousand year period who didn't all know each other. Many of the prophecies Jesus fulfilled were out of his control. It was impossible for him to have intentionally fulfilled the place of his birth for example.

THE REJECTION OF THE MESSIAH

I asked myself, if the evidence from their own Scriptures was so overwhelming, why did the Jews reject Jesus as the Messiah? The answer was they didn't, not all of them anyway. It was mainly the ruling Jewish religious leaders who rejected Jesus. They were waiting for a king to rule on earth who would deliver them from Roman oppression. I didn't have time to dig into all of the details, but evidently these leaders misunderstood some of the prophecies, and they were protecting their power and control over people, which the teachings of Jesus disrupted and exposed.

The New Testament clearly documents that many Jews *did* believe in Jesus as the Messiah, including a few of the religious leaders. Jesus was buried by Joseph of Arimathea, for example, who was a high ranking religious leader. Nicodemus was another religious leader who became a believer. The early church was also composed almost entirely of Jews. Christianity evidently started off very Jewish.

SUMMARY

The weight of the Old Testament evidence added a heavier burden on my heart and mind. Jesus not only matched the identity of the Messiah above all odds of probability, but I also found the entire basis for the Christian doctrine of the crucifixion embedded in Jewish religious practices and their own Scriptures.

I tried to determine whether I was somehow misinterpreting these prophecies. Was I reading into them something that wasn't really there? Were the skeptics right, who claim Christians have gone back and scoured the Hebrew Scriptures to deliberately find post hoc similarities to the New Testament? I looked over everything carefully and had to admit the answer was no. I was haunted by one fact. Why are there so many different things that any diligent researcher could find in the Hebrew Scriptures which match the life of Jesus? How could I explain away many pictures that are not really open to interpretation?

I wanted a way out if I decided to stop pursuing this. I felt as if I was living in a movie. It was a very strange feeling to find such a compelling witness for the reality of God in a book that was over two thousand years old—a book I had never given any credence for most of my life and didn't see anyone reading. Could this be real? How could it be? Logically, I felt obligated to concede to the weight of evidence, but another part of me just couldn't come to grips with what this would mean for me, my family, and the world in which I grew up.

I never expected this when I set out to find ammunition against my Christian neighbors. The New Testament and now even the Old Testament had an overwhelming amount of evidence for its veracity. If I was potentially going to base my beliefs in God from these documents, though, I needed to investigate the documents themselves.

Chapter Six

The Investigation Phase IV:

The Historical Evidence for the New Testament

THE UNIVERSITY PROFESSORS

I decided to examine the historicity of the New Testament. I began to analyze the Bible as a historical document, microscopically, since I was a doctor and had conducted scientific research. It was time to put emotions aside! Was the Bible a historically reliable document? Could I trust what was written almost two thousand years ago? Is the Bible that I am reading today the same as what was originally written by Matthew, Mark, Luke, and John? Did they actually write these documents?

That same day I got an advertisement in the mail from a company that sold audio lectures of college courses at major universities. I was surprised to find that there was a section on the Bible. They had two courses just on the New Testament from two different universities. I figured, *Where better to start than listening to lectures on the New Testament from college professors at major universities?* They were heads of their departments with many degrees and publications in their field. I could relate to their academic background, and I was sure that anyone with a Ph.D. in the New Testament would know the facts and tell the truth.

I started listening to both of them on my iPod, but I quickly had a profound sense that they didn't believe the New Testament described true historical events. The more I listened, the more depressed I became. My heart was losing any possible hope of an answer to the meaninglessness of this world. My mind, however, was elated. Part of me felt sick inside, while paradoxically another part of me was glad. It was a strange battle going on that I couldn't control.

My mind didn't want to accept the accountability that belief in a creator would entail, while my heart desired the answers that one would bring. My heart thirsted for eternal life, but my mind was holding on to its own self-centered life. My mind, however, had a heavyweight champ on its side: fear. I was afraid of the implications of absolute truth, as shown in the Bible, since I was raised entirely in a culture that rejoiced that absolute truth didn't exist.

One professor said that the historical evidence for Jesus was lacking. He firmly asserted that none of the four Gospels (Matthew, Mark, Luke, and John) were written by eyewitnesses but by people living later who invented and doctored these stories to convert people to Christianity. He noted that the actual early documents don't have their names on any of them. The titles like "The Gospel According to Matthew" were later additions that only appear in our modern Bibles.

As I listened, he began to list many discrepancies among the four Gospel accounts of Jesus' death and resurrection. Luke, for example, stated that the women saw two men in the empty tomb of Jesus, while Matthew stated it was one man. He went through at least ten to fifteen examples like this. Each one felt like a .357 magnum had hit me in the heart.

He also said that historians could only establish what likely happened in the past, and by definition, a miracle is the least probable explanation. As a result, historians can't claim that a miracle probably occurred. The miracles from the Bible also invoked God, and he maintained that historians can't know anything about God.

I felt as if I had been hit with a 1-2-3 knockout punch. He seemed to destroy the historical credibility of the New Testament by pointing out discrepancies and showing that miracles are not even subject to historical analysis. My heart that was devastated because I really wanted an answer to this world, death, and the meaninglessness of evolution, but my mind was in opposition.

My mind reasoned, *These professors know the truth. They have degrees, publications, and years of experience in the New Testament. There is no possible way that they could be wrong about Jesus and the Bible. Sure, the writers of the Bible were sincere and believed in what they wrote, but that doesn't mean those events actually happened!*

I kept listening. I decided to try out the other professor. She presented the characters of the New Testament as though they were fictional characters, which I thought was odd. They were described like made-up people in nice stories that religious people had invented. Some of their lives were true, but other aspects had been tainted over the years as the stories got changed. Something inside of me just didn't feel right about her statements. *Was it my emotions?* I wondered. How did she know what was true and what was false?

In frustration, I stopped listening to her and returned to the first guy, starting where I had left off. I noticed he was now a bit sarcastic a few times. It was the tone of his voice and the way he made a couple of statements. I sensed he had an axe to grind, but I couldn't imagine why. It was very subtle, but I caught it and was surprised. He sounded like he had a hidden motive. I perceived bias creeping out. History should be an easy place to present facts without bias and emotion.

This professor then pivotally taught in one of his lectures that Jesus did not claim to be God. *Why would the professor say something that was completely false and easily verifiable?* At that moment I saw a big red flag. My heart leaped off the mat from its near knockout blow and proclaimed, "This is not true, and you know it!" My heart was yelling at both me and the professor. I knew it wasn't true, and certainly there was no way the professor could have missed the obvious. A passage I had read in the Bible came to mind:

"My Father, who has given them to me, is greater than all; no one can snatch them out of my Father's hand. I and the Father are one."

Again the Jews picked up stones to stone him, but Jesus said to them, "I have shown you many great miracles from the Father. For which of these do you stone me?"

"We are not stoning you for any of these," replied the Jews, "but for blasphemy, because you, a mere man, claim to be God." (John 10:29-33 NIV)

It was perfectly acceptable if the professor didn't personally believe that Jesus was actually God, but why would he state that Jesus never made that claim? Why wouldn't he state the obvious and let people decide for themselves?

These clues were critical, since I was close to packing it in. Something was fishy, and I suspected a hidden motive with the professors. I decided to look elsewhere for information. Some very valid points were raised that demanded answers, but did I have all of the facts? I planned to revisit this issue in more detail once I had more information.

THE NEW EVIDENCE THAT DEMANDS A VERDICT

What about that big book by Josh McDowell, *The New Evidence That Demands a Verdict?* I had already found in there a lot of critical information about the resurrection of Jesus, and I hadn't even read a fourth of it. I was not impressed with the academicians and their assessment of the New Testament. I wanted to see what further evidence the title of the McDowell's book was talking about. I wanted facts and sound historical analysis.

I did some more digging on the internet and discovered that the contents, references, and conclusions reached in this textbook were not without debate. I found entire web sites devoted to refuting almost every aspect of this book. Many of the commentators seemed quite upset in their rebuttals, which made me question their motives. I decided to keep reading and keep an open mind to both sides of the argument.

Following is a summary of what I learned from Josh McDowell's textbook, and the critics thereof on the internet.

If the New Testament really described actual history, then it should be evaluated like the rest of history.

What tests are applied to historical documents to determine if they are accurate or reliable? I learned that three tests are used: the bibliographical test, the internal evidence test, and the external evidence test.

The Bibliographical Test [34]

The original manuscripts of the New Testament are no longer in existence. Today only copies of copies have survived. The bibliographical test answers the question "How reliable are the copies?" The answer is based upon two pieces of information: 1. The total number of copies in existence. 2. The time interval between the original and those copies. In other words, if Matthew was written in 60 A.D. and the earliest copy that we have was dated 200 A.D., then the time interval is 140 years. An ancient document is more reliable if there are many copies in existence with a short time interval. Possessing a lot of copies allows for comparisons between them to look for changes and determine how accurately the text has been preserved. The closer in time the copies are to the original, the less chance for changes and errors over time.

I was immediately blown away to discover that the New Testament is the most historically attested ancient book of all time. It literally embarrasses any other piece of ancient literature by leaps and bounds. Not only are there far more manuscripts than other ancient historical writings, but the time gap between the original manuscripts and their copies was far shorter!

I found out there are more than 20,000 copies of New Testament manuscripts. I could not believe it—**twenty thousand!**[35] The next best piece of ancient literature, *The Iliad*, has only 643![36] Most ancient writings that are accepted as historical fact today don't even have a hundred! More than this, the dates of the copies of most other ancient works are over 1,000 years after the actual historical events took place. The time interval for the New Testament manuscripts was as low as 60 years.[37] Now I was *really* suspicious. "Why isn't this a well-known and publicized fact? Why isn't this taught in school?!" I shouted aloud in my office. That data alone was so profound it almost seemed like an intentional cover-up or suppression of evidence by our modern society.

I also discovered that the Scriptures for both the Old and the New Testaments were preserved through time with 99.5% accuracy.[38-39] Yes, there were some copying errors and possibly some intentional changes over the years, but none of them affected the main message at all. The vast majority of them would not even be noticed in translation.

The critics of McDowell claimed that there aren't any originals in the handwriting of the purported author, the actual authors are unknown, and there is a three hundred year time gap between the first entire Gospel manuscript and the time it was supposed to have been written. They also pointed out that a small error rate does not necessarily validate the historical accuracy by itself.

Another major objection to the large number of New Testament manuscripts was a lack of *independent* corroborating testimony, because many of the copies are merely copies of earlier ones.

These were valid points that I took to heart, but compared to any other historical records I had to concede the Bible surpassed them all by a landslide. By their standards ancient history courses would cease to exist.

The Internal Evidence Test [40]

Surprisingly, the bibliographic test demonstrated to me that the copies in existence today are exceptionally close to what was originally recorded by the authors of the New Testament. They were well preserved and barely altered even after two thousand years. I could now trust that what I had read and analyzed in my modern New Testament was very close to what was originally written.

If the New Testament I was reading was well preserved, then how reliable was the information itself? This next test determined the credibility of historical documents. If historical information is not accurate or trustworthy, then it doesn't matter how many copies you have or how well preserved they are. Well preserved copies are useless if the historical information they contain is not credible.

The internal evidence test determines credibility by analyzing the authors themselves, their ability to tell the truth, the possibility they falsified information, and any internal errors, inconsistencies, or facts that are simply false in the information they recorded. An important principal here is called Aristotle's dictum: "*The benefit of the doubt is to be given to the document itself, and not arrogated by the critic to himself.*"[41]

1. *Errors, Changes, and Discrepancies*

The bibliographic test had highly suggested that the New Testament was well preserved even though it contained minor copying errors and possibly some intentional changes. Most of these errors were unnoticeable after translation, and those remaining did not affect the major doctrine being presented. There was a lot of debate about this subject, however. Some highly regarded critics stated that some of the changes or additions did attempt to deify Jesus. I analyzed many of them and had to disagree. Even if these verses were added, changed, or even deleted the basic doctrine of the New Testament was clearly still there in a unified manor in many different places.

What about the inconsistencies, though? The university professor had pointed out many discrepancies among the four Gospels when they described the same event. If there were valid and multiple irreconcilable discrepancies, then the New Testament could fail this test. Aristotle's dictum does not hold true if there is a strong reason to doubt the work being examined.

I investigated each of the discrepancies that the professor mentioned in his lecture. I analyzed them myself and also used a textbook that deals with this very topic.[42] I was very surprised to find that many of them had very simple explanations. Four different people reporting about the same event will frequently describe that event differently and choose to include or exclude different details.

Matthew, for example, says the women who first arrived at the empty tomb of Jesus saw one angel. Luke states they saw two men in "shining garments." So which is it, two men or one angel? I quickly realized it could easily be both. Two angels in shining clothes were at the empty tomb of Jesus. Luke chose not to use the word angel, even though he inferred it by describing their clothing as "shining garments."

Matthew, on the other hand, could have simply chosen to focus on the words of one of the angels. He also never specified that there was *only* one.

I also discovered that none of these discrepancies were at the heart of the narrative but involved minor details. It was now clear to me that the university professor was only presenting one side of the story. He listed minor discrepancies not central to the story without any other possible explanations and then used the discrepancies to discount the main message. It almost seemed as though he was looking for a reason to reject the New Testament. *Why would he do that?* If someone didn't do some digging on his own he might just accept what the professor said.

Simon Greenleaf was a famous professor at Harvard Law School who wrote a book that examined the reliability of the four Gospels by applying the rules of evidence used for the court system. After examining the discrepancies among the four biographies of Jesus, he said this:

> *There is enough of a discrepancy to show that there could have been no previous concert among them; and at the same time such substantial agreement as to show that they all were independent narrators of the same great transaction.*[43]

The discrepancies were actually complimentary descriptions by different reporters and easily explainable. He made the point that if the four accounts were exactly the same in their details then they would be criticized for collusion or copying.

The university professor's assertion of discrepancies among the four Gospels as a reason to doubt their authorship and authenticity just didn't hold up. I couldn't honestly find a problem with this part of the internal evidence test.

The next aspect to evaluate was the New Testament authors themselves, their ability to tell the truth, and the possibility that they could have falsified information.

2. *The Authors of the Four Gospels*

The original writers of a historical document are of paramount importance. What was their ability to tell the truth? How close were they to the events they were describing? Eyewitness testimony is the best. Historically, this is as close as you can get to the events and is an excellent reason to accept the accounts as legitimate.

The critical question for the New Testament is "Were the four Gospels really eyewitness testimonies?" The New Testament claimed to be written by eyewitnesses or people like Luke who compiled the testimonies of eyewitnesses, but the university professor adamantly challenged this claim. I also needed to determine "Were the writers of the New Testament biased by their religious beliefs? Did they falsify their biographies of Jesus to support their new religion and gain followers?" If the accounts were made up and doctored by religious people, then it didn't matter how many copies there were, how well preserved they were, or even if they were internally consistent.

This was critical for me. I was dealing with accounts describing someone claiming to be God, holding the answers to eternity. I had to have assurance that I could trust Matthew, Mark, Luke, and John as the true and accurate authors. The University professor had mentioned that none of the four Gospels contained the name of the author. He claimed that these were added later. What evidence was there for or against their being the authors?

Early Church Attestation

I learned that the early church attested and clearly documented that these men were the authors.[44] This was not final proof that they were, but it was documentation. Several men recorded and mentioned the authors of the New Testament in their writings. These were Christian authors, however, and could have been biased.

I found an interesting fact that suggested these early Christians, however, did not just accept any writing as Scripture even if it claimed to have been written by an apostle of Jesus. The early church, interestingly, refuted and rejected many other writings allegedly written by the apostles with their actual names on the works because they determined that they were not genuine.[45]

This was ironic. The church accepted the four Gospels as written by Matthew, Mark, Luke, and John despite their names *not* being cited in the works but then rejected other "Gospels" that *had* their names written on them. This was a strong witness that they were very careful and astute about accepting authorship as genuine. The chance for bias was still there, but I felt better about them now.

I also discovered that there was nothing in history to the contrary. There was no known controversy over the authors of the four Gospels. No one during this time period questioned their authorship. Since

Christianity was so controversial and faced fierce opposition, I found it odd that there wasn't any refutation of the authorship or legitimacy of the four Gospels.

If Matthew, Mark, Luke, and John did not write these accounts, then the conspirators did a poor job of picking false authors. Matthew, a tax collector, would have been hated by many people, since tax collectors were despised even by fellow Jews. Mark was a disciple of Peter who supposedly wrote Peter's account of the life of Jesus. Luke was not mentioned during the life of Jesus and was not a Jew. Why wouldn't the Jesus' followers pick Peter, whose name had a lot of weight and notoriety? If they were going to forge the accounts, why not use the name of the author in the document? This would be the obvious motive and method to make a better forgery.

Eyewitness Testimony

So far I hadn't found any clear reason to reject the authorship of the four Gospels. There was clear documentation in history that these four were the authors and nothing to the contrary. The claimed authors also didn't fit the profile of forgery. The authors of Luke and John directly mentioned that they were eyewitness themselves or had received eyewitness testimony. The author of John's Gospel, for example, clearly stated that he was an eyewitness.

Jesus did many other miraculous signs in the presence of his disciples, which are not recorded in this book. But these are written that you may believe that Jesus is the Christ, the Son of God, and that by believing you may have life in his name.

This is the disciple who testifies to these things and who wrote them down. We know that his testimony is true. (John 20:30-31; 21:24 NIV)

John also affirmed this in one of his letters that was also a part of the New Testament.

That which was from the beginning, which we have heard, which we have seen with our eyes, which we have looked at and our hands have touched—this we proclaim concerning the Word of life. The life appeared; we have seen it and testify to it, and we proclaim to you the eternal life, which was with the Father and has appeared to us. We proclaim to you what we have seen and heard, so that you also may have fellowship with us. And our fellowship is with the Father and with his Son, Jesus Christ. We write this to make our joy complete. (1 John 1:1-4 NIV)

The author of the narrative bearing Luke's name clearly stated in the first few sentences that he used eyewitness accounts and personally affirmed them.

> *Many have undertaken to draw up an account of the things that have been fulfilled among us, just as they were handed down to us by those who from the first were eyewitnesses and servants of the word. Therefore, since I myself have carefully investigated everything from the beginning, it seemed good also to me to write an orderly account for you, most excellent Theophilus, so that you may know the certainty of the things you have been taught. (Luke 1:1-4 NIV)*

This didn't tell me who actually wrote them, but it would have been something easily verifiable by adversaries during the time these works were written. If Jesus really did all of the miracles in Israel that the New Testament recorded, then droves of people were healed and witnessed his ministry. This would have been the biggest event in all of human history.

If it were manufactured and a lie, Luke's statement would have been foolish and unsustainable in the early church days, when the church faced opposition. Luke the physician clearly traveled with Paul, and would have had ample opportunity to travel to Israel and conduct his research and interviews. Luke noted that *many* people had written accounts about the life of Jesus. This meant that when he did his research, he found a lot of material to examine. These were eyewitness accounts handed down from the first, which would be the disciples and people who witnessed Jesus. If Jesus really did the miracles and was God, then scores of people would have wanted to document what happened. It was easy for me to pretend I was there and realize this would be a natural thing to do.

The Medical Language of Luke

If Luke really wrote his Gospel and the book of Acts like Christianity claimed he did, one might expect him to use some medical terminology. Being a doctor myself, I know we like to use medical terms, even in everyday life, because they can be very descriptive and full of content. I found that in 1882 a man named William Kirk Hobart wrote a book called *The Medical Language of St. Luke*.[46] He showed that indeed the books of Luke and Acts are filled with medical language not found anywhere else in the New Testament.

In Luke chapter 1 verse 2, for example, Luke used the Greek word "autoptes," which is translated "eyewitness." This was a medical term used to describe someone seeing for themselves by firsthand observation. Our word for autopsy comes from this Greek word. The books of Luke and Acts are uniquely filled with words like this that are not used anywhere else in the New Testament. These medical terms are found only in those two books.

This did not prove to me that Luke actually wrote these two books, but it did prove to me that one man who was likely a physician wrote both books. The chance of a coincidence seemed unlikely. This was a very important piece of internal evidence for the New Testament. A later author trying to forge or invent stories based upon religious bias would not be able to pull this off.

3. Jesus—Legend or Religious Invention?

I couldn't find any credible evidence that the four Gospels were not written by Matthew, Mark, Luke, and John. The facts and circumstances actually attested that they did write them. The last area to examine was the content of the four Gospels. Did the authors of the four Gospels invent the doctrine of the resurrection and Christianity? Was Jesus the result of legends and stories passed down for many years by religious people, as the University professors had asserted? This was critical, because even if the authors and their witnesses were genuine eyewitnesses, the Gospels would still fail the internal evidence test if the authors falsified their information.

Since Matthew, Mark, and Luke were written during the time that eyewitnesses to the events described were still alive, including hostile eyewitnesses who wanted to destroy Christianity, McDowell and others argued that it was highly unlikely that anyone could get away with lying about the facts. The opponents of Christianity would have been able to refute and discredit the information written in the Gospels. Many people in Israel would have seen the miracles and heard the teachings of Jesus and be in a position to directly verify or challenge what was written.

I really expected to find some evidence of the opponents of Christianity challenging the claims of the apostles of Jesus, but I couldn't find any! There was zero evidence that the authorship or content of the four Gospels was ever challenged or disputed by anyone. History was silent here. This was shocking to me because the four Gospels recorded the alleged miracles and resurrection of Jesus Christ. These occurrences were not normal, everyday historical events. One would expect some type of challenge or refutation of such claims.

The apostles, however, took it one step further. They threw it in the face of their adversaries that they also knew these things to be true.

"Men of Israel, listen to this: Jesus of Nazareth was a man accredited by God to you by miracles, wonders and signs, which God did among you through him, as you yourselves know." (Acts 2:22 NIV)

I had to admit that in the New Testament the Jewish religious leaders were documented to have personally witnessed and tested the miracles of Jesus. They interviewed a man blind from birth who received his sight. They also questioned his parents to confirm that he was born blind.[47] In the book of John, they wanted to kill Lazarus after he had been resurrected from the dead because his resurrection caused many Jews to believe in Jesus.[48] In the book of Acts, a lame man was healed in the temple by the apostles Peter and John.[49] They were thrown into jail by the religious leaders. This is what the religious leaders said:

When they saw the courage of Peter and John and realized that they were unschooled, ordinary men, they were astonished and they took note that these men had been with Jesus. But since they could see the man who had been healed standing there with them, there was nothing they could say. So they ordered them to withdraw from the Sanhedrin and then conferred together. "What are we going to do with these men?" they asked. "Everybody living in Jerusalem knows they have done an outstanding miracle, and we cannot deny it." (Acts 4:13-16 NIV)

This kind of statement would have been vehemently challenged and exposed if it were a made-up story. The Jewish religious leaders would quickly claim that this never happened, but they never did. I had to admit that the silence of the religious leaders was very intriguing. I realized that if they really did witness the miracles of Jesus, then this would explain their silence. I had not thought about these events in the Bible in this manner until Josh McDowell brought them to light for me. This was strong evidence against the possibility of the four Gospels containing falsified or exaggerated information, but I wanted more.

It also didn't make sense to me that later Christians invented the doctrine of the resurrection. For what benefit or purpose? From what motive? Their own doctrine insisted that the resurrection was essential.

The apostle Paul himself asserted that if Jesus wasn't raised from the dead then Christianity was useless.

> *For if there is no resurrection of the dead, then Christ has not been raised either. And if Christ has not been raised, then all our preaching is useless, and your faith is useless. And we apostles would all be lying about God—for we have said that God raised Christ from the grave. But that can't be true if there is no resurrection of the dead. And if there is no resurrection of the dead, then Christ has not been raised. And if Christ has not been raised, then your faith is useless and you are still guilty of your sins. In that case, all who have died believing in Christ are lost! And if our hope in Christ is only for this life, we are more to be pitied than anyone in the world.*
>
> *But in fact, Christ has been raised from the dead. He is the first of a great harvest of all who have died. (1 Corinthians 15:13-20 NLT)*

Paul wasn't somebody who was converted by other Christians and somehow naively believed in the resurrection of Jesus based upon traditions he heard. Paul claimed to have seen the resurrected Jesus in person. I couldn't help but think, *Why would he pretend that Jesus was resurrected and then proclaim Christianity is sham without the resurrection unless it actually happened?*

Something else occurred to me. The early Christian church didn't have a New Testament, like we have today, until many years later. Their "Bible" was the ancient Hebrew Scriptures that have been discussed earlier. The New Testament records that many people believed in Jesus based upon his fulfillment of the prophecies about the Messiah from the Hebrew Scriptures. In other words, many people were being converted without having the four Gospels in hand to read, study, and analyze. When these people were told about Jesus, they were being taught from the Hebrew Scriptures.

The convincing argument and legitimacy for the first generation of conversions was the ancient Hebrew Scriptures. I had already seen for myself how these prophecies of the Messiah were uniquely fulfilled by Jesus against all odds of probability. They were so powerful because they stood *independent* of the New Testament stories by at least four hundred years. This directly contradicts the notion from the university professors that the doctrine of Christianity was the result of myth and legend developing over many years by religious people.

If the doctrine of Christianity was invented by religious people many years later, then how could I explain this same basic doctrine being prophesied and pictured throughout the Hebrew Scriptures? It would be entirely different if, out of the blue, people claimed that God visited earth, died for our sins, and then was raised from the dead. I would be much more suspicious about this sudden new religion if it had absolutely no basis or background.

What I had learned and verified for myself, however, was that Christianity could viably find its origins and roots throughout the ancient Hebrew Scriptures, because Jesus perfectly matched the identity of the Messiah. Even the precedent for a sin sacrifice was found throughout the Hebrew Scriptures. It was thus completely fallacious to state that Jesus was a myth or legend that formed over many years.

The New Testament states that it is all based upon the prophecies and pictures found in the ancient Hebrew Scriptures. They witnessed the revelation of what had been prophesied about over four hundred years before it happened. The fact that I could today verify that these prophecies and pictures were real, legitimate, and uniquely fulfilled by Jesus eliminated the theory of a myth or legend forming over years. You can't say something was invented many years later when the basic story and doctrine you are criticizing was prophesied and recorded hundreds of years before it happened.

It was very apparent to me that the professors conveniently avoided discussing any of this. They acted as if these theories and doctrines did suddenly appear years after Jesus died, and they made such statements without foundation. It was clear from my analysis that the New Testament can't be isolated from the Hebrew Scriptures (Old Testament) when the New Testament makes claims that it is entirely based upon the fulfillment of them. These professors ignored evidence from the Hebrew Scriptures.

> *For I delivered to you first of all that which I also received: that Christ died for our sins according to the Scriptures, and that He was buried, and that He rose again the third day according to the Scriptures. (1 Corinthians 15:3-4 NKJV)*

The early Christians claimed that the death and resurrection of Jesus Christ was "according to the Scriptures." I learned that Paul always appealed to the ancient Hebrew Scriptures when telling someone about Jesus Christ. Paul wrote the book called Romans in the New Testament, which many feel is the most important book of doctrine in the Bible. Paul directly quoted the Hebrew Scriptures 72 times in this book. In all, the New Testament has at least 343 direct quotations from the Hebrew Scriptures and 2,309 allusions to them, and yet the university professors claim Christianity was the result of legend and story telling?[50] Simply quoting Scriptures didn't necessarily prove anything, but it was clear that the apostles' doctrine was intimately linked to the Hebrew Scriptures.

I had to admit I was astounded to find almost everything but the actual name of Jesus in the prophecies of the Messiah. I couldn't make a case, either, that the Christians were reading into these Scriptures what they wanted to see. The prophecies and pictures were exact and clear. It just didn't make any sense to claim that their doctrine was the result of myth and storytelling.

Jesus even made the claim that he was the God of the Jews written about in the Hebrew Scriptures!

"You are not yet fifty years old," the Jews said to him, "and you have seen Abraham!"

"I tell you the truth," Jesus answered, "before Abraham was born, I am!" At this, they picked up stones to stone him, but Jesus hid himself, slipping away from the temple grounds. (John 8:57-59 NIV)

I learned from my study Bible that "I Am" was the name of God given to Moses by God.

Then Moses said to God, "Indeed, when I come to the children of Israel and say to them, 'The God of your fathers has sent me to you,' and they say to me, 'What is His name?' what shall I say to them?"

And God said to Moses, "I AM WHO I AM." And He said, "Thus you shall say to the children of Israel, 'I AM has sent me to you.' " (Exodus 3:13-15 NKJV)

Jesus told the Jews that he was the great I AM, their very own God. This is why they tried to stone him. His claim didn't necessarily make it true or convince me either, but I couldn't ignore the intimate connection between the New Testament and the ancient Hebrew Scriptures. This definitively eliminated the possibility that the New Testament doctrine was a result of a legend and storytelling over many years.

I wasn't about to become a religious zealot, but I also wasn't willing to surrender my logic and ignore the facts.

I was very irritated that University professors would teach on a topic of potential eternal significance and not present all of the evidence and facts. If they were going to raise these tough questions, why wouldn't they also offer some possible answers? Certainly they would expect objections and have rebuttals prepared. I don't have a religious degree, yet I found many key facts and alternative explanations that they conveniently left out.

In summary, I found that the New Testament passed the internal evidence test. This felt really weird because the deeper I investigated, the more compelling the story became. I didn't expect this at all. At the outset the New Testament seemed like a religious fairytale, but I was discovering it actually stood on very firm historical and analytical ground. The errors and changes were not significant and the discrepancies were not necessarily discrepancies at all. Prophecies and pictures even demonstrated that there was a startling harmony between the Hebrew Scriptures and the New Testament.

I couldn't find any credible evidence that the four Gospels were not written by Matthew, Mark, Luke, and John. There wasn't any evidence to the contrary but many compelling arguments for their authorship that I couldn't escape. The possibility that they falsified their accounts due to religious bias did not hold up, even though it seemed at first glance to be an obvious explanation. The absence of a logical motive and the presence of hostile witnesses, who remained silent even when challenged by those they wanted to destroy, was very convincing. The four biographies of Jesus even included many details that a surreptitious author would naturally avoid, like women discovering the empty tomb.

The university professor's theory that these four biographies of Jesus were the result of legend and storytelling over many years fell apart. I had to face the fact that Jesus not only matched the identity of the Messiah written about at least four hundred years prior, but the New Testament doctrine was identifiable in those same Scriptures. I had a hard time swallowing this because it seemed impossible. I moved on to the final test.

The External Evidence Test [51]

This final test looks for outside historical sources to confirm or disprove the events recorded in a historical document. What other sources in history exist that can comment on the authenticity and accuracy of the works in question? Was Jesus mentioned in history outside of the New Testament? Can the names of people and places mentioned in the Bible be confirmed by archaeology and other ancient writings? These seemed like excellent questions to me.

1. *Archaeology*

Archaeology was the first area I examined. I was surprised to find that there were entire books documenting how archaeology had confirmed countless facts, people, and places mentioned in the Bible.[52-53] I was intrigued that no known archaeological discovery has ever proved a biblical reference to be false.[54]

And there have been thousands of such discoveries! I had already learned that Luke was noted to have been an excellent historian. I looked deeper now at these claims.

Luke, the physician, supposedly wrote the Gospel of Luke and the fifth book of the New Testament called Acts. In his writings he mentions many specific places, dates, and rulers' names. Archaeology has confirmed and authenticated his material.[55]

Sir William Ramsay set out to disprove the writings of Luke by personal firsthand archaeology and research in the actual areas Luke mentioned. He ended up completely reversing his opinion and even made several new discoveries to support Luke's history. Luke's work was so detailed and accurate, it confirmed he must have been a contemporary of the events he was describing.[56]

I read about several incidents where historians questioned Luke and judged his work as unreliable because they didn't believe some of his facts that couldn't be confirmed at that time. Eventually, later archaeological discoveries vindicated Luke and made the modern historians reverse their positions. Other facts in the Bible recorded by other writers have also been substantiated by modern archaeology.

Pontius Pilate, for example, the man who sentenced Jesus to crucifixion, was not believed by many to have been an accurate historical figure in the time of Jesus. In 1961, however, a stone inscription bearing his name was found that authenticated his existence and title in the proper time frame.[57]

I was satisfied that archaeology supported many of the Bible's facts where it could. It didn't prove that the religious doctrine was true, but it did confirm that it was accurate and reliable in documenting people, places, and dates.

2. *Other Ancient Writings*

I now turned to other ancient writings. I first looked at Christian writings to see what existed, even though there was an obvious potential for bias in them. Several documents from the second century documented and confirmed the authorship of the Matthew, Mark, Luke, and John. Papias, writing around 130 A.D. from Hierapolis (modern day Turkey), noted that Mark recorded Peter's information and that Matthew also authored one of the Gospels.[58]

Irenaeus, who was taught by a man named Polycarp who personally knew the apostle John, made some very strong statements about the authorship of the four Gospels. He declared that *"So firm is the ground upon which these Gospels rest, that the very heretics themselves bear witness to them."* [59] Neither of these men proved that the authorship was factual, but it did document that there was no question about their authenticity back then.

Jesus is also mentioned in non-Christian ancient writings. In the ancient Jewish writings called the Talmud he was accused of performing sorcery, which in itself was confirmation that Jesus was doing something extraordinary.[60] It also documented that Jesus was crucified on the Passover and that the religious rulers desired to kill him. This one was particularly convincing, because it was written by people who did not believe Jesus was the Messiah.

Tacitus, a Roman historian, mentions the crucifixion of Jesus under Pontius Pilate. He also recorded that Christians had a "mischievous superstition," which likely alluded to the resurrection.[61] Josephus, a Jewish historian living in the first century, produced many writings that confirmed historical details from the Bible.[62] Pliny the Younger, a Roman author and governor in Asia Minor from the first century, mentions Christians worshipping Jesus as God.[63] Lucian, a Greek writer from the second century, wrote sarcastically about Christians believing they were immortal and that their leader was crucified.[64]

The critics of McDowell challenged many of these references and their reliability. The arguments were long and a little suspicious to me. It seemed that they were trying to find any argument possible to discredit him. I did appreciate, however, reading alternative views on this subject.

The New Testament passed this final test in my assessment. There were archeological and non-Christian sources to support the accuracy of the New Testament and the general descriptions of Jesus and early Christian doctrine. I was frustrated by the discrepancy between the amount of information readily available compared to the numbers of times that it was taught to me during my life, which was almost zero. It just seemed like this information should have been taught to me at some point in my education. Something just wasn't sitting right with me. It was fascinating to me even though I wasn't a Christian. Why weren't Christians talking about it and proclaiming it? *Did they even know?* I wondered.

THE UNIVERSITY PROFESSORS REVISITED

The New Testament had clearly passed all of the tests used for regular history and even surpassed other ancient historical documents in a stunning and surprising fashion. It was strange to me that we had more documentation on the life and events of Jesus than anyone else in all of ancient history by a landslide. It seemed that it shouldn't or couldn't be true, but yet it certainly appeared that it was.

My next step was to email one of the New Testament University professors that I had listened to, who didn't believe the New Testament was historical reality. I knew a lot more now and wanted to see what she would say. I asked her, "Why don't you believe the New Testament is literally true as written?" The professor was very gracious to answer my questions.

She claimed that the writers of the New Testament were not objective. Their religious beliefs affected their views of historical reality. This surprised me because the disciples of Jesus had no idea what was about to happen. Their religious beliefs at the time Jesus was crucified were shattered. They were expecting Jesus to be a military Messiah who would save Israel from the rule of Rome. They were not expecting God in the flesh as a sacrifice for the sins of the world. They were not focused on sin and eternity but on their present lives. If anything, their religious beliefs were turned upside down. To proclaim Jesus was God was blasphemy to the Jewish religious system. Her statement made absolutely no sense and didn't mesh with the facts.

I asked the professor, "What do you believe?" She said she couldn't know since she wasn't there. The problem was that she wasn't teaching the New Testament as if she didn't know. She did not present all the facts in her lectures. I learned that her position of "I cannot know" is called agnosticism. Basically, agnostics believe that they can't know the truth about God. This also struck me as very odd. If the New Testament was leaps and bounds more attested to and more sound than any other ancient historical documents, why wouldn't she believe it? If the same methods and standards used to document other historical events were applied to the New Testament, it should be undeniably accepted as true by someone who is an expert in this area. Most of the things that are accepted as fact about ancient Greece and Rome, for example, have a paucity of data and support compared to the New Testament, and yet those historical events are not questioned.

Caesar's Gallic Wars, for example, have only ten copies and the oldest is nine hundred years later than when these events actually occurred[65]. Bruce Metzger, an expert in the New Testament, wrote *"The works of several ancient authors are preserved to us by the thinnest possible thread of transmission... In contrast...The textual critic of the New Testament is embarrassed by the wealth of his material."*[66]

It was clear that there was a changing of the standards used to evaluate biblical history. Why? Because God and miracles and many other things people *don't want to believe* are described in the history of the New Testament. This was becoming more suspicious to me, because I had just learned how the New Testament blows away any other documents describing ancient history.

Let's look at the professor's contention that you can't know truth if you aren't there. Here's an example: How did Julius Caesar die?

A.   He hanged himself.
B.   He had a heart attack in bed.
C.   He was stabbed to death in the Roman Senate.
D.   He had a chariot accident.

C is the correct answer. A, B, and D are false. The correct answer excludes the others. We don't as a society say, "There is no correct, knowable answer" or "It's okay if you believe A and I believe D and another B. It's nice that we all have different opinions." Truth is exclusive by nature. I was frustrated with this professor, because I knew that Jesus either rose from the dead or He didn't. Only one set of historical events has occurred on this earth.

Now it was clear to me that these professors I had listened to were not objective at all. They ignored the historicity of the Bible, and one of them denied the plain doctrine of the New Testament that Jesus claimed he was God. The standards used to define ancient history were suddenly and suspiciously changed, I suspected, because the New Testament contained miracles and supernatural events. Something was wrong but I didn't know what. I felt really weird inside, because it seemed like an intentional denial of obvious facts guised and supported by the aura of academia, degrees, and scholarship. I really felt that it was a conspiracy, but why?

One last point further opened my eyes to see that something funny was occurring in the university classrooms teaching the New Testament. One professor said historians can't know anything about God and that miracles can't be historically proved because they are the least likely possibility. The problem with his statement is that Jesus was supposedly raised from the dead by God. If the professor couldn't know anything about God, then the professor certainly couldn't say it didn't happen or that it was the least likely possibility. You can't have it both ways.

I wasn't a believer in Jesus either, but I realized that if God existed then miracles wouldn't really be miracles. They would be nothing for God and not unlikely at all. The professor's own belief and statement destroyed his own position! Wasn't this just basic logic? I was angry because I felt that I had almost been duped. What if the resurrection of Jesus is true? Because of their biased and agenda-based teachings, these two professors could have ruined my potential discovery of the truth! I was infuriated that they were falsely legitimized by the cloak of academia.

I wondered if they wanted to avoid rejecting Jesus as God by trying to hide from the fact that Jesus made this claim. In other words, if you could convince yourself that Jesus never claimed to be God, then you might feel better about rejecting him. I knew this simply because it had crossed my own mind! Something inside of me didn't want to have to make a decision about Jesus. He presented me with a decision that no one else in history ever had or could. I had an inner motive to hide from this decision. Admittedly, I found myself condemning these professors for not accepting the New Testament as literal history, based upon a landslide of information, yet I had not accepted it myself. Why? What was holding me back? I wasn't sure.

Were the professors just trying to be politically correct? Perhaps it wouldn't be a popular decision for a college professor to openly support Jesus Christ as God, especially in an age where people file lawsuits over the display of manger scenes during Christmas. I had an intriguing thought: *Who devotes themself to a career trying to prove that something isn't true?* I couldn't think of any other profession in the world where this was the case. Who gets a degree in something that they don't believe in? How can a person hold a degree in the study of the most attested document in ancient history and then claim either that they don't believe it or that it isn't accurate?

My gut and heart knew something was drastically wrong here. I had a hard time swallowing that this kind of behavior and misrepresentation of the truth could be occurring in our universities. They weren't even presenting the evidence and letting people decide for themselves. I had researched this with an open mind and unbiased heart and had even started out against Christianity and the Bible. As I contemplated all of this, I thought I might have realized what was actually happening.

The evidence was overwhelming that the New Testament was true and represented accurate historical facts. Everything I could find confirmed that Jesus actually rose from the grave. This was something I never expected nor heard about. I thought deeply about the implications of all this being true in our world and culture. It was here that the motives to attack and even misrepresent this part of human history became apparent to me. If the New Testament was really true then I knew our world was way off base. I wondered, if you wandered far enough away from the truth, could this cause you to do almost anything to hide from it? I was afraid and in unbelief.

Admittedly, I wasn't ready to accept it as true either, even though everything from my heart to my research told me I should. I also realized that if I couldn't decide then, in effect, I was still rejecting Jesus. I was uncomfortable with this truth because of his claims to be God who died to save me. There was even a part of me that wished I could believe the professors and find an escape hatch for my conscience in their teachings. I did agree, however, that due to the possible implications of Jesus being God, the Bible deserved the utmost scrutiny. Since I wasn't ready to accept everything, I kept reading.

THE CASE FOR CHRIST

I wanted to hear from experts who would present fair and unbiased evidence. *The Case for Christ* by Lee Strobel was my final book.[67] I was immediately captivated because Lee was not initially a believer in Jesus. That sounded eerily familiar. He was a reporter who investigated "the case for Christ." His wife became a Christian and he was afraid his life was going to be boring.

I feared she was going to turn into some sort of sexually repressed prude who would trade our upwardly mobile lifestyle for all-night prayer vigils and volunteer work in grimy soup kitchens.[68]

Lee Strobel was not a Christian, and he investigated all of the difficulties of Christianity in an unbiased manner. He interviewed thirteen top-notch, well-respected scholars in all areas of Christianity. Each one addressed a different aspect of the evidence for Jesus and answered major questions about Jesus. I was stunned by their presentation of the evidence and their answers to many difficult and pointed questions, many of which I had not even considered before. Their answers were credible and logical and more than satisfied my critical mind. I was also surprised to find that academic people actually believed in Jesus. Strobel's book is summarized in the table below.

Type of Evidence	Question Answered	Expert Interviewed
1. Eyewitness Evidence	Can the biographies of Jesus be trusted? Do the biographies stand up to scrutiny?	Craig L. Bloomberg, Ph.D.
2. Documentary Evidence	Were Jesus' biographies reliably preserved for us?	Bruce M. Metzger, Ph.D.
3. Corroborating Evidence	Is there credible evidence for Jesus outside his biographies?	Edwin M. Yamauchi, Ph.D.
4. Scientific Evidence	Does archaeology confirm or contradict Jesus' biographies?	John McRay, Ph.D.
5. Rebuttal Evidence	Is the Jesus of history the same as the Jesus of faith?	Gregory A. Boyd, Ph.D.
6. Identity Evidence	Was Jesus really convinced that he was the Son of God?	Ben Witherington III, Ph.D.
7. Psychological Evidence	Was Jesus crazy when he claimed to be the Son of God?	Gary R. Collins, Ph.D.
8. Profile Evidence	Did Jesus fulfill the attributes of God?	Donald A. Carson, Ph.D.
9. Fingerprint Evidence	Did Jesus—and Jesus alone match the identity of the Messiah?	Louis S. Lapides, M.Div., Th.M.
10. Medical Evidence	Was Jesus' death a sham and his resurrection a hoax?	Alexander Metherell, M.D., Ph.D.
11. Evidence of the Missing Body	Was Jesus' body really absent from his tomb?	William Lane Craig, Ph.D., D.Th.

12. Evidence of Appearances	Was Jesus seen alive after his death on the cross?	Gary Habermas, Ph.D, D.D.
13. Circumstantial Evidence	Are there any supporting facts that point to the resurrection?	J. P. Moreland, Ph.D.

After finishing Mr. Strobel's book all of my questions and objections had been answered. I was relieved, excited, and also apprehensive at the same time. Just when I said to myself "Whew! It's over!" my mind was bombarded with thoughts. *Was I ready for the next step? What would that mean? Would I have to carry a Bible around if I did accept it as true? How could I face The Bible Woman at work? Would I have to get on my knees and pray every day? Would I have to go to church? What about drinking, swearing, and partying? Was this going to be boring? Would people think I was weird? Would I be like the neighbors I detested? What was I doing?* I didn't have the answers, but I knew it was time to make The Decision.

Chapter Seven

The Decision

Honey? What are you doing? You have done nothing, but work on your computer and read for weeks. Can't you put that aside and come talk to me?" my wife Ruth called down forlornly from the bedroom.

"Okay. I'll be right up," I replied. I trotted up the stairs with my mind ready to explode from information overload. The pressure reminded me of medical school, when we had to learn hundreds of new facts and concepts per week.

I walked into the bedroom and saw her sitting on the bed. The kids were sitting on the floor watching television.

"I'm done!" I exclaimed.

"Good! Finally! What have you been doing all this time?" she asked bluntly.

"I have been reading that book you gave me," I said sheepishly.

"Book? What book?"

"That one about the guy who didn't believe in Christianity. He set out to prove it wasn't true and then became a believer," I muttered. Ruth had been looking disinterestedly at something on the bed and was talking to me with her head down until I mentioned which book I was reading. She immediately looked up in surprise. Most of my reading had been on the computer or late at night, and she didn't know what I had been up to.

She was staring at me. "What do you think?" she asked, a big curious grin spreading across her face.

I began to feel uncomfortable. "I have a lot to think about," I replied. There was silence for fifteen or twenty seconds. I think she was expecting me to say more, but I didn't. *Why is she grinning?* I wondered.

"You have a funny look on your face, and you have been very quiet lately. Are you okay?" she queried.

"I am exhausted and I need to go to bed," I replied curtly. I had been very subdued and pensive for the past few weeks, and she had noticed it. Everything I was reading and researching was so far from the world that I grew up in that it had affected me. I went to bed without further explanation and fell asleep right away.

The next day was Saturday and I slept in. I awakened to the sounds of toy tractors racing through the house. "Rrrrrrrr. Rrrrrrrrr. Ehhhhh. Ehhhhh," our two boys grunted and growled. The kids had a birthday party to go to and were excited. I was looking forward to staying home. They left around eleven in the morning. I got up, went downstairs, and turned on the gas fireplace.

I was eager to think about everything while there was peace and quiet in the house. I immediately noticed that strange feeling was still with me and all around me. I could sense something was different around me, but I didn't know what. It felt as though someone was there, but I knew I was just being weird. I watched the flames flicker and dance in the fireplace as I began to review everything.

My reading and research were over. It was time to decide. What was I going to do with Jesus? I found myself in a place that I never expected to be in. I had started off as an angry neighbor seeking to prove the hypocrisy of Christians from their own Bible and ended up having to decide if Jesus Christ was God.

The New Testament had taken me completely by surprise. I wasn't expecting the message that God became a man and visited earth in order to die for my sins because he loved me. At the outset this seemed outrageously farfetched, but the deeper I went, the more and more it became credible. I had eyewitness accounts that firmly withstood the most probing questions I could think of or find. The prophecies from the ancient Hebrew Scriptures were an inescapable witness that a Messiah (savior) was coming. Jesus matched the identity of this Messiah beyond all probability.

Although the resurrection story seemed at first glance to be wishful thinking or a religious fairytale, it quickly became an intriguing and inescapable dilemma. The best explanation of the evidence surrounding the resurrection was that *Jesus actually rose from the dead!* I couldn't account for the circumstances surrounding this alleged event in human history. Men were transformed, lives were reversed, and adversaries were silenced without any logical explanation except the daunting conclusion that Jesus actually rose from the dead. Shockingly, the university professors had it completely backwards. After honestly and thoroughly examining the evidence, the resurrection was clearly the most likely possibility.

It was very difficult to admit this to myself because the supernatural was involved. My mind kept trying to find some way to discredit the resurrection, but my search had only deepened my heart's conviction that it really happened. The harder I tried to disprove the resurrection of Jesus Christ, the more convinced I became that he actually did it.

The Bible, surprisingly, was the most historically attested ancient document in all of history. It passed all of the tests, was well preserved, and was able to withstand the most difficult questions and inquiries. I kept asking myself, *If the evidence is so unmistakable, why isn't everyone a Christian?* My mind and heart were consumed with everything I had read and learned. Even though I wanted it to be true in my heart, my mind insisted I must investigate every escape hatch possible. Every time I thought of one, however, it closed as quickly as I found it.

I was torn because my research, logic, and the facts all led me to believe Christianity had to be true. Another part of me, however, kept wondering why I hadn't heard more about Jesus and Christianity in a real way, except for a handful of times, in thirty-six years. *Could something of infinite importance that is so available really be ignored or lost in our world?* I asked myself. This seemed ludicrous. *What about evolution? How could I explain all of the other religions in the world? Would I become one of the Ski Trip weirdoes? I can't become a Christian! People will laugh at me,* I thought.

I was more afraid of what this would mean for my personal life than the intellectual decision itself. I didn't want the label "Christian" or the goody-two-shoes lifestyle that I thought Christianity was. I didn't want to have to face people's questions if they saw me in church. Could I still go out and have fun? How could I tell people that I had decided to become religious? Wouldn't they think I was weird, weak, or trying to hide from a big mistake?

I felt like an intellectual seesaw going up and down. Every time I got comfortable with one side of the argument, I reverted back to the other. Something wasn't adding up. I couldn't reconcile the evidence, Scriptures, and the strong case for Christianity with the world in which I grew up. Either Jesus wasn't really God or the world was way off track. The discrepancy greatly troubled me.

My heart and mind were at war over believing the New Testament. What about the miracles? Miracles were hard to accept and seemed impossible or fictional. I had a very difficult time accepting a supernatural explanation when the world I had grown up in was completely naturalistic. Even though a miracle was the best explanation of the evidence for the resurrection and the emergence of Christianity, something in my mind didn't want to accept it.

Then, like a ton of bricks, it hit me. I had taken God out of the equation! I was analyzing the Bible as if he didn't or couldn't exist, because my entire life experience in the world had shown me God was irrelevant and unknowable. If he did exist, however, and Jesus was really God, then miracles were no longer miracles. If the Bible was true, then God could easily "speak" the universe into existence. It wouldn't be hard for God to do anything at all. The "impossible" was now easily possible.

All of the hard questions went away *if* God was a fact. It was completely illogical for me to evaluate a book all about God without considering him as real. This helped me swallow the idea of miracles. The only problem was that if God was real then why did the world ignore him, argue about him, and come up with so many different ideas about who he was?

I was tired, frustrated, and confused. I felt weird spending so much of my time reading about Jesus and the resurrection. No one I knew ever mentioned the Bible or Jesus, and now I was spending all of my free time in religious stuff. Every time I put off the decision it haunted me. I knew that deciding I couldn't decide was really rejecting Jesus, because indecision *is* a decision. I couldn't stop thinking about everything I had read and studied. I decided it was time to go one way or the other. I knew I wasn't contemplating intellectual suicide or a blind leap of unfounded faith. I was amazed at the amount of information, facts, and evidence that underpinned Christianity and the Bible. Without this I would have long ago dismissed it as just another religion. If I decided to believe, however, I could feel very comfortable with the basis for my new faith.

Then something inside of me said, *This is all just an intellectual exercise. What's the big deal if you decide to believe in Jesus and start attending church? If you have decided it's true from your analysis, then isn't that enough? There isn't any present day reality to all of this anyway! You're wrangling over ancient history and doctrines about God.* The conflict within me was raging.

"Greg? Greg? We're home," Ruth yelled as she opened the garage door. I didn't answer since I was still deep in thought. She saw me on the couch and continued, "What are you doing? Why aren't you answering me?"

"Sorry, I was daydreaming. Did you guys have fun?" The sound of trampling little footsteps now filled the room as my two boys raced in from the garage holding their gift bags from the party. They immediately dumped them on the kitchen table and ransacked the contents like starving bears.

"The kids had a great time. What did you do?"

"I stayed on the couch and vegged out."

"You seem a little strange and quiet. You never relax," Ruth answered.

I didn't really want to talk about this with anyone, not even Ruth. I wasn't ready to discuss it.

"I'm fine. I'm just thinking about a lot of stuff. I'll fill you in later."

"Okay. I'm going shopping with Kim for a few hours. Watch the kids for me." I played with the boys the rest of the day. My mind needed a good rest and distraction.

That night I had to go to the airport. Ruth's sister was flying in from out of town. It was about six o'clock and I was down in the basement reading the Bible again on my laptop. Pondering a particular passage from John, I read the words over and over.

Now Thomas (called Didymus), one of the Twelve, was not with the disciples when Jesus came. So the other disciples told him, "We have seen the Lord!"

But he said to them, "Unless I see the nail marks in his hands and put my finger where the nails were, and put my hand into his side, I will not believe it."

A week later his disciples were in the house again, and Thomas was with them. Though the doors were locked, Jesus came and stood among them and said, "Peace be with you!" Then he said to Thomas, "Put your finger here; see my hands. Reach out your hand and put it into my side. Stop doubting and believe."

Thomas said to him, "My Lord and my God!"

Then Jesus told him, "Because you have seen me, you have believed; blessed are those who have not seen and yet have believed."

Jesus did many other miraculous signs in the presence of his disciples, which are not recorded in this book. But these are written that you may believe that Jesus is the Christ, the Son of

God, and that by believing you may have life in his name. (John 20:24-31 NIV)

If this account was true then this was a man who actually saw God in person and lived with him. He was writing to the world to let them know what happened. It must have blown him away later in life as he looked back and realized what he had witnessed.

I felt like Thomas who wanted to actually see to believe, but then I focused on what Jesus said. I felt as if he was talking to me. *I am someone who has not seen Jesus, but I can still believe*, I thought.

I finally decided, *Okay, I believe it. I can intellectually accept Christianity. Now I can go to church. It won't kill me. What do I have to lose?* I was a little nervous when I took this step in my mind. My heart raced, and I felt very jittery making this decision.

"Greg? Greg! You need to leave to pick up my sister," Ruth yelled down into the basement.

"Okay. I am going." As I drove the car it was now dark outside and the car was silent. Normally I had the radio blaring. I was still deep in thought. I had the urge to actually say "I believe" out loud to myself even though no one was around. The feeling around me was stronger than ever. For some reason, I hesitated to say the words out loud, even though I had said them in my mind just a moment before.

As I pulled out onto the main road I said aloud in the car, "I believe. I believe that Jesus died on the cross for my sins and was raised from the dead." The moment I said this I felt strange and peaceful at the same time. Had I just become religious? I headed towards the airport and thought about how my life might change.

I decided I would go to church, wear the appropriate clothes, learn from the sermons, and try to be a nicer guy. God would see that I was being a good boy and let me into heaven someday. He would see and understand that I was making a conscious effort to be a Christian, and God would be pleased. No problem. What was so weird about that? As I thought about it I felt better. I can do this Christian thing!

I didn't think that there was anything else to Christianity. Everything I had read about had happened so long ago that I just couldn't know—for absolutely certain, anyway—until I died. I knew I had to have faith. I needed to simply trust my own research and heart and accept it. I was glad it was finally over, but was it? I had no idea this was just the beginning.

Chapter Eight

The Awakening

It was Monday morning and I was racing to work. The light turned green and the car in front of me didn't move right away. "You idiot! Green means go! Just step on the gas and move it!" I yelled at the vehicle in front of me. He finally moved forward, taking his time. In annoyance, I tailgated him until there was an opening. At last! I whipped into the left lane and passed him. "Yes!" I exclaimed. I showed him.

I pulled up to the next light and another car was on my right. I stared at the red light and covertly watched the intersecting signal light for cross traffic. This would give me notice on when that light was about to turn and provide me an edge. I saw it turn yellow and revved my engine with one foot and kept the other foot on the brake. As soon as our light turned green I floored it and shot out in front. I glanced into the rearview mirror and saw that the guy on my right had been left behind in the dust. I pulled into the right lane sporting a victory grin.

THE HOLY SPIRIT?

I arrived at work and went into the lab to my computer. Tammy, The Bible Woman, was at her desk reading. She got up, slowly moseyed over to me, and asked, "How is your Bible reading coming?" I figured she might inquire about that when I saw her approaching, and I had a ready response. I wasn't prepared yet to tell anyone I had decided to become a Christian or that I believed in the Bible.

My reply was short and to the point, "Good. I have read a lot and now I am digesting it."

With a funny look on her face, eyebrows slightly but noticeably raised, she airily said, "I pray that the Holy Spirit will reveal Himself to you." Then she walked away. It was as if she was hinting to me that she knew something was going to happen. I had no idea what she meant, but I was too embarrassed to ask. Mulling her statement over in my mind, the words nagged at me throughout the rest of the day. *What did she mean?*

Late that night I was working in my home office after everyone was in bed. Her words echoed in my mind. "I pray that the Holy Spirit will reveal himself to you." I suddenly became a little spooked. *What*

Holy Spirit? I was still having that intense feeling of a presence surrounding me, but now it seemed more noticeable since she said that. I was freaked out. *Is something going to happen to me? Is something going to appear?* I worried. *Am I being silly?*

Suddenly I spun my chair around and looked quickly behind me to ensure nothing was there. *Whew! The coast is clear*, I thought, sighing with relief. A few minutes later I jerked my gaze up to the ceiling to see if I could see something. I didn't know what to expect and was acting crazy. *Get hold of yourself!* I admonished myself mentally. I didn't recall anything significant about the Holy Spirit from my Bible reading, from The Ski Trip, or during the incident at Marco Island.

Subsequently, every night when I worked late alone in my home office, I thought about what Tammy had said. I had a feeling that something was going to happen, but I didn't know what.

THE PATIENT

The next week I had a new patient who really set my mind reeling. Let's just call him The Patient. It was Monday morning and the office was already buzzing with patients and nurses. The nurse said to me, "We have an 'add-on' for today." I looked at the schedule and noticed a man's name written in blue ink underneath the regular list of typed patient names. The normal routine was to first tend to the regularly scheduled patients. I completed that in about thirty minutes then proceeded to room number four, where the "add-on" was waiting for me.

He was tall and slender and sitting upright on the medical examining bed, facing me. He was fifty years old with short, receding gray-brown hair. His lanky legs and feet hung off the edge of the bed, swaying casually, and his arms were folded in his lap. His eyes were deep blue with an unusual glimmer and light in them, which immediately got my attention. I looked more closely and was mentally jolted when his eyes reminded me of The Ski Trip kooks. His eyes were fixated on me in a slightly uncomfortable way, but, conversely, his smile was warm and inviting.

I turned my attention to his medical chart. He was a skin cancer patient, which was my specialty. I started the normal routine by reviewing pertinent information in his paperwork and medical history. I noticed he worked for a church. This got my attention for a different reason—because of my decision to become a Christian.

"So you work for a church?" I asked.

"Yes, sir," he replied simply, showing little emotion. His glimmering, intense eyes looked right through me, making me feel uncomfortable.

When I started to examine his skin he just lay there staring up at the ceiling. He had a very unusual sense of peace about him. He wasn't the least bit concerned or curious about his skin cancer; I found that very unusual. Most people were nervous, curious, or fidgeting in their chairs and had a lot of questions.

"Do you have any questions or concerns?" I asked.

"No, sir, everything will be fine," he replied, still staring at the ceiling.

There was something very unusual about him. The nurse was standing behind him (he couldn't see her), and she shrugged her shoulders and gave me the *I have no idea what's up with this guy* look.

I left the room while the nurse prepared him for surgery. He had a small skin cancer on his left temple. When I returned to perform the first stage of the procedure, there he was, lying peacefully, staring upwards without a care in the world. He was calm and had a relaxed smile and appearance. He turned and looked at me as I began to put the drape over his face. He didn't say anything but gave me a strange look. His eyes and expression radiated with immense compassion.

This guy is looking at me like one who is full of love! I thought. Not a perverted love, but a caring love. It reminded me of my grandmother's warmth and the delight she used to take in me. My heart rate instantly shot up and I had an immediate desire to get away from this man. When I put the drape over him, which exposed only the small area on his forehead, the nurse sensed my bewilderment and gave me a perplexed look. *What is up with this guy? Why am I affected?* I wondered.

I removed the first stage of the skin cancer and left the room. After he was bandaged up, I didn't go back into his room, to see how he was doing, as I normally would have. I was still a little freaked out by this guy. The skin cancer sample removed from his skin was sent directly to our lab for pathology. About thirty minutes later the pathology was ready for me to analyze under the microscope. Fortunately, his skin cancer had been completely removed by the first stage and he didn't require more surgery. *Let's get him out of here*, I thought.

I told the nurse, "Get him ready for discharge. The wound is so small we will let it heal on its own. He won't need stitches."

When it was time for his discharge I had to return to the room. He was sitting up in the medical chair waiting for me. A small white bandage was on his left forehead. I told him the good news, and all the while he continued to look at me with *that look*. It is hard to describe it exactly, but I sure felt it. He didn't say or ask anything. He just stared. Then suddenly and unexpectedly he looked me dead in the eyes and asked, "Have you accepted the Lord Jesus Christ as your Lord and personal Savior?"

I was stunned and, for once, speechless. My stomach dropped into my pelvis. I felt as if I was on the descent cycle of the worst roller coaster of my life. The blood drained from my face; I turned white and felt an internal pressure building inside of me. And it was all happening so suddenly. *Why is he asking me this?!* I couldn't speak. I was frozen. He was looking at me as if he somehow knew what had I been up to for the past several weeks. I glanced over his shoulder at the nurse, who stood behind him. Her eyebrows were raised high and her mouth gaped open. She was completely slack-jawed. In my ten years of being a doctor, I had never had a patient say something like this so completely out of the blue.

"Uh. Uh. I have to go, uh, back to the, uh, lab," I stammered. I flew out of the room as quick as I could and went straight to the kitchen. I collapsed in a chair there. I was in a cold sweat with my heart beating out of my chest. I poured myself a cold glass of water and chugged it down. I began to feel that same presence around me again. It wigged me out, but I was at work and forced myself to become composed.

"What was that about?" the nurse asked when she came into the kitchen, The Patient's chart in her hands.

"Is he gone?" I asked.

"He's gone. I just walked him out."

"Good. I need to get back to work," I said, then stood up. I didn't want to talk about it with her and used the busy work schedule to escape. Luckily, it was a particularly hectic day, which helped me get it out of my mind. The feeling of a constant presence, however, never left me from that day forward.

That night when I got home Ruth knew something was wrong. "What's up with you? You are acting strange," she inquired. It must have been the silence. I usually came home quite talkative. I didn't answer her and just left her standing there baffled. I went out on the porch to ponder everything that was happening. I began to focus on what The Bible Woman had said to me that day: "I hope the Holy Spirit reveals himself to you." *What did she mean? What did she mean?* I wondered. "She probably doesn't even know!" I muttered, consoling myself.

I felt something in the air, especially when I was alone—as if something or someone was there. It swirled about me in a strange aura that I could only feel and sense. It was peaceful and warm, but at the same time, I was a little anxious since I didn't know what it was. I didn't tell anyone, especially Ruth. I knew everyone would think I was bonkers if I told them. Happily, she left me alone and didn't press the matter, but I knew she was curious.

Usually when I came home, I wanted peace and quiet, but this time our rambunctious kids were for once a delightful distraction. Ruth and I went to bed early. I didn't tell her that part of the reason I was going to sleep early was so I wouldn't have to be in my office alone. I was a little spooked about "the presence."

THE NEXT-DOOR NEIGHBOR

The next day I was outside in the yard and the next-door neighbor came over. We chatted and he invited me to go to his church that Sunday. "I want you try the church I have been going to. They simply teach the Bible and worship God," he said to me. I was surprised because we had not talked about God and he didn't know about The Investigation.

"I don't know," I replied sheepishly.

"You don't have to wear a suit. You can wear jeans and a T-shirt if you want to," he stated, his excitement growing. I think he noticed my relief when he mentioned the required clothing. He figured I was a little more interested now. He continued, "They even have a coffee bar and espresso machine!"

That's all I had to hear. I loved coffee, wasn't crazy about dressing up, and had already decided to go to church but was embarrassed to initiate it on my own. I also didn't want to show up somewhere and have people I knew ask me a bunch of questions like "What are you doing here?" I didn't want people to know I had been reading the Bible and researching Christianity.

"Okay. I'll go," I replied.

"Great. You can follow me over. It's right around the corner."

"I'll see you then."

I walked into the house and wondered how I would tell Ruth. I felt embarrassed and weird telling her. She was in the kitchen area sitting at the table with the kids. "David asked me to go to church on Sunday. I don't know if I want to go."

I was lying, since I actually did want to go, but I wanted to sound unsure and not too eager.

"Really? Are you going to go?" she asked, surprise written all over her face. I think she was pleasantly shocked.

"What do you think?" I replied, sticking to my tactic of letting her think I may not want to go, putting the final decision on her.

"I think we should all go," she said.

"Okay. I'll let him know."

I hurried out to the yard knowing she would think I was giving David my answer. I didn't want her to know I had already said yes.

CHURCH

Sunday arrived and I put on a pair of jeans and a polo shirt. Ruth wore a pair of slacks and a blouse. I gathered up the kids and we all got in the car. I pulled the car behind the neighbor's, who was waiting for us. On the way there I was a little jittery and a few butterflies were in my stomach. After all, our prior experiences at church had not been very good.

It was only a short distance to the church; it was right down the road, in fact. When David turned into the parking lot I thought he had made a wrong turn. "Honey, he's pulling into a strip mall," I said.

She pointed and said, "No. Look there. The sign says 'Calvary Chapel.' There is a church here." It was a church, but there was no steeple, stained glass, or big white front doors. The building was a large, long, single-storied structure with people streaming into two entrances at the front. The parking lot was packed, and they even had guys directing traffic. *Do this many people really go to church?* I wondered. I also noticed almost everyone was carrying a Bible. Why would they bring a Bible to church? I had only been a few times in my entire life, but I didn't recall people bringing their own Bibles.

When we walked up to go in, I immediately felt at home. *I can't believe I don't feel uncomfortable*, I thought. The people here were not like any I had ever experienced before. A lady greeted me at the door with a glowing smile on her face. "Welcome," she said as she handed me a flyer.

I smelled the good aroma of fresh ground coffee and headed straight for the coffee bar, which was immediately on the left once I entered the building. I could hear and smell the espresso machine brewing and the milk frothing. *Aaaah, music to the ears!* It didn't seem totally right in a church, but it was heaven sent to me!

I ordered a latte and watched everybody coming in. Smiling faces, jubilant hugs, and a peaceful and warm ambience surrounded me. I was instantly jealous inside. *Why are these people so happy? I have it all and yet I am miserable.* Baffled, I tried to analyze some of them and judge them to make myself feel better.

That guy is a geek. Oh, look! Here comes Holly Hobby in her dress. And gracious! Get a load of this guy. He's a jubilant pansy, I gloated inside. I was beginning to feel a little worried about whether I could really pull off this church thing. I wasn't like these folks.

The music started. It was flowing underneath the closed doors straight ahead of me. I headed that way, opened the doors, and entered the sanctuary with Ruth and David, our neighbor.

I instantly felt an immense sense of energy and joy. Everyone seemed excited and engaged. During the worship people were closing their eyes and raising their hands. At times everyone was clapping their hands. I could tell they were experiencing something, but I didn't know what or how. It seemed very weird, but at the same time it was alluring and it drew me. It was, however, very orderly. They seemed very grateful and reverent of God. I could sense they were fulfilled and satisfied, something I had never found and was always looking for. *How could this be?* I wondered.

The jealousy returned. The woman on the stage was singing with her eyes closed, and the bongo drums guy was looking up at the ceiling with a huge smile on his face. These people can't have what I have. *They don't have the education, training, or knowledge that I do,* I thought. The music was interesting, but it seemed to go on forever.

The pastor finally came out after the last song ended. He taught a forty-minute lesson directly from the Bible. He went verse by verse through a section from the book called Matthew. Everybody was following along with their own Bibles. Now I knew why everyone had one! I had only been to church twice in my life, but his message was different. The previous guys did a lot of talking, but this man was more of a teacher. He explained each sentence and helped everyone understand what was being said in the Bible. He didn't offer a lot of his own opinions, which I liked. He strictly relied on what the Bible said.

At the end he talked about "receiving Christ." He kept using that phrase, as if a transaction was necessary between man and God. It didn't make sense to me. *What does he mean by telling us to personally receive Christ?* Jesus died two thousand years ago and is up in heaven. *How can I receive him?* I asked myself. *In fact, hadn't I already done this when I decided the Bible was true and agreed to come to church?*

Overall, I actually enjoyed the service. I was irritated by the congregation's collective joy and peace, but I didn't let that get the best of me. Nobody was pushy, intrusive, or looking at me like I was new or different. I liked the coffee bar thing and enjoyed being able to wear everyday clothes. I had always thought it was hypocritical for people to dress up for church and then go home and act like everybody else. I told my wife, "I think I can go here once a week." She was glad and David was ecstatic. *Why is he so happy for me? What does it matter? Why would he care if I go to church?* I wondered.

THE MELTDOWN

The next day something strange happened. I was in our home office working late. Everyone was asleep. I wasn't able to concentrate because I couldn't stop thinking about Jesus and the Bible. I was still a little spooked about the Holy Spirit. The presence was still with me, and getting stronger. It was weird and comforting at the same time. The Patient's words were coming up in my mind, "Have you accepted the Lord Jesus Christ as your Lord and personal Savior?" *Isn't that what the preacher asked us to do, as well?*

Suddenly I started thinking about my bad habits, recalling specific incidents from the past when I had wronged someone or said mean things. I started remembering in detail, beginning from childhood on into adulthood, becoming more horrified and disgusted with myself as I reflected. Scenes began to flow uninterrupted through my mind. I tried to shut them out, but they kept coming—in graphic splendor. I watched, seeing clearly, transfixed, and knowing it was all true.

"You're a loser and a wimp! You dress like a sissy!" I railed to a new boy on the elementary school playground. "We don't want you to play with us," I jabbed. The boy ran away in tears. "What's the matter?! Are you running to your mommy?" I yelled after him.

"Hey, Doug. Let's ditch Chris. He's in the bathroom and won't know where we went," I said to my friend when I was in the fourth grade.

"You're ugly. No guy will ever like you!" I jeered at a girl in the eighth grade. Her face contorted as if she had been shot. She stared at me in disbelief and began to shake in sorrow. I smiled at her discomfort.

"I can't believe you cheated on me!" My tenth grade girlfriend sobbed. "How could you do that to me? Don't you understand that I love you?" she asked with tears running down her face. She was balling so hard she couldn't catch her breath. I wasn't fazed.
"I like her better," I coldly replied.

"I can do a much better job for your nightclub. This DJ you have sucks! Hire me and I'll show you how it should be done," I said to a potential employer. I was in college at the time. I got the job. The other guy lost his.

"Daddy, will you come out and play with me?" my four-year-old son asked with a ball in his hands.
"Not right now! Can't you see I'm busy?!" I yelled. He dropped the ball and ran away in tears.

"What is wrong with you?!" Ruth asked me.
"There is nothing wrong. Shut up and leave me alone! Why do you keep nagging me?" I retorted. "You're always on edge and so short-tempered."
"You keep snapping at me," she sobbed.
"Stop crying and get out of here. I can't deal with ___ right now!"
"Fine!" she yelled as she slammed the door behind me.
"Women are a pain in the ___" I mumbled to myself.

"You dummies! What in the world are you doing! Get the ___ upstairs to your rooms right now!" I yelled at my two sons, ages four and five. They ran upstairs crying and howling.
"Mommy! Mommy! Daddy is yelling at us again." I was downstairs trying to pick up their toys that were strewn all across the floor. Ruth came running down the stairs.
"What's the matter with you? You are always yelling at them."
"I have had a long day at work. Leave me the ___ alone," I snapped.

One by one the reel continued to roll in my mind, just like a movie. It was a horror film and I was the star. I was beginning to see how I had been cruel, unkind, jealous, prideful, unforgiving, and unloving for as long as I could remember. I understood and saw myself from a new perspective. I put my elbows on the desk and rested my forehead on my hands. I began to weep at the monster I had been for so long in so many situations. It was as if someone was showing me who I really was. I didn't like what I saw.

The pain of the truth pierced me through and crushed my heart from sorrow. Tears became a torrent and sobs became howls of anguish and grief. I then sensed the presence of God in an unexplainable way for the first time in my life. He stood before me in my mind, and I was afraid. I sensed a terror inside because I knew I was a sinner dead in my sins before a holy God. I shuddered at how fallen I was and began to shake.

I ran to the bed behind me and fell on my knees. I let it all out so loud that I can't believe I didn't wake up the whole house. I was quivering in fear and sorrow. I stuttered between sobs, "Oh, God! Forgive me. Please forgive me. I am so wrong. I am so wicked. I am sorry, so, so sorry! Jesus, please help me!"

I continued unabated, "I don't want to be this way anymore. Change me. Oh, Jesus, please change me! Make me the person you want me to be. I believe you died on the cross for my sins. I have sinned against you. I didn't know. I really didn't know..." I wept in anguish.

This went on for at least ten minutes. I was crying so hard my words were disjointed. I had surrendered. I had thrown myself at the mercy of God, and begged to be forgiven like a condemned criminal before a judge. I could somehow feel God's power, which made me cry harder. I hadn't planned to have an emotional episode and certainly didn't want to, as a proud and successful, professional, adult man. The words just came out. Something came over me that made me repent, surrender, and beg for mercy. I had no concept that I was accomplishing anything other than a private emotional meltdown. This prayer, however, was a critical turning point in my life.

At last my emotions subsided. I had let it all go. I slowly regathered myself. I felt really weird and embarrassed, even though I was alone. I tip toed into the bedroom, certain Ruth would be waiting to ask me what was going on. She was asleep. I climbed into bed, preparing to sleep. As I lay there I felt an immense sense of profound peace. It was more than ordinary peace and something I had never experienced.

Wow. I had no idea what a good cry and emotional meltdown could do for me, I thought. I went to bed unaware that anything special had happened. I slept like a baby. I had no idea I would never awaken the same again.

Chapter Nine

The Transformation

THE FIRST FEW MOMENTS

In the morning when I woke up, everything was completely different in every conceivable way. I will never be able to adequately explain what it was like. In magnitude, it was comparable to seeing for the first time after having been blind since birth. I felt as if I had awakened from a dream that had lasted thirty-six years.

"Eh-eh-eh-eh!" the alarm clock squawked at 5:30 a.m. I was slowly awakening but was dazed and confused. I reached over and turned off the alarm. I sat up on the side of my bed and sensed that something was radically different. *I feel a tremendous peace. I don't feel worried and stressed about my day like normal. The tension seems broken and the pressure weighing down on me has lifted,* I thought.

I moved through the still dark bedroom and into the shower. The warm water hit my head and flowed down my back and stomach. *What is so different?* I soaped up and lathered up my hair. I closed my eyes and let the water wash the shampoo away. Suddenly it came to me. *My mind is silent!* The usual freeway traffic jam of thoughts and anxieties were gone!

I realized at that moment that for most of my life, from the time I woke up, my mind started racing with all kinds of worries and concerns. *The mortgage is due; the kids are sick; my stocks are going down; I have to go the bank, pick up my laundry, get to the gym, prepare slides for a talk, get the toilet fixed, and have the oil changed...*

These types of thoughts had bombarded my mind for years within seconds of opening my eyes. Today they were gone! For the first time I could remember, the confusion, stress, and frustrations of a rat race life weren't on my mind, and it felt great! The normally overcrowded road in my mind was peacefully and serenely quiet and empty. "This is weird but awesome," I mumbled to myself.

I squeezed the last bit of toothpaste on the brush and began the brushing sequence. I had the habit of brushing my teeth in the shower. I moved the brush up and down while the warm water continued to flow over my head. It was then that I made another startling observation. *I feel like I am content, but what is that?* A brand new happiness was embedded in my heart that didn't make any sense to me. *I just woke up. I haven't purchased anything or had anything happen to me to make me feel this way. Why am I feeling this way?* The feeling was familiar, but in a different context.

This feels like the day I got behind the wheel of a new BMW M-3 convertible for the first time. When I first got that awesome piece of racing engineering, I had zeal in my life and a kick in my step that was incredible. I looked forward to living each day because I knew I would get to drive and be seen in my hot new car. The problem was, that feeling only lasted for a few weeks, and truthfully, it began to fade in a few days.

But now I am feeling that same way for no reason within minutes of getting out of bed! I normally rolled out of bed grumpy, disenchanted with life, and dreading another day of work. This was strange but admittedly desirable, just like having a clear and quiet mind was.

The last part of my shower routine was shaving. I began to stroke down each side of my face and tapped the razor on the tile to clean it out. I marveled at how different everything was. I had experienced similar feelings in the past, but they were always related to something I had bought, won, or been given—something tangible.

I quickly thought of another sensation that was similar. *This is just like a good buzz! I feel as if I just drank two glasses of wine—the first two!* I was feeling relaxed with a gentle euphoria and excitement about my situation, like good wine brought me. *This is a rather crazy time to feel this way, though—I am simply taking a shower!*

Wine was always the one thing that seemed to ease my tension, clear the cares of life, and bring me a happiness and sense of joy. It seemed to fill the void in my life, but it never lasted. To compound the issue, I got headaches and a hangover the next day. Today was different. I was taking a regular ol' shower and feeling terrific for no discernable reason. Baffling! I hadn't had any alcohol. I had just awakened. It was the early part of the work week and not a Friday—a day when I could at least look forward to the weekend. There wasn't a new car in the garage or a vacation round the corner. *Maybe I just need a good shot of espresso*, I thought. *A caffeine jolt might clear up my mind so I can figure out this thing.*

I got out of the shower, got dressed, and went downstairs. I kept waiting for my mind to clog up and the pressure to return, but that didn't happen. I brewed a quick shot of espresso and chugged it down. I stood there for a minute or two expecting the rush of caffeine to awaken me out of this pleasant but strange nirvana. Nothing changed. I quickly brewed another shot, gulped it down, packed my bags, and got into the car. I felt as if I was getting ready for a trip I had been eagerly anticipating all year, but I was headed to work, not Vegas. In the few days leading up to a Great Vacation, I always experienced a similar euphoria, joy, and excitement about the coming trip.

THE FIRST DAY AT WORK

I got in the car and started to drive to work. The urge to race to get there was gone. The traffic didn't tick me off. A guy cut in front of me and I didn't beep the horn or give him the finger. I forgot my cell phone, but I wasn't frustrated. When I pulled up to the red light at the signal limit line, I didn't feel the urge to floor it to beat the guy next to me. "This is weird," I said aloud. Has Mario Andretti become Mister Rogers?

When I arrived at work these feelings got stronger, and my unexplainable personality changes became more noticeable. The schedule was overbooked, but I didn't care or blame the nurses. I even had a difficult and demanding patient but didn't lose patience with her.

She was the first patient of the day. I opened the door and saw a little old lady sitting in the exam chair with a white piece of paper clenched in her hand. She was glaring at me with an urgent stare. The moment I entered the room she took control of the conversation.

"Now, Dr. Viehman, I have a list of things I want you to go over," she said in a demanding way shaking the list at me. Such a list is always a bad sign to doctors. However, instead of thinking, *Oh no! A list!* I said, "Sure, what can I do for you?" The crazy thing is that I knew I was actually being sincere. I wanted to help her and answer her questions. I didn't feel irritated, put out, or hassled by her!

I felt a very intense love and caring attitude towards her. It was as if something was within me empowering me to be kind to this difficult and demanding patient. I didn't have to act or pretend, either. It was real! Normally I would *act* nice if I could, but in my heart I'd be thinking *Get me out of here!* Instead, I was puzzled. *Why do I like this woman?*

The nurse could tell I was way out of character and gave me a look that asked, "What's the matter with you?" I didn't feel or act like I normally did, but this was me. It was a very strange feeling to suddenly feel like a new person, living in the same body.

I drove home after work very perplexed. My usual daily knapsack filled with anxiety, frustration, emptiness, impatience, bitterness, and selfishness was no longer on my back. It felt as though a huge weight had been lifted from my life. I was content for no reason. In the past I always relied on something, someone, or someplace to keep me satisfied. But now I felt a joy in my heart about my life without any specific reason for it. I had the strange conviction that somehow the void, hunger, and thirst in my life for bigger, better, and more were gone. Could it really be?

I always left early in the morning before anyone was up. When I arrived home I saw Ruth for the first time since this had happened to me. I came through the garage door and she was in the kitchen.

THE FIRST NIGHT AT HOME

"Hi, honey. I'm home," I said. She was cooking dinner and the kids were playing on the floor. When she turned around and looked at me, I saw her in a completely different way. I felt a desire to spend time with her and talk, which was not normally the case. I sensed an appreciation for her that was new. In the past I had taken her for granted. This all occurred in an instant.

The same thing happened when I saw the kids. "Daddy!" they yelled and ran towards me. I hugged them and suddenly had a very strong realization that I was *dad* to two precious children. My thoughts centered on them and their needs instead of my typical self-centered impulses.

I was having deep, strange, and new thoughts. The boys returned to their play while Ruth continued to cook. I sat peacefully in the kitchen and took it all in. I was seeing my family and my role for the first time, with a new perspective that was outside of the moment-by-moment living. It was almost as if someone was showing me my life and how short and fragile it was. I had a desire to make the most of every moment instead of squandering them. Then it hit me. *I feel like Emily Gibbs from* Our Town *or Ebenezer Scrooge from* A Christmas Story! It's as if I was looking down on life with a new appreciation for the everyday routines that are so easily taken for granted. *I am approach-*

ing forty and my life has gone by in the blink of an eye. I can't believe how easily I have taken my life and my family for granted, I groaned inside. I had never thought I didn't appreciate life during those precious moments before, but now somehow the truth had been revealed to me—in full force. My heart was crushed and I could only observe my family and marvel.

While we were eating dinner, a sudden dread came over me as the thoughts continued to escalate. Guilt, shame, and sorrow filled my heart as I watched Ruth and the kids at the dinner table. Something as simple as a dinner together could be missed for the miracle that it really was. *Why am I thinking this way? What has happened to me?* I wondered. I continued to stare at them as I took everything in. I started thinking about the past, and a new set of flashbacks began to play. There were four of us there, but I was the only one who could see the accusing visions come into mental view.

"Greg, we are going to see your grandmother this weekend," Mom said to me in high school.

"I'm not going. I'm sleeping over at JB's house," I replied.

"You should really go. She is getting older and you might not see her too many more times."

"Nah. I don't want to go. It's boring over there."

"Greg, your grandmother has died. The funeral is next weekend," Mom said on the phone. I was in Durham, NC, during my residency in dermatology.

"I can't come up. I'm too busy and it's too far away," I said.

"Greg! She is your grandmother."

I wanted to go but didn't want to see another dead person. I didn't want to see her house empty that had filled my memory banks for years. I selfishly hid from death and didn't go.

"Honey, come on inside and spend some time with me. Just talk to me," Ruth said at a party.

"Nah, I'm staying out here with the guys. Go back inside. We're having a good time," I fired back. She went back in. *"Man! Can't we have some peace and relaxation around here?"* I said to the group as I chugged down a beer.

"Yeah. Wives are a pain in the ____" one guy snickered. Everybody laughed.

"Greg, I forgot to get your dry cleaning today. I'm sorry," Ruth said sheepishly.

"What the ___ is wrong with you? Can't you do anything for me? You don't even have to work!" I railed.

"How many hot dogs would you like for dinner?" Ruth asked me while I was diligently studying for the dermatology board examination.

"I don't care! Just make me some. I'm busy studying," I snapped.

"Can't you just tell me how many you want?" She implored.

"I'm busy and I don't care. Don't ask me again!" I said, gritting my teeth and clutching a coffee cup.

"Greg, calm down. I need to know how many you will eat," she politely replied.

I stood up in rage. "If you ask me one more time I will pour out this coffee on your white carpet!"

She didn't flinch. "How many hot dogs?" she calmly inquired.

I looked her dead in the eye and poured out the black coffee onto the white rug. It descended like a black waterfall. "I told you to leave me alone!" I yelled.

"Daddy, can we play with the tractors tonight?" our three-year-old son asked.

"No, not tonight, son. Your mom and I are going out with friends."

"Da-Da, will you come down to the sand box with us?" our two sons asked.

"Not now. I have to train for a triathlon today."

The visions from my past faded and suddenly I wasn't hungry—even though I had eaten little food. In a matter of seconds I realized how incredibly insensitive, arrogant, selfish, and demanding I had been for many years. My heart was sinking and tears began to well up in my eyes. I fought them off by getting up from the table and putting the plate in the sink. I spent the rest of the night playing with our two sons and talking to Ruth. I felt better.

Everyone went to sleep and I stayed up late in the office, which was in a spare bedroom. I marveled at what had happened to me in just one day. *I feel as if I have been drugged. It's as if my old self has died and come back as a new person. What is happening to me?* I was confused and a bit scared, but glad at the same time. *My family is young. I am still young. It isn't too late! I can still make changes in my life,* I promised myself.

THE NEXT THREE DAYS

I went to bed and slept like a peaceful baby for the second night in a row. The next day was the same as the first. I was more comfortable, though, and more familiar with some of the changes. I was enjoying the sense of peace and serenity, since I had always been wound so tight previously. It was still hard for me to believe I wasn't dreaming. This was evidently for real. On day three I started waking up scared. I was afraid I would go back to my old self. I thought it couldn't last much longer, whatever it was.

"Eh-eh-eh-eh!" the alarm clock squawked at 5:30 a.m. With my eyes half shut, I reached over and turned that horrible noise off. *Is the peaceful feeling still there? Am I still different?* I immediately thought as I began to wake up. *What if it's gone? What if I go back to my old ways and self? What will I do?* I worried.

I got up, went into the bathroom, and stood looking at myself in the mirror. The boxers I was wearing were twisted. A bad hair day was staring me in the face. I looked like a punk rocker. Somehow none of that fazed me. *I feel at peace and I'm not anxious to get to work. This is a good sign*, I thought. I quickly realized I was still the new man. "Yes!" I exclaimed. "Yes!"

Every morning I kept waiting for *him*, the old me I didn't like anymore, to return, but he never did. *What in the world is up?*

A NEW TONGUE

On the fourth day I realized that something else very profound had happened to me. I had missed it during the first three days because I was so confused and overwhelmed. It was early morning and I was getting ready to go to work. I chugged down the usual morning espresso and began to load up a backpack for work. "My wallet! Where is my wallet?!" I said aloud in despair. I ripped the house and car apart in a frenzy and couldn't find it! I rifled through the backpack, stripped down all of the jackets and clothing, and ransacked the kitchen, where I usually kept my keys and wallet.

In the past I absolutely abhorred losing my wallet or keys. It drove me crazy. This time was different, though. I wasn't as upset, but that wasn't what got my attention. For some reason, I was no longer cursing. My sailor's tongue was silent when it normally would have been firing off cannons of profanity. I suddenly stopped my panicked search mission and stood dead still for a moment. I replayed the last three days mentally and realized I had not uttered one profane word! I was so shocked that I simply got in the car and began driving to work, not caring about the wallet.

Cuss words had been a part of my normal everyday vocabulary since the fifth or six grade. My thoughts flashed back to the "Christian" summer camp, where I had learned most of the words.

"Hey, Andy, would you pass the ___ peas, please!" We were eating in a large dining hall filled with tables of eight. All of the kids in one cabin ate together at their own table.

"___ you, Viehman. Get it yourself!" he replied.

"Okay, you ___," I railed.

"Watch your mouth, Viehman, or I'll kick your ___!" the counselor fired back."

I had used cuss words as adjectives, nouns, and adverbs *all* of the time. I didn't even think about it. When something went wrong, I uttered blasphemies using the word "God" or "Jesus" even though I didn't believe in God. Without thinking about what I was saying, the words came out automatically.

When I arrived at work I sat down at my desk. I jiggled the mouse to wake up the computer screen, but nothing happened. I normally would have immediately said a cuss word or mentioned Jesus in a derogatory way, but I was silent.

I went under the desk to try to see what was wrong with the computer and nailed my head on the way back up. It felt like a sledgehammer had bonked me. "Ow! Ow!" I yelped in pain, but the normal swear words didn't come out. I suddenly realized I wasn't purposefully holding back the words, either. I wasn't biting my tongue or concentrating on not saying these phrases. They were simply gone from my vocabulary after twenty-three years of training!

I stayed on the floor rubbing my head and wondered what was happening. I was still under my desk. I was so amazed I didn't get up. "What has happened to me? How can this be possible?" I quietly whispered to myself. I tried to think of possible causes for everything I had been experiencing for the past four days. *Why am I feeling content? Why are the cuss words gone? Why am I being genuinely nice to people who normally irritate me? Why do I have a feeling of peace and serenity?* Question after question raced through my mind. I stayed under the desk for at least five minutes pondering everything and searching for answers.

My first intuition was that this new personality was a self-induced euphoria from a good cry. *Maybe I am feeling this way because I got a lot of junk off my heart when I had the "meltdown."* I remembered that I often felt better and more relaxed after a nice weep. I hadn't had a lot of major emotional crying episodes in my life, but the few big ones I did have seemed to relieve pressure. These new changes and feelings I was experiencing, however, were too radical for that explanation to make sense.

I next considered a pharmacologic effect. *Maybe the beta blocker pill I take every day to prevent migraines had mistakenly gotten switched out for Valium*, I thought. This seemed like a good hypothesis, but how likely was the pharmacist to make that kind of blunder? Valium is a medication that can produce calmness, a sense of peace, and a slight euphoria. I had only taken it once before, during a laser procedure to fix near sightedness, an operation I needed so I wouldn't have to wear glasses. Valium slurred my speech and made me a little slow, yet I wasn't experiencing those symptoms at all, so this possibility didn't fit with everything I was currently experiencing. However I couldn't think of anything else that had the power to affect me so dramatically. All day at work I tried to think of other explanations, but nothing else came to mind.

When I got home I immediately ran up the stairs to check the migraine prescription bottle, to see if the pills had been accidentally switched, since this was the best theory I had. I raced into the bathroom and opened the closet. I fumbled through the bottles in anticipation. I picked up the bottle in question and quickly opened it. I emptied it onto the counter, spilling a few on the floor in the rush to examine them. I stooped over to get a close up view of the markings on a few pills. They were beta blockers, not Valium! I was half disappointed and half excited. I wanted an answer, but I didn't want my new behavior to be merely drug related.

I stood there holding the bottle for a few minutes. The best idea I had come up with to explain everything was gone. Even though I was a physician, I had no diagnosis for myself. I was flabbergasted. Shouldn't a person really know himself at my age—enough to know why such a dramatic change would occur?

I thought about the Bible, but figured the radical changes had nothing to do with religion. How could they? I had decided to believe in Jesus and go to church, but that decision couldn't explain what had happened to me. If God was real and Jesus died for people's sin almost two thousand years ago, how could there be any direct relation to me in the year 2003? How could that explain what was happening to me?

THE TESTING

Okay, Greg, put your medical mind to work, I forced myself to think. *How can I single out a specific change I have undergone and develop a way to test it?* I put the bottle down, pondered a moment, and it hit me. I would put the "cussing change" to some extreme challenges.

The Television Test

I went downstairs and turned on a football game. I loved to watch football. It was easy for me to get wrapped up in a game even if it wasn't a favorite team. It was customary for me to cuss and yell at the TV when the team I liked was losing or blowing it. Luckily, a team I liked a lot was playing. They were already losing and it was just the first quarter, but nothing came out of my mouth. Their offense was stagnant, but I sat there mute! I had no desire to utter profanity at the quarterback.

In the second quarter there was an interception by the other team, but still no reaction was brewing inside of me. This was crazy! The impulses, anger, and words were gone. I even tried to muster them up, but I couldn't. They weren't in me anymore. I felt as if I was watching the game with someone else.

The Despised Neighbor Test

The next few days were just as strange. The old me wasn't coming back, and explanations were still elusive. I decided to take our yellow Labrador, Daisy, for a walk to think things through.

"Come on, girl. We're going for a walk. Wanna go for a walk?" I said to her. She was lying on her side like a dead cow, but sat right up at the word "walk." She tilted her head at me the second time I said it, and then started wagging her tail. She went right to the door. "Let's go, Daisy," I said, and off we went.

I wanted to be alone with Daisy primarily so I could think, but unexpectedly we ran into a neighbor—one I despised. Every time I had previously seen this guy I felt animosity and wanted to avoid him. I was walking along in deep thought over my puzzling situation when suddenly there he was right in front of me.

"Hey, Greg. How's it going?" he asked with a smile. There was a long pause as I stared at him. I could not understand why I wasn't angry, spiteful, or cursing this guy in my mind. Disconcertingly, it was even worse than that! *Oh, no! I am feeling a friendship with this guy, a bond for absolutely no reason!* I tried to muster up some envy or something evil to bring up the more familiar emotions I usually had for him, but they were absent. *Something within me likes this guy now,* I marveled. *But come on. I know I don't like him. I know I don't!*

Fifteen minutes later we were still talking and having a good time. I walked away feeling like an alien. *Was I possessed with a sappy geek? Was I now a chatty, cheerful dweeb interested in spending time with people?* I didn't plan on telling anyone what was going on or they would think I was crazy. I feared the medical board would take away my license—citing schizophrenia or some psychological disease.

The Internet Shopping Test

The next day I realized that my desire to constantly search for and buy things was absent. That urge to have something new coming in the mail was gone. In the past I shopped online all of the time to find the latest thrill. I was either waiting for something to arrive or searching for the next item to acquire. I decided to test my new feelings by getting online. I fired up the computer and went to Polo.com, a favorite shopping site.

All right! A new blue rugby had just come in, but I felt no draw. I didn't want it. Custom polo shirts were on sale, but I wasn't interested. Shoes were 25% off, but I didn't even click on that icon. The motivation and excitement weren't surfacing no matter what I looked at. "This is crazy!" I said. "I know I should want to buy something."

That was all I could take. I had to put this thing to the test one more time. I knew myself better than anybody, so I devised the ultimate test. If I passed this one, then I was convinced of one thing. I was going to see my internal medicine doctor! There had to be a medical answer.

The Walmart Test

It was Christmas time, and the stores were going *bananas*—customers in droves. I got in the car and drove to the local strip mall. I could hear the *Mission Impossible* theme playing in my mind. When I pulled in, cars were everywhere and parking spots seemed a mile away. Normally, I would have driven away, but the congestion didn't bother me at all. I wasn't angry, frustrated, or cursing. A guy almost backed into me, but I didn't care. My middle finger was paralyzed for some reason—I couldn't get it to go up! I parked out in Timbuktu and began the long walk in.

I did a quick check. The tension was missing. The sour puss attitude was gone. Even the desire to get in and out of there *fast* didn't show up. I strolled through the parking lot dodging crazy Christmas shoppers. I didn't have a care in the world. I kept waiting for even one of my old behaviors to rear its ugly head, but they were strangely kept at bay.

I walked into Walmart. It was chaos! Long lines, crashing carts, fighting parents, and stressed-out faces filled the place. Anyone who shopped here at peak season was nuts! The *Mission Impossible* music started again. This was it! This was The Test! I hated lines and crowds, and I was extremely impatient. The old me would not survive this without a temper tantrum or fits of rage and frustration. It was on! The bedlam inside started right away.

Kids were crashing into me. Shopping carts were running over me. Frustrated and stressed-out voices and expressions surrounded me. This should have provoked the old me to come back, but that's not what happened! I didn't think, *You little twerp!* Or *That son-of-a-___.* I didn't say "Get out of the way!" or "Gee. Just knock me over next time!"

I gave it a few minutes, but I didn't erupt. Okay, I finally admitted to myself that I had passed part one of the test, so I decided to buy something and try the cash register test. I grabbed the cheapest item I could find—a pack of gum. The registers were so crowded I could hardly see the checkout area. The ends of the lines were barely visible and extended back into the clothing section. A hoard of people was pushing towards the registers like a cattle call. Under normal circumstances my blood pressure would have been highly elevated—through the ceiling—but there I stood at the end of the line without a care in the world!

My fists weren't clenched. My jaw wasn't grinding my teeth into dust, and I didn't instantly hate the people in front of me. In fact, I was so amused by this, I started laughing! I burst into hysterical gales, annoying everyone around me. "I don't care!" I said, smiling in response to their quizzical stares. "I really don't care!" I said even louder. The man in front of me cared. He turned around, narrowed his eyes, curled his lips, and gave me a death look. That didn't faze me either!

I walked out to the car after about thirty minutes in line and was dumbfounded, giddy, and confused. I had always hated being uptight over stupid things but could never control it. *How could that impatience and short fuse have just disappeared?*

I drove home in a trance, taking it all in. Those first few days after I experienced these changes were the strangest days I had ever lived. Mentally, I began using medical reasoning to analyze everything. *The very nature of my existence has been changed,* I thought. Religion, emotions, feelings, desires, and even the deepest yearnings can't produce this. I decided I needed a Diagnosis.

Chapter Ten

The Differential Diagnosis

I came home from Walmart and found Ruth and the kids upstairs watching TV. "What were you doing, honey?" she asked.

"I went to Walmart," I replied.

"What did you get?"

I hesitated and didn't respond immediately. "A pack of gum."

"A pack of gum?" she inquired.

"It's a long story."

"Greg, you're acting strange. What's up with you? You have been quiet, nice, and talkative lately, but also spending a lot of time alone. I don't understand."

"I'm fine. I just have a lot on my mind. I'm going into the office for a while."

She knew I was different but didn't know what I had been up to. I wasn't ready to talk about it yet. I wanted a diagnosis first, and I needed to be alone to think about it. I walked into the office and sat in a chair. I got out a pad of paper and a pen and placed them on the desk.

The physician's analytical and scientific mind within me began to work. I decided to analyze the situation just like any other medical problem. In the medical field a diagnosis is made by first taking a thorough history to elucidate the signs, symptoms, and circumstances of the illness. A complete physical examination is then performed to look for clues and findings that will help pinpoint the diagnosis. After a thorough history and physical examination, a differential diagnosis is formulated. The differential diagnosis is a list of possible diseases or causes for the symptoms that the patient is having. Appropriate diagnostic tests can then be ordered to help find the correct diagnosis.

I became my own patient. I decided to take myself through the medical diagnostic process to find out what was happening. The signs and symptoms I was experiencing were so unusual, I had to do this alone. I feared a regular doctor would either not believe me or think I was crazy and report me to the medical board. I went through each step of the workup and recorded the results and findings. I began with the history, which included signs and symptoms.

THE HISTORY, SIGNS, AND SYMPTOMS

The symptoms had started suddenly two weeks ago upon awakening after the emotional surrender I had gone through the night before. I first experienced unexplainable peace, contentment, and satisfaction that was independent of the circumstances. I discovered that morning that I didn't need anyone or anything to be content. The emptiness, loneliness, and void in my life had disappeared for no apparent reason. Since then, I had a joy about life and each day, even though there wasn't a reason to feel that way. In order to experience this in the past, I always needed a specific event to look forward to or something that I received. Now I had this feeling all the time. The desire to constantly buy and accumulate things had vanished. The peace and joy that I felt squelched these cravings.

The constant pressure, stress, worry, and anxiety I normally experienced had also vanished. My attitude was no longer cynical and bitter. Depression, misery, and irritability were replaced with a peace that transcended understanding.

That same morning I also noticed patience combined with a lack of frustration in situations that usually had me flustered. This was followed by a sincere and genuine love for people I didn't like and those I had heretofore viewed as weirdoes who usually irked me. I wasn't merely *acting* nice and kind either. It was genuine and coming from the heart. I felt as though I somehow had a new heart. I wanted to do the right thing even if it inconvenienced me. My prior typical desire to irritate, belittle, berate, and criticize others was gone. Except for wondering about their absence, I didn't even think about these things, much less act upon them.

I sensed a profound sensitivity to Ruth and our children that was new and life changing. I suddenly became aware of how I had neglected them and selfishly squandered precious moments. I was deeply grieved and had a strong desire to change and be a better husband and father. I wanted to focus on them instead of myself. The subtle motives behind my actions that were selfish and devious were also strangely revealed to my conscience.

I had been a selfish giver and selfish taker my entire life. My outward actions may have appeared nice, but the true impetus behind them was selfish. I was giving in a cunning way in order to get something or to advance my own agenda. I selfishly took what I wanted from life. I did what I wanted when I wanted at everyone else's expense. Everything had revolved around me.

That part of me now appeared to be absent. I was suddenly aware of selfish motivations for the first time in a way that grieved me. In the past I subconsciously knew what I was doing, but I did it anyway. Not only did these behaviors bother me, but I was able to stop them and make changes. I had a newfound power to be unselfish that I couldn't explain.

That first night I came home, for example, I spent time with my wife and kids instead of squandering time alone on the computer or in front of the television. I didn't do it to avoid "the dog house" or to put time on the "father clock" to get points, but because my heart truly desired to.

This sensitivity and awareness of selfishness was also present when I made mistakes. Even though I had a radical change overnight, I was far from perfect. I continued to have bad thoughts at times, and I didn't always do the right thing. I was dramatically improved but still riddled with problems. The difference was that I was now *aware* of my reprehensible behavior. In the past I was not only blind to it but proud of it. But now if I say or do something wrong, a dreadful feeling comes over me until I rectify the situation. It's almost as if the feeling "knows," because the dread only goes away after I apologize. It is a lot easier now to say "I am sorry" and "please forgive me." I rarely uttered these words before.

The most perplexing sign, though, was a complete exclusion of all cuss words from my vocabulary. I used to use them all the time in sentences as nouns, verbs, and adjectives. They flew off my lips automatically, but now they didn't come out even in stressful situations. All of these signs and symptoms appeared suddenly and on the same day.

I didn't feel sick, tired, or systemically ill. My energy and overall well being were actually improved. There were no signs of mental illness, cognitive problems, or unusual thoughts or behavior—other than my positive changes. The one medication I took daily for migraines had not been mistakenly switched at the pharmacy. I hadn't changed dietary habits or alcohol consumption. There was no history of travel or exposure to unusual substances or situations. I didn't take illicit drugs or herbal supplements. No one else in my family or at work had mentioned experiencing similar symptoms.

The only thing different before the symptoms started was a recent interest in the Bible and Jesus Christ. I had spent countless hours studying and answering every question I could think of while examining the validity of the Bible. Right before the symptoms started I had made a recent intellectual decision to be a Christian.

On the night directly preceding the onset of the symptoms, I had an emotional meltdown and cried out to God for help and forgiveness. It was a moment of introspection and realization of my sins. I made the conscious decision to believe that Jesus Christ was God and that he died for my personal sins and was literally resurrected. I reflected on my meltdown and remembered that I had personally engaged Jesus by begging for change and forgiveness.

At that moment, however, I didn't notice or feel anything different. I figured I had become emotional from religious studies. That night I had slept like a baby for the first time in many years. The next morning was when the new symptoms suddenly appeared.

The signs and symptoms didn't seem to be temporary but had persisted for two weeks without any noticeable changes. They were not getting better or worse but were stable. They were not intermittent; I had them all of the time. The symptoms were completely original; I had never experienced them before. Other people, especially at work where one's personality is on full display and under a microscope, could tell something was different about me.

THE PHYSICAL EXAMINATION

The next part of the diagnostic process was the physical exam. This is a direct examination of my actual body looking for clues to the diagnosis. I had a spare set of medical instruments in the home office closet. I kept them handy for when I was on call.

The physical examination was completely normal. I examined myself since I couldn't and didn't want to tell anyone what was going on. Blood pressure, temperature, and heart rate were normal. Lymph nodes were not enlarged, and the thyroid gland was non-palpable (normal). The heart and lungs sounded normal, and the abdomen was without any findings. I didn't have a rash, any areas of tenderness, or other visible findings. A self-directed neurologic examination was also completely normal. Reflexes, balance, and other tests for the brain were without abnormal findings. The results of the physical examination were unremarkable.

THE TESTING

The next part of the process was testing. Testing is a way to reproduce signs and symptoms or to directly measure or examine parts of the body. I was afraid to see our personal doctor and tell him what was happening with me. I knew he would think I had lost it. Thus I couldn't order any blood work or imaging studies. I wanted an MRI of my head to look for a brain tumor, but I had to do without it.

I had, however, already tested each and every symptom to see if they were reproducible and consistent. The Walmart Test demonstrated several things: I had patience, which was brand new. I wasn't negatively affected by long lines or crazy Christmas shoppers. Anger, hatred, frustration, and a short temper did not surface even under stressful circumstances.

I learned a few things about myself in the process. I was selfish! My impatience was really the outward expression of a selfish heart. I am special and shouldn't have to wait—right! I want immediate service! Even anger, frustration, hatred, and a short temper were all related to an egocentric personality. I hated people in front of me in lines because they made me wait. Frustration and anger were likewise the manifestation of selfishness when I was not being immediately served and satisfied. I understood for the first time that these characteristics were all linked to a narcissistic personality where everything was about me.

The Despised Neighbor Test proved I had love and concern for people I previously didn't like. My reaction to a demanding little old lady in the office with "a list" confirmed this new attitude toward other people. I was completely out of character. I felt love for the unlovable and was unperturbed by things and people that were irritating.

The disappearance of cuss words was tested by hitting my head, losing my wallet, and watching a favorite football team lose on TV. None of these situations elicited a single profane word.

The peace, calmness, sense of serenity, and satisfaction I felt were also sticking around. Screaming kids, nagging nurses, and even arrogant drivers who cut me off in traffic didn't conjure up the old self. I was actually being tested continually, yet passing! Almost every situation in life was a validation for this new person I had become.

Finally, the Internet Shopping Test didn't evoke the slightest urge to buy. The desire to constantly purchase things was strangely absent.

Now it was time for an analysis of the data I had collected. I went downstairs and made a shot of espresso so I could work late. I went into the basement and closed the door. My wife and kids were sleeping and I didn't want to wake them. I brought my textbook of medical and surgical diseases with me for reference.

THE ANALYSIS OF THE SYMPTOMS

This was a perplexing problem to evaluate because all of the changes I felt at first glance appeared desirable! I was trying to diagnose what could cause me to change so suddenly and dramatically for the better.

I started by closely analyzing the symptoms. I wrote them all down and looked for patterns or ways to group them together. I discovered the symptoms could be split into two categories: new symptoms that suddenly appeared and old symptoms that suddenly disappeared.

I not only had lost bad behaviors but somehow had concurrently gained new, good behaviors. I had never considered my old ways to be "symptoms" until now. I always thought worry, anxiety, anger, and emptiness, for example, were normal. Now that they were gone, however, I thought it was important for them to be considered in the diagnostic process. In some diseases it's possible to have symptoms for so long that they become normal. Once the disease is cured and they disappear, it becomes evident that they were symptoms all along. Everything that had changed in me, old and new, was now part of the diagnostic puzzle.

I listed every single aspect that had changed. I mulled over the list for a while and realized I could subdivide them into two categories: symptoms that affected or involved other people and those that mainly affected me or were experienced internally.

I organized everything into a table to help the diagnostic process. I totaled at the bottom all of the old symptoms and new symptoms to quantify the changes. The table appears on the next page.

I. Symptoms Related to Self	
Old Symptoms Gone:	**New Symptoms Present:**
Emptiness, Void, Unsatisfied, Discontent, Disenchanted (life is vain)	Peace, Fulfillment (life complete), Satisfied, Content
Loneliness, Desolation	Love, Peace
Miserable, Depressed, Discouraged, Cynical	Joy
Worry, Anxiety, Tension, Pressure	Peace, Calmness
Impatience, Demanding, Intolerant	Patience
Covetous, Greed (acquiring for self), Self-indulgent, Gluttony	Benevolence (giving to others), Peace
Negative, Pessimistic	Positive, Optimistic
II. Symptoms Related to Others	
Old Symptoms Gone:	**New Symptoms Present:**
Anger, Short Temper/Tantrums, Hasty	Joy, Self Control
Callous, Cruel, Unconcerned, Offensive, Inconsiderate, Curt	Kindness, Caring, Concerned
Hatred, Dislike, Envy, Jealousy, Despise, Disdain, Snobbery, Condescending, Ridicule, Disparaging, Scornful, Rude, Unloving, Unfriendly, Antagonistic, Animosity, Annoyance, Unforgiving, Slanderous	Love
Unthankful, Ungrateful, Unappreciative	Goodness
Bitter, Irritable	Agreeable, Pleasant
Stubborn, Unyielding	Love
Competitive Pride (desire to surpass others)	Uncompetitive Humility (desire to enjoy others)
Total # Different Symptoms: 62	**Total # Different Symptoms: 16**

As I studied the table I noticed several things. First, the old symptoms were bad and detrimental, while the new ones were good and beneficial. More profoundly, the old symptoms were more complicated and numerous than the new ones. Sixty-two old had been replaced by only 16 new! The new symptoms were simpler.

I had been miserable, depressed, angry, negative, short-tempered, and unhappy, for example, but now joy alone replaced all of them. Worry, anxiety, tension, frustration, loneliness, emptiness, and feeling unfulfilled and disenchanted with life were replaced with an indescribable peace that transcended my understanding. Two new symptoms replaced a plethora of old ones.

I couldn't understand how this could be, but it was true in almost every category. There seemed to be a lot more ways to do things wrong or experience life negatively than the converse. The new symptoms simplified my life! Part of the peace I was experiencing seemed to be emanating from simplicity in my mind, heart, and relationships.

This was interesting information, but I sensed that there was more to discover from the table. I looked it over for thirty minutes and searched for answers. I felt that I was working with a jigsaw puzzle comprised of many different symptoms that somehow fit together to form a picture. The table organized the pieces but didn't put them together. I knew the symptoms were interrelated, like pieces of a puzzle, but I wasn't able to fit them together yet.

I had lived with the old symptoms for a long time and the new ones for only two weeks. I knew the disappearance of the old was somehow directly related to the appearance of the new. Finally, something came to me that unraveled the mystery and solved the puzzle.

THE REVELATION OF THE SYMPTOMS

The very core of my old symptoms was the first grouping in the table. The emptiness, void, and feeling that life was meaninglessness were the heart and driving force for all the other old symptoms, both personally and in my relationships. Everything originated with that core set. This group of old symptoms was the nucleus that controlled all the others. I started making a diagram to link and interrelate them. The pieces fit together perfectly.

The void and emptiness caused me to covet things and have greed, because I thought materialism and life experiences were the cure. These things, however, required money, which forced me to focus on my career and self-achievement. If I got a good job that paid a lot of money, I could buy and experience the things I was missing to fill the void. Once I finally had them, however, I ended up frustrated, irritable, and bitter because they didn't fill my heart the way I thought they would. This sparked the desire for bigger, better, and more, which only compounded the entire cycle.

My craving for bigger, better, and more things required more and more money to buy or experience them. Each time they failed to satisfy and fulfill, the result was more agitation, frustration, and misery. This became a feedback loop that had no end. This cycle was the impetus for every hobby, vacation, car, watch, clothing, lust, and interest in my life. Everything directly or indirectly was a result of feeling desolate and unfulfilled in life. I had never realized this until now.

This endless and futile process to fill the vacancy in my heart caused a self-centered and self-indulgent life that resulted in callousness and unconcern for others. I didn't have the time, energy, or room for anyone but myself.

Once I reached a certain level of success I began to experience worry, fear, and anxiety. I was now able to understand the reason. My entire quest to be fulfilled in life through self-pleasure, self-achievement, and self indulgence was like a raging fire that had to be constantly fed. The more I fed it, the bigger it got. At a certain point, I understood that if something happened to me, my career, or the money stream, I wouldn't be able to feed the fire anymore. If the money stopped or I couldn't continue to feed the fire, the void would be exposed. I would have to face the truth that I was unsatisfied with life despite having everything I could ask for. The fear was emanating from the emptiness and void. The raging fire was kept burning to keep me distracted and occupied so I could forget about the hole in my heart.

The combination of this vicious cycle and its consequences produced tension, depression, cynicism, and bitterness. I'd worked my entire life to reach the top, but I found it emptier than where I began. Everything I had achieved failed to enrapture me and take away the void. I had always looked forward to all of the things I would buy and experience someday, but once I had them there wasn't anything left to give hope. The result was a paradox of misery from success.

This entire personal situation then set the stage for my treatment of others. Every single wicked characteristic I displayed towards people emanated first from my misery. Anger, a short temper, and sarcasm exhibited because I was taking out my personal anguish on others. Cruelty, hatred, and criticism resulted in tearing other people down to build myself up. Competitive pride was an attempt to compare, surpass, and feel superior over others in order to quiet my own internal pain. I continued to fit all of the pieces together. The void and emptiness were the root cause and origin for everything.

I was blown away at how easily I now understood the origins and pathways that led me to become the monster that I was. The new symptoms provided the revelation that interrelated all of the old ones. If the origin for the bad was a state of internal emptiness, then my new state of feeling fulfilled and complete eliminated the root cause for all of the others. It broke the cycles before they could even get started. The diagram illustrated to me how changing the core affected everything else, personally and relationally.

Now that I felt joy, peace, and satisfaction in life I didn't have to chase things, people, money, or experiences any more. This removed the frustration, bitterness, and misery that their failure to fulfill me had always caused. I was free of the vicious cycle and consuming fire that had usurped all of my time and energy. The raging fire of covetousness, greed, and self-indulgence was extinguished. I didn't have to feed it anymore. A huge burden and tension had been lifted from me. These changes drastically simplified my life in just two weeks.

Internal euphoria, which was now present and independent of my situation, which I defined as joy, also drastically affected my relationships. It empowered and changed them from the inside out. I didn't have to take anything out on others, tear anyone down, or feel superior since I felt fulfilled just as I was! I didn't need to focus on myself anymore. I was free to concentrate on others, especially Ruth and the kids. Personal peace and satisfaction directly guillotined that wretched part of my character.

The pieces of the "symptoms jigsaw puzzle" fit together perfectly. I put them together by making the diagram that interrelated all of the old symptoms (next page). This illustration was the completed puzzle of my old symptoms. Just like puzzles I had solved as a kid, the pieces once put together formed a picture. I saw my own heart. The diagram illustrated what made me tick in every aspect of my life. The symptoms and changes affected my attitude, motives, desires, thoughts, feelings, emotions, and conscience. Every aspect of my life, personality, and character had been changed. This meant I had a new heart since the day I awakened as a new person. How was this possible? Any diagnosis would have to explain all of this. I had a gut instinct there wasn't going to be a medical answer, but I still wanted to consider the possibilities and rule them out.

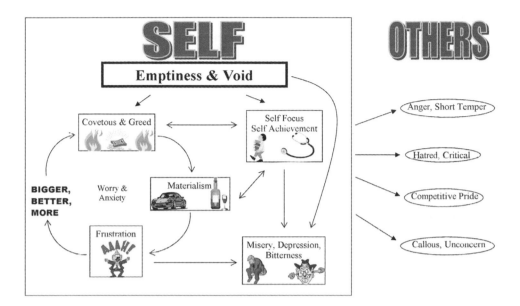

THE DIFFERENTIAL DIAGNOSIS

I made a list of possible diagnoses. I included some that were unlikely and did so to make sure I was comprehensive in my analysis.

The differential diagnosis included the following: psychiatric disease, a self-induced euphoria from an emotional meltdown, a drug or external substance, hormonal imbalance from endocrine disease or cancer, and brain cancer.

Psychiatric disease didn't make any sense because my cognition, thoughts, emotions, and actions were all normal. I wasn't frantic, overexcited, or hyperactive, which mania can cause. My speech was not rapid or fragmented, either, which is characteristic of this disease.

A self-induced euphoria seemed like a good candidate at first, until I began to think about the type of symptoms I was having. *You just can't change like that,* I said to myself. Emotions, feelings, and reactions to situations—like anger, for example—are deeply wired within the brain and nervous system and mediated by chemicals and hormones. I knew as a doctor that the radical changes I was experiencing equated to radical changes in my brain, nervous system, and body chemistry. These processes work at the molecular and cellular levels in the body. I needed a diagnosis that matched the symptoms and one that could account for changes in body chemistry and nerve activity.

Drugs, alcohol, and other substances that can change moods and bring a false sense of peace or relaxation work at the cellular level in the body. This was exactly the reason I suspected a drug or foreign substance at the outset of my investigation regarding the new me. Valium might have been a good candidate, but I didn't take any. I checked my prescription, a daily beta blocker for migraines, but it couldn't produce these symptoms. It was also correctly prescribed and not mistakenly switched out at the pharmacy. Marijuana was another drug that could produce some of these types of symptoms temporarily, but I didn't use it.

If I was truly changed in the absence of outside agents entering my body, and having eliminated all that were relevant, I decided that internally produced substances were the next candidates to examine.

Chemical and hormonal imbalances from endocrine disease or cancer can internally produce many changes. These didn't fit, however, because of the sudden onset and wide range of dramatic symptoms I was having. Thyroid, adrenal gland, and pituitary gland diseases can cause emotional and psychological symptoms, but not this suddenly or comprehensively. It didn't make sense for any cancer-related hormone or substance to affect such a wide variety of emotions and personality traits. It certainly didn't explain a love for people I didn't like. *How could anything selectively target bad language?!* I asked myself.

Brain cancer was extremely unlikely for the same reasons. I didn't have headaches or neurologic symptoms.

After all of this, I still had no diagnosis and no candidates left that seemed reasonable. What now? I had a new heart but had no idea how I got it. I didn't know what to do or think.

Chapter Eleven

The Preliminary Diagnosis

It was eleven o'clock at night. Everyone was asleep and I was still in the office at home. I stared out the window at the empty street below. I was a prideful physician who understood the human body, but I didn't have a clue what was happening to my own existence. My heart was troubled and perplexed by this enigma. I was tired and wanted to go to sleep, but I felt that I was missing something. I was captivated by how all of my symptoms fit together, even though I didn't have a diagnosis. I decided to keep going until midnight and then call it quits. I went back to the basics of medical diagnosis. The history is always critical. I felt it was important to go over the circumstances surrounding the onset of my symptoms one more time, in case I had missed something.

The last time I was "normal" or my old self was when I went to bed that night after crying out to God, I thought. The Bible and Christianity were the only new things introduced into my life, but I had not considered them in The Differential Diagnosis. I decided to pick up the Bible and do some reading. This was the first time I had read the Bible since the symptoms started. It had been about two weeks. I randomly opened the New Testament to Romans chapter six and began to read.

I immediately noticed that the Bible was more clear, understandable, and interesting. A lot of sections that I had read the first time through hadn't made sense or had seemed extraneous. Now, however, I felt that I could understand what was being taught. The words came alive and their message was clearer. They had a personal application and impact that was new. It was a strange and intangible feeling within me. It was similar to getting my first pair of glasses. I could now "see" and read with more clarity than before. This was strange. Once I started reading I couldn't stop. I had a new urge to keep reading the Scriptures.

I was instantly intrigued, because Romans chapter six teaches that something literally happens to a person when he becomes a believer. The Apostle Paul, the author of the book, stated that the "old man is dead" and that a Christian has been "set free from sin." I kept reading this section since it resonated with me. Both of these statements seemed familiar. I had already experienced being set free from sin, ever since I was changed. I felt that my old self was gone or dead. For the past week I had been a different person in every conceivable way. The old Greg Viehman was practically dead in my life. Paul elaborated on this concept by stating that the old self has been "crucified with Jesus" and "raised to walk in the newness of life." In a crazy way, I felt that this too described my symptoms. What in the world did Paul mean? Could what he described be the answer?

My heart was racing and my palms were sweaty. I had a profound sense that I was onto something. The things I was reading seemed to describe what I was experiencing. I read Romans chapters seven and eight searching for more information. Chapter seven teaches that Jesus is the answer for those struggling with bad behaviors that a person normally can't control. This concept matched my symptoms, but I didn't understand how Jesus could be involved until I read chapter eight.

This chapter keeps mentioning that the Spirit of God lives *within* Christians. It even defined a true Christian as someone who has the Spirit of God living within him. I read this passage over and over again.

> *But you are not controlled by your sinful nature. You are controlled by the Spirit if you have the Spirit of God living in you. (And remember that those who do not have the Spirit of Christ living in them do not belong to him at all.) And Christ lives within you, so even though your body will die because of sin, the Spirit gives you life because you have been made right with God. The Spirit of God, who raised Jesus from the dead, lives in you. And just as God raised Christ Jesus from the dead, he will give life to your mortal bodies by this same Spirit living within you.*
>
> *Therefore, dear brothers and sisters, you have no obligation to do what your sinful nature urges you to do. For if you live by its dictates, you will die. But if through the power of the Spirit you put to death the deeds of your sinful nature, you will live. For all who are led by the Spirit of God are children of God.*
>
> *So you have not received a spirit that makes you fearful slaves. Instead, you received God's Spirit when he adopted you as his own children. Now we call him, "Abba, Father." For his Spirit joins with our spirit to affirm that we are God's children. (Romans 8:9-16 NLT)*

What did this mean, that God's Spirit lives within them? How could this be? I looked for more verses and found this one. My study

Bible has references for verses on similar topics, which made it easy for me to research these ideas.

> *And now you Gentiles have also heard the truth, the Good News that God saves you. And when you believed in Christ, he identified you as his own by giving you the Holy Spirit, whom he promised long ago. The Spirit is God's guarantee that he will give us the inheritance he promised and that he has purchased us to be his own people. He did this so we would praise and glorify him. (Ephesians 1:13-14 NLT)*

I read this over several times and tried to apply it to me. I focused on the key phrase "when you believed in Christ." This moment of believing seemed to be a critical point in time when a Christian receives the Holy Spirit, whatever that meant. I reviewed my Christian journey looking for clues.

I had first *intellectually* believed in Jesus, but then a week later I personally cried out to him for forgiveness and change. I did not feel significantly different after intellectual belief, but I woke up a different person after repenting and surrendering to Jesus with my whole heart the night before. *Does this mean that I have the Spirit of God living within me?! Is that possible? Is there a current day reality to Christianity? Could this explain my change?* I asked myself. My heart was fluttering with excitement. I kept digging. I found another verse where Jesus talked about the Holy Spirit.

> *"If you love me, obey my commandments. And I will ask the Father, and he will give you another Advocate, who will never leave you. He is the Holy Spirit, who leads into all truth. The world cannot receive him, because it isn't looking for him and doesn't recognize him. But you know him, because he lives with you now and later <u>will be in you</u>." (John 14:15-18 NLT, emphasis added)*

The Bible was expressly saying that I was saved and that the Holy Spirit of God was now living within me. This was a mind-blowing possibility. *If salvation actually results in a literal change in a person's existence, then this might be the answer*, I thought. I had a preliminary diagnosis of "saved," but I needed to understand how this worked and if it could explain my symptoms. What did "saved" mean? How did I get saved? Jesus referred to the Holy Spirit as "him," a person. Whoa! How could he be within me? Who is the Holy Spirit? How could this account for the symptoms I was having?

It had gotten very late and I needed to sleep. I was so enthralled that I wanted to keep going, but my eyelids were closing from the lead weight of fatigue. I got into bed. My mind was racing with thoughts and questions. I couldn't wait for tomorrow. I knew I was onto something big, but I had no idea just how unfathomably colossal it really was.

Chapter Twelve

The Disease of Sin

The next morning was a half day at work. As soon as I finished I went to the local bookstore. I wanted to find out more about the Holy Spirit. I walked in and headed for the religious section. I was delighted to find a book called *The Holy Spirit* by Billy Graham.[69] I purchased it and raced home to do some studying. It was just past noon, the kids would not be home until three o'clock, and my wife was out, so I had the house to myself. I went up into the office and reviewed everything I had discovered the day before. I made some quick notes in preparation for reading.

I opened the new book and began quickly scanning the chapters for pertinent information. Medical school had taught me to quickly find and assimilate facts. I was too excited to start reading from the beginning. Right away I found a few new concepts that changed everything.

Mr. Graham stated that the root problem for all of humanity was sin. When a person is "saved" he is rescued from a state of sin. I didn't fully understand what "sin" was, but I realized he was implying that sin resulted in bad behaviors and actions in people. Jesus was like a "cure" for the "disease" of sin. If Graham was right, then what had happened to me was actually a cure, not a weird sickness. If so, I wanted to start completely over in the analysis, because if the Bible was true then I had the entire diagnostic process backwards.

Before The Transformation occurred in my life, I thought I was healthy and normal. The first morning I awakened as a new person, however, I became worried that I was sick and abnormal because of the symptoms I was having. I figured that my new behavior, personality, and conscience pointed towards a disease state since it was so sudden, radical, and unexplainable. I tried to diagnose what was wrong with me from the symptoms I was having.

If Billy Graham was correct, however, then I had it all backwards. Before I was saved I actually had been sick and diseased with sin for my entire life without knowing it. The symptoms I was having after The Transformation were really signs of the cure from Jesus Christ. I was evaluating the results of my salvation as a disease, not knowing I was saved or what "saved" even meant!

If sin is like a disease then I had actually started off sick and infected with sin, but thinking I was normal, and ended up cured and saved without knowing it, yet had interpreted these changes as abnormal! Could I have lived an entire life with an undiagnosed disease of sin, thinking I was normal? Was it then possible that I had been saved and cured of sin without knowing it, thinking I was abnormal?! This possibility was so out of the realm of anything I ever expected or could comprehend that I was in shock. If this were true then my entire concept of my existence would have been wrong since I was a child. I had to find out if this was really possible. I needed to take a hard look at myself prior to The Transformation, when (as I now understood it) I supposedly had the disease of sin.

I updated the preliminary diagnosis to "saved" from a disease of sin. Could this diagnosis really make sense and explain everything to the point that I could believe it? I dove into Mr. Graham's book and the Bible, and searched for answers and information. I found a plethora of information to help me revamp the diagnostic process. I needed to redefine the disease, symptoms, cure, mechanism of the cure, and results of the cure. Once I had these definitions and descriptions, I would be able to match them up with my situation and see if they adequately explained what had happened to me.

THE NATURE OF MY EXISTENCE

The original disease that the Bible said I was suffering from since birth, without realizing it, was "sin," but what is sin? I had already admitted to myself that I had sinful actions, but there was evidently a lot more to it than just bad behavior, according to the Bible. In order to fully understand the disease of sin, I first needed to learn what the Bible stated about my own existence. What makes up a human being?

I discovered that human beings are supposedly made up of a physical flesh body with an internal spirit/soul that exists forever. Thus man consists of both body and spirit/soul. The body is physical and tangible. It allows us to interact in a physical world. The spirit/soul, as explained in the Bible, is intangible. If man has a spirit/soul, this would be the source of the real person. I thought of an analogy that made this easier to understand.

The physical body is like the hardware of a computer, while the spirit/soul is analogous to the software. The hardware is the outer, visible, and physical housing that interacts with the world like our physical bodies do. The spirit/soul of man, or "software," manifests itself by living within the physical body, or "hardware." The hardware of a computer will break down and suffer wear and tear like our bodies do. However, the software that runs inside the computer does not physically break down and can be inserted into a brand new computer "body."

The software contains the information and language that makes the computer function, just like the spirit/soul would be the source of thoughts, emotions, and personality. The software, or spirit/soul, would be the real source of life. A computer with just hardware will seem like it is "dead." It won't turn on or work, but if you put software in it, then it turns on and comes to "life."

Man = flesh body + spirit/soul   or   Man = hardware + software

This supposed "spirit/soul" part of man was something that was never explained to me on The Ski Trip or at Marco Island. I had never even considered such an idea. Evolution, biology classes, and medical school had clearly taught me that man *only* consisted of highly evolved organic matter (the physical body) and nothing more. I was willing to temporarily tolerate this idea of a spirit/soul within man because it seemed to answer some questions I had about the human body.

I had always wondered in brain anatomy classes during medical school how a human brain consisting solely of organic matter could have love, emotions, memories, feelings, and a conscience. It just didn't make sense or seem possible. This was a question that no one could answer for me, either. Modern science doesn't have a clue how this works.

The idea of a spirit/soul living within the body, however, did make sense and provided answers to these difficult questions. Even though this seemed farfetched, it was paradoxically more plausible than molecules being the sole cause for emotions and personalities. I knew that chemicals and nerves within the body *affected* some of our emotions and feelings, but they couldn't be entirely *responsible* for them. How can chemical matter make me love my family and be willing to die for them? How can nerves and chemicals know when I have done something wrong and make me feel guilty about it?

I suddenly understood that if humans really have a spirit/soul then this would mean that *my* personality, memories, love, thoughts, and emotions were coming from my spirit/soul which inhabits my body. Although this was a radical concept, it made sense—*if* it were true. In addition, I realized that this meant that *I* was eternal and more than "evolved organic soup." This was very appealing to my heart, which had been searching for eternity and answers. *Wow! Could I really be an eternal spirit?* I pondered in awe.

Now that I understood what the Bible taught about my existence, I could understand the disease of sin.

THE DISEASE OF SIN

I quickly found myself back with Adam and Eve in my quest to comprehend sin. I read in Genesis, the first book in the Bible, that the first two people were literally created by God. When they disobeyed God they were radically changed for the worse. They became physically and spiritually separated from God. Their prior connection to God was severed; they were disconnected from him. This "fall" also resulted in a dramatic change in their bodies. Separation from God resulted in a new state of existence where physical death entered the world. The human body was now susceptible to decay, injury, and eventually death.

I began to understand during my study of Genesis that from this point forward all human beings were born separated from God in a fallen body that would eventually die. If the biblical account is true, then this state of separation from God in a "fallen flesh body" is the condition of sin or "sinful nature." Separation from God is also called a state of spiritual death in the Bible. If so, this would mean I was born spiritually dead and separated from God in a state of sin.

Disease of sin = separation from God = spiritually dead

Sinful man = fallen physical body separated from God + eternal spirit/soul separated from God

The computer analogy helped me understand the disease of sin. A person is analogous to a personal computer that was originally intended to be connected to the giant all powerful mainframe computer (i.e., God). The connection, however, had been severed by sin. I had been unplugged from the intended connection and couldn't have proper communication. Sin was like a virus that the mainframe could not allow in its presence. The virus caused the connection to be cut. I was quarantined from the mainframe computer, or separated from God. In order for me to be reconnected, the virus of sin would have to be completely removed.

I was still dubious about how Adam and Eve caused the fall of all mankind, separating us from God, and I wanted to understand this aspect of sin better. This was an entirely new concept for me. While it was true that I couldn't physically see God, I wondered about his presence in my life. It wasn't hard for me to believe that I was separated from God, since I hadn't seen him or sensed him, and I certainly hadn't had much exposure to hearing people talk about him. Given this almost complete lack of exposure, the separation concept made perfect sense.

If sin was my original disease before I was saved, then what were the symptoms of this disease? Did I have these symptoms prior to The Transformation? In probing for answers to these questions, I would need to look into the symptoms of sin.

Chapter Thirteen

The Symptoms of Sin

All diseases have symptoms at some point in their history. The symptoms are a sign of a larger problem in the body. Chest pain, for example, is a symptom of heart disease. When the arteries that feed the heart become clogged the heart can't get enough oxygen. The sensation of chest pain is a manifestation of an underlying primary problem in the heart.

If sin is like a disease then I surmised that it too would have symptoms. If so, what are the manifestations of separation from God? Would the symptoms of sin match up with the symptoms I had before The Transformation? These were important questions that needed to be answered.

I searched the study Bible and found a verse which specifically addressed this issue.

The acts of the sinful nature are obvious: sexual immorality, impurity and debauchery; idolatry and witchcraft; hatred, discord, jealousy, fits of rage, selfish ambition, dissensions, factions and envy; drunkenness, orgies, and the like. (Galatians 5:19-21 NIV)

I was shocked when I read this because it sounded like the old me. I kept searching and discovered that anger, jealousy, lying, lust, impatience, greed, pride, and many others were all the result of separation from God. Selfishness was the primary manifestation of the sinful nature. This piqued my interest because I had already discovered that selfishness was a major problem before I was changed. Sin and its side effects seemed to match my situation exactly.

I always thought these symptoms of sin, however, were "normal human nature" because everyone had them. I realized that if "normal human nature" was really a sinful nature resulting from separation from God, then humans are born with two major problems. Not only are we separated from God, but the separation itself results in a whole host of other problems like selfishness, pride, loneliness, and death.

The Bible was claiming that this world and our existence are fallen (i.e., it's not supposed to be this way). If this is true, then I was born with something drastically wrong with me. This was difficult to swallow. Something had always seemed wrong, but I could never put my finger on it. *Could this be the reason I was frustrated with life?* I wondered.

The intriguing concept to me was that sinful behaviors are a *result* of a state of sin or separation from God. Bad behavior is a symptom that I am a sinner. Sinful actions are not the root cause but symptoms of the disease. Just like chest pain, the symptoms of sin are a sign that something is wrong at a much deeper level. Sin is the root and sins are the fruit. Separation from God has side effects. The personal computer malfunctions because it is disconnected from the mainframe.

I had to admit, no one had to teach me to lie or be selfish when I was a child. I had also personally witnessed this early behavior in our boys while they were toddlers. They were born with selfish and sinful tendencies. I had good evidence that humans are born with these characteristics. I always knew that these behaviors were wrong, but since everyone was like this I figured that's just the way we are. I never considered that there could be a defect in our existence that causes them.

Separation from God is also supposedly the reason people feel empty, alone, unfulfilled, and unsatisfied. The personal computer that was designed to be connected to the mainframe is missing the interaction and exchange of information it was designed to have. It can try to create programs to fulfill itself but they will never satisfy. The personal computer will be "lonely" and "unfulfilled" because it is disconnected. The Bible claims that people were originally created to live with God and worship him. It says that we were not originally designed to live an independent life in a state of separation.

This doctrine really hit me hard, because as crazy as it sounded, separation from God was a reason and explanation for many of the things that had constantly plagued my heart. I had felt empty inside for as long as I could remember. I felt disconnected and unfulfilled. I had everything but nothing could satisfy me! *Why?! How could this be?!* I lamented for years. I kept asking myself as I pondered the concept of separation from God, *Could this really be the reason?* If I have tried everything to find fulfillment then maybe I'm not missing "something" but *Someone*. This was the first time in my life that I had discovered an explanation for these feelings.

I immediately went back to the diagram that I had made (see Chapter Ten) which explained and interrelated the old symptoms I had before I was transformed. This diagram illustrates how a state of emptiness and void in my life was the central control center for all of my problems and symptoms, both personally and relationally. If separation from God resulted in emptiness and a void in people's lives, then I had good evidence that I had been separated from God my entire life. All of my symptoms matched the disease of sin. It was a strange feeling to realize that something could have been intrinsically wrong with the nature of my existence for as long as I had lived.

At this point, I had an explanation for sinful behavior and for the void I had experienced up until The Transformation. With the possibility of an eternal spirit/soul being a part of our existence, I also had a reason for how humans have emotions, love, a conscience, and personalities. I was amazed at how cohesive and internally consistent these biblical doctrines were. They seemed to answer many questions and match my circumstances at several different levels, which shocked me.

The disease of sin and its symptoms were a match for my situation, but what about the cure? If the new me was a result of receiving the cure for sin, then I needed to see if this explained The Transformation. What is the cure? How does it work? What are the results? How does someone get cured? These were the next questions I wanted to answer.

Chapter Fourteen

The Cure for Sin

THE CURE FOR SIN

I had already studied Jesus as the sin solution during The Investigation. To refresh my memory, I reviewed what I had learned. I had first admitted I was a sinner when I realized that I had lied, stolen, cheated, and done a lot of bad things. The penalty for my sins was eternal death or eternal separation from God. Because God is sinless and perfect he cannot tolerate any sin in his presence. I could not go to heaven unless my sins were completely removed. I needed a perfect, sinless standing, like God.

God as a righteous judge has to judge my sin, but as a loving God he also wants to forgive me. Jesus became the solution by dying in my place so God could forgive me but still punish sin. God was then able to give me a perfectly clean slate just as if I never sinned.

During my investigation stage, I hadn't yet realized that I was *already* separated from God since birth—that I was spiritually dead. I did not understand that my sinful actions were a *symptom* of a sinful nature or the disease of sin (separation from God in fallen flesh body). The problem was much larger than just my bad behavior.

The cure for sin would thus have to solve three major problems: the death penalty for sin, separation from God, and the sinful behaviors that result from it. A cure for sin would need to provide payment for the death penalty and a reconnection to God, and it would need to establish a new nature. It was obvious that I couldn't be reconnected to God until the penalty was paid and I received a sinless standing.

The initial investigation explained the first major problem, but not the second two. Jesus paid the penalty for sin, and thus the possibility of the removal of the record of sin, by dying on the cross. But how did Jesus also provide the reconnection to God and create a new nature that had power over sin?

These last two problems were the mechanism for the cure and its results. I had to understand both to see if the cure for sin matched The Transformation.

THE MECHANISM OF THE CURE

In medical diseases it's important to understand, when possible, how a cure corrects the problem. This allows the physician to know what to expect and to evaluate progress.

If the disease of sin separated me from God, then the cure would reconnect me to him. Jesus would be The Reconnection to God. The personal computer would be plugged back into the mainframe, allowing communication and information exchange. I was astonished that this is exactly what I found in the Bible and in Mr. Graham's book. What blew me away in wonder, awe, and even a little fear was the mechanism of The Reconnection.

When a person cries out to God in repentance for change and forgiveness by trusting in Jesus Christ, several things actually happen at this specific moment in time. First God declares this person righteous-as though he has never sinned at all. Because Jesus became sin for all of mankind, God is able to declare a person righteous even though he is a sinner past, present, and future.

This declaration from God allows the personal computer to be reconnected to the mainframe. The personal computer doesn't have to be separated and quarantined anymore, because the virus of sin has been dealt with. What blew me away is that God himself is The Reconnection. The Holy Spirit, who is God, enters the believer's body and joins with the believer's spirit to end the separation. This means that at the moment of salvation God actually dwells within the existence of the believer. This transaction is what "saved" actually means. Just like in medical diseases, the cure has to enter the body to produce the results.

Wow! Now it all fits together, I thought. When I first made The Preliminary Diagnosis of "saved," I didn't understand the Holy Spirit, but now I did.

Salvation is not just a prayer to God, but it triggers an actual transaction from God. Christianity isn't only something you believe but something you become. The moment a person sincerely cries out to God, he forever changes the very nature of the person's existence. He or she is reconnected, alive, and restored by God living within the person. *This would be incredible if it were true*, I thought.

After having been told that God didn't exist, that He couldn't be known, I marveled at the thought that He could actually be living within me. Whoa! These realizations made me want to read and study more. If the disease of sin separated me from God, making me spiritually dead, then The Reconnection meant that I was now spiritually alive! Eternal life means that not only will I live forever, but I am reconnected to God right *now*. If this is true, eternal life with God started immediately—from the very moment I was saved. The following Bible verse brought a lot of these concepts together.

> *You were dead because of your sins and because your sinful nature was not yet cut away. Then God made you alive with Christ. He forgave all our sins. He canceled the record that contained the charges against us. He took it and destroyed it by nailing it to Christ's cross. (Colossians 2:13-14 NLT)*

Saved = spiritually alive = man's spirit + Holy Spirit (union/connection)

Saved = Holy Spirit in you = eternal life = The Reconnection to God

What was absolutely tantalizing was that if Christianity was reality and God is now inside of me, it could easily explain the impossible set of changes in me that occurred overnight. Until now I couldn't understand how I could be different at the molecular level with a new set of emotions, feelings, conscience, and even love for those I didn't like, *but* the power of God within me made it easily believable *if* it were true.

If I really had the Holy Spirit within me and I had passed from spiritual death to eternal life, then I would actually *expect* some noticeable changes from this transaction. The next question was "What are the observable and tangible results of being saved and having the Holy Spirit within?" I needed to determine if the results of salvation matched the changes I had experienced in The Transformation.

THE RESULTS OF THE CURE

When I was a resident doctor I had a stomach ulcer which caused abdominal pain. Once I was cured, however, the pain went away, my appetite increased, I slept better, and I gained some weight back. I experienced results and changes from the cure.

What were the results supposed to be from receiving Jesus Christ, the cure for the disease of sin? Did I have any of these signs of being truly healed by him?

I was very anxious and curious to study and understand the results of the cure. This would prove to me whether or not salvation is a real transaction that produces results from the Holy Spirit. The disease, symptoms, and cure for sin are all subjective biblical doctrines, but results are objective and tangible. The symptoms of sin, for example, were present in everyone I had ever met, and thus it was hard to believe this was a disease state affecting the entire planet.

I understood that Jesus is the cure, but all of this could easily be a matter of opinion or biased personal belief. If Christianity is nothing more than labeling everyday human behavior as "sinful" along with an intellectual belief that Jesus died to forgive these sins, then there is no way to know it is personally true for me today. I could easily sit in church and trust in my research on Jesus and the resurrection to feel good about my Christianity, but there would be no way to *really* know it was true.

If, however, something actually happens to a Christian who receives the cure of Jesus Christ, then everything changes. If there are genuine and observable results from the cure, then there is personal proof that it really worked. Just like in the medical field, the old symptoms of the disease should fade away and there should be signs that the cure is working.

I was fascinated with the possibility that this cure might actually be working in me. It was something I never expected. Because I hadn't expected any changes, I wanted to try church again, but this time I was equipped with an intellectual belief in the truth of the Bible. God had been so absent from my life and thoughts that I didn't even know change was possible. Throughout my entire life and the culture I had observed, church attendance seemed sufficient. I didn't think there was any way for people to know for sure that there was a God or that people could truly be saved from sin. I was still not convinced that my salvation was a reality, and I figured I'd have to wait until I died to find out for sure, and then if I was wrong, well, I wouldn't lose anything.

I remembered reading Josh McDowell's testimony, which described his anger dissipating over time after accepting Jesus as Lord and Savior by praying to God. I distinctly recalled not understanding how this was possible. How could his personality change from a prayer? My medical degree and knowledge of science precluded any link between a single prayer and a complete change of personality and emotions. These are deeply wired within the brain and nervous system in biochemical pathways that are poorly understood. Socialization from the modern world eliminated any ability to understand the relationship between the two. In my mind, it had to be a self-induced psychological change empowered by a religious belief. I did not understand anything about the Holy Spirit at this time, however. I was really curious now, because maybe Josh did change from being saved.

I used the study Bible and Billy Graham's book to find the answers. The Holy Spirit of God is not only the means of The Reconnection but also the source of power to change a person's life.[70] God not only came to save mankind from the penalty of sin, but he also wanted the believer in Jesus to have power over sin *before* the person died—in fact, while he was alive. Billy Graham explained that God knew that simply forgiving sin would not be enough, since the same individual making the same mistakes would remain.[71] In my case, the same Greg Viehman would roam the earth with all his bad qualities still in place. God knew that help, guidance, and power were needed, since we can't change on our own. The Holy Spirit is the solution to this problem.

If God living within me is the power to change, then what types of changes should I expect? I asked myself. These changes should correlate with the new symptoms I experienced after The Transformation.

God's Love: Unselfish Giving

I learned that God is love, but not the type of love I was accustomed to. God's love can be defined as unselfish giving. Unselfishness that focuses on other people should be a hallmark of salvation if God is now really living within me. This immediately got my attention, because I had already concluded that I had a new and unexplainable power to be unselfish not only in my actions but in *the motives* behind them. I recalled feeling a power within me to be a different person. I found a verse which listed some of the "symptoms" of the Holy Spirit living inside a person.

> *But the fruit of the Spirit is love, joy, peace, patience, kindness, goodness, faithfulness, gentleness and self-control. Against such things there is no law. Those who belong to Christ Jesus have crucified the sinful nature with its passions and desires. (Galatians 5:22-24 NIV)*

This list blew me away, because I had actually felt and experienced each and every one of these. I felt a love for people I didn't like. Joy and peace were an amazing combination of a euphoria and contentment that couldn't be put into words. Patience is unselfish waiting, which The Walmart Test validated. I also experienced and felt true kindness, unselfish niceness. I thought about the past and realized how often I had acted nice, but there was a veiled selfish motive behind it.

Before The Transformation I was faithful in my responsibilities, but they too were selfishly motivated. Now I sensed an unselfishness empowering my dependability. Before I was changed I lacked self-control and gentleness. I was impulsive, short-tempered, and explosive at times. Ever since I woke up that day after crying out to God, however, I had self-control. It wasn't perfect, but it was profoundly new and powerful. It was an unselfish strength that was under control versus the old me who was selfishly out of control.

The common denominator was a new and immediate sense of unselfish others-centered giving. When you have been completely self-absorbed and the epitome of the narcissistic personality disorder most of your life, then you profoundly notice unselfish motivations suddenly appearing on the scene. I could feel them coming from within me but didn't know how or why. I was stunned that this short list seemed to explain and elucidate many of the changes I was experiencing.

The Old Man Is Dead

There was something else in this verse about the Holy Spirit. I was struck by the reference to the sinful nature being dead. This was similar to what I had already learned in the New Testament book of Romans chapter six. This chapter teaches that when a person is saved his old nature dies. I clearly felt that my old personality, bad habits, and evil desires were gone. I was still tempted to do and say many of the things I used to, but now I was able to say "no" and make better choices. I was also aware of these situations and able to think them through before acting. Before I was changed I never thought about what I was doing. I acted rashly as things came up, but now I had an acute awareness of sinful actions and thoughts that was brand new.

Gradual and Ongoing Results

I discovered that the results of the cure could be dramatic and immediate like mine, but most people experience a gradual change. I wasn't perfect overnight by any stretch of the imagination, but I was radically transformed. I didn't know why some people have immediate changes while others experience a more incremental process. I couldn't find an answer to this question in my study Bible or on the Internet.

It was also clear that "the cure" isn't perfected until a person dies and goes to heaven. Even though I now had power over sin, I would still continue to screw up and make mistakes. Notes from the study Bible explained that believers have to continue to grow in their Christian walk to make continued progress and have victory over sin in their lives. I recalled parts of the Bible where even the Apostle Paul discussed his struggle over his sinful nature. I didn't fully understand this yet, but it certainly seemed to be true since I had never met a perfect person before.

Spiritual Understanding

Another result of the cure is an ability to better understand spiritual concepts and the Bible. The Holy Spirit living inside a person supposedly enables him or her to discern and comprehend the Bible itself in a new way.

> But the man who isn't a Christian can't understand and can't accept these thoughts from God, which the Holy Spirit teaches us. They sound foolish to him because only those who have the Holy Spirit within them can understand what the Holy Spirit means. Others just can't take it in. But the spiritual man has insight into everything, and that bothers and baffles the man of the world, who can't understand him at all. How could he? For certainly he has never been one to know the Lord's thoughts, or to discuss them with him, or to move the hands of God by prayer. But, strange as it seems, we Christians actually do have within us a portion of the very thoughts and mind of Christ. (1 Corinthians 2:14-16 The Living Bible)

This immediately rang true. The moment I picked up the Bible after praying to God for forgiveness and change, I noticed a difference. I understood it better and craved to read it. It wasn't that I couldn't understand it prior, but now it seemed clearer, like going from blurry vision to 20/20. I simply couldn't get enough, and this never went away. It became like food. I didn't understand how or why I felt this way. The Bible claimed that this was a sign of the Holy Spirit within me.

An End to the Void

Finally, I learned that people who are saved experience an end of the void, loneliness, and emptiness in their lives. The reason given is that we were created for God and only he can fill our hearts and fulfill our lives. Salvation brings an end to the separation. It is analogous to being reunited with someone you love after many years of separation. The moment you reconnect, everything changes. I marveled that this could be the reason I no longer felt this way.

SUMMARY

Everything I had studied and found in the Bible about the disease of sin, the symptoms of sin, the cure for sin, and the results of the cure matched what had happened to me temporally and experientially. My diagnosis, according to the Bible, was salvation by Jesus Christ resulting in a reconnection to God by the Holy Spirit with a resultant new nature. I had been saved from the disease of sin.

> *Therefore, if anyone is in Christ, he is a new creation; the old has gone, the new has come! (2 Corinthians 5:17 NIV)*

The cure for sin solves all three major problems: the death penalty for sin, separation from God, and the sinful behaviors that result from it. Jesus Christ provides the payment for the death penalty. The Holy Spirit is The Reconnection to God and establishes a new nature with power over sin.

The only aspect I still needed to examine was receiving the cure. I wanted to make sure that my history lined up with a biblical definition of salvation. If Jesus was the cure for sin, then how does someone receive the cure? Had I really received the cure, according to the Bible?

RECEIVING THE CURE

Receiving the cure is surprisingly easy. It is almost too easy. A person must believe in his heart that Jesus is fully God, who died in the person's place for his sins, and rose again the third day. The person must admit he is a sinner who has sinned against God and personally call on Jesus to forgive him. Most importantly, the Bible is clear that a person must repent of his sins and desire to change. Repentance is a turning away from old behavior and going in a new direction. It is not merely remorse or regret for bad behavior, but also a desire to change that culminates in actions of change.

As I thought about this, I replayed in my mind what had happened to me. I first *intellectually* believed in Jesus after finishing The Investigation, but I didn't notice any changes. By historical analysis and faith I had found a God I could believe was real, but I had mentally kept him in the realm of intellectualism. My new faith, at that point, was based on my personal journey that had completed a detailed examination of the evidence, because I trusted my own judgment.

Nothing I had ever seen or heard in the world suggested a current knowable reality to God. Growing up in the absence of God in a society ignoring God does not lead to any expectation other than church attendance defining Christianity. Did I really believe it actually happened, though? Did I actually believe that God walked the earth in human form, died on the cross, and was resurrected the third day? I did, but it seemed so long ago, untouchable, and personally impractical to me. If the Bible was right, then the absence of changes at this first stage made sense, since I had not yet repented and still viewed Jesus as intellectual doctrine. I believed in my mind but didn't personally engage God from my heart to forgive and save me.

That night in my office, however, I did everything the Bible said was required to be saved. I moved from the intellectual stage to a personal, heartfelt surrender to God. I believed Jesus was God and that he was resurrected the third day. I saw myself as a sinner, cried out to Jesus, and deeply desired to change. I was immensely grieved over my past behaviors. I feared God and called out to him in complete surrender. Now I was discovering that God's definition of belief is more than just believing in his existence, but having complete and utter trust in him, placing everything at his feet, and putting your faith into action. It's like looking at a chair and knowing it is a chair versus actually sitting in that chair and trusting that it will hold you.

The crazy thing is that I didn't say or do anything on purpose. I wasn't intentionally saying certain words or reciting a religious script that night. My heart just came out of me. I had set out to prove Christianity was a bunch of religious hypocrites and not reality. When I did cry out to God, I didn't expect anything. I had no idea that God personally heard me. If I had received the cure, then I didn't even know it.

It also occurred to me that I could have easily stopped at the stage where I intellectually believed in Jesus and the basic Christian doctrine. It was about one week before I actually personally cried out to Jesus asking for forgiveness and change. I could have continued on with an intellectual Christianity, especially since I had no idea there was anything else to it.

This is like having the medicine in hand but never taking it. I can hold an antibiotic in my hand and intellectually believe that it can heal me, but I have to actually take it for it to work. I wondered if there were a lot of people out there in the land of Christianity like this—people who believe in the medicine but never personally take it into their bodies to receive the cure.

It was unmistakable that I had received Jesus, the cure for sin, according to what the Bible taught. I matched all of the requirements.

THE REACTION TO THE CURE

These were radical concepts for me to ponder. This was something I never expected nor even thought was possible. As I read and studied, something within me witnessed to my heart and mind that these things were true. I felt dramatically different in every way. All of my signs and symptoms matched those of salvation by Jesus Christ. Then all of a sudden it hit me. A veil lifted and I finally got it. "Oh, my goodness! I have truly been saved. God's Holy Spirit has been given to me!" I shouted out loud.

The night that I cried out to God, he heard me, saved me, and filled me with the Holy Spirit. "That's what The Bible Woman had been talking about!" I exclaimed. She had said, "I pray that the Holy Spirit reveals himself to you." That explained how I felt love for those I didn't like and the source of unselfishness permeating my thoughts and motives. I was feeling the Holy Spirit living within me. This was mind-blowing!

At this moment in time I became acutely aware of the reality of God's presence within me and all around me. I realized that God not only heard what I said, but now actually dwelled within me. I said to him, "Father. Are you really there?" He didn't say anything back, but I knew he was telling me, "Yes. I am here, and have always been with you." I felt that I had awakened from a dream that had lasted thirty-six years. I was so excited; I literally didn't know what to do.

This is incredible! This is personal proof that Christianity is reality, not religion! I thought. *My faith is based on a new existence and not just intellectual acceptance of doctrine.* This was shocking and completely unexpected to me in today's age of reason dominated by tolerance, agnosticism, and naturalism. I went from God unknowable to God within me!

The Implications of The Cure were a series of tidal waves that kept knocking me over. My entire life, thought process, and concepts of reality were changing faster than I could comprehend. I kept saying

"Whoooa! I didn't expect Jesus Christ to be *that* real and present. No one told me that his Spirit is put inside you at salvation." Everything I was doing in life and had ever been taught were so far from this truth. I literally could not believe it, but this was just the beginning. Many more tidal waves were headed my way.

Chapter Fifteen

The Final Diagnosis

THE FINAL DIAGNOSIS

The final diagnosis was salvation from the disease of sin by Jesus Christ. I had exhibited the signs and symptoms of sin since I was born and never even suspected they were a sign of separation from God. In my attempt to prove Christianity nothing more than a religious institution of hypocrisy, I ended up becoming a believer myself. An intellectual acceptance of Christianity with plans for weekly church attendance was forever changed when I cried out to God one night in my bedroom. What I thought was an emotional meltdown resulting from too much religious reading was actually a transaction of eternal significance.

I had been saved that night and didn't even know what salvation was or that it's an acute reality. The Holy Spirit of God joined my spirit, reconnected me to God, and gave me a new nature. I went to bed absolutely oblivious to all of it.

Upon awakening I found myself radically changed in every conceivable way with no logical explanation. I thought I was diagnosing a disease state when the symptoms I was having were from the cure not the disease. I had it reversed and created a spiritual comedy of comedies! In reality, I'd had the disease of sin my entire life and hadn't realized it. Then I got cured and I didn't know that, either. I had been trying to diagnose what was wrong with me when I was actually diagnosing the cure! Because my behavior changes were so drastic, all I could think was that there was something wrong with me. Instead, I found that for the first time in my life I had been made right with God.

Overnight, God went from distant, unknowable, or non-existent to my Savior who lived within me and all around me. I was saved from the disease of sin by Jesus Christ and was now experiencing the beginning of eternal life, or The Reconnection to God. My heart told me it was true and my symptoms were not explainable by anything else known to man. They perfectly matched the disease of sin, and my changes lined up exactly with biblical salvation from the cure of Jesus Christ. I was a walking miracle in a culture that said they didn't exist. I was living proof that Jesus is God and the answer to heaven and eternal life. I had The God Diagnosis.

I was extremely excited. I couldn't wait to tell all my friends and share the Good News with them. I could hardly sleep that night. I was sure they would be thrilled. Boy, was I in for a shock!

Chapter Sixteen

The Confession of The Cure

"Greg? We're home. Where are you?" my wife called.

I looked at my watch and saw it was after six. I had completely lost track of time and didn't realize that over five hours had passed. I had been completely absorbed for several days finding a diagnosis. I had been studying day and night every free moment. "I'm upstairs in the office. I'll be right down." *What would I tell her? How could I explain everything?* I wondered. *Would she believe me?*

"What did you do all day?" she asked.

"I'll tell you later tonight. It's a long story."

"Just tell me now. Don't be weird. You have been reading in seclusion for days."

"We need to have peace and quiet. After the kids go to bed."

"Okay," she agreed.

The rest of the night I was pensive and apprehensive. I knew she had been attending Bible study, but I didn't know where she stood. I wasn't certain if she was saved or understood the reality of Christianity, since we had not discussed it. I kept thinking about what to say. My heart rate ramped up as the time approached. Finally, the kids went to bed and the moment came. By now my heart was pounding.

I walked into the bedroom. Ruth was sitting in the bed reading. I got into bed and sat up against the headboard using a few pillows to support my back. "Ruth, you know that book you bought me that I started reading? The one about the Bible?" I said hesitantly.

"Yes. Why?" she said as she put down what she was reading and gave me her full attention.

"Well, I finished it. In fact, I have read the entire New Testament, and studied it in detail. I know I mentioned this to you earlier, but I never told you what I was up to."

"Go on," she said expectantly.

"Well, I decided I could believe in Jesus. I realized I could go to church and do the Christianity thing."

"That's great. I thought you had been acting a little different. Do you want to keep going to the church that David took us to?"

"Sure, but wait. There's more. About two weeks ago I stayed up late in the office. I became convicted of the problems in my life and personality. I broke down and cried out to God asking for forgiveness and change." She was staring intently at me. "Ruth, God did something to me. He actually changed the nature of my existence. I woke up a different person. I have spent every moment since that day trying to figure out what happened to me. Now I know—I was saved. The Holy Spirit has been given to me. God now dwells within me, as incredible as that is, and is changing me. Everything is different."

She didn't say a word for a few moments. She was studying my face to see if I was serious. "Wow. That's awesome! I have become a believer also, but I have not experienced what you are talking about."

"You have to believe me. I am not crazy or some religious weirdo now," I interjected.

"I do. I do," she said, but I sensed a trace of doubt in her expression.

"I am sorry for the way I have treated you," I sobbed as my eyes filled with water. "I was wrong. Please forgive me. I am so sorry. I am going to make it up to you. I'm not going back to my old self," I cried.

She hugged me and said, "I forgive you. It's okay."

"No! It's not okay. I was a miserable, arrogant, prideful, self-centered, egotistical jerk to you, the kids, and many people I know," I stuttered, fighting off sobs in between my words. "This is all so crazy. How can God be that close to us and real, and yet nobody is talking about it?! There is something really wrong, Ruth! Something is drastically wrong. I don't think a lot of people realize what real Christianity is. I had no idea even after studying it that God indwells someone who is saved. I can't comprehend the magnitude of what this means for my concept of reality. Do you realize I have lived my entire life spiritually dead, separated from God? I never said one word to him, and yet he was right there all around me. He heard what I said that night. *He heard me*! How can God hear me out of billions of people on the earth? Think this through, Ruth. Let it sink in! We don't know anything about our existence. This storybook life we have lived has been a mirage and façade hiding the truth. Almost everything I was taught about the truth of our existence and purpose in life was a lie. I think our entire culture is built upon a Great Deception.

"I didn't expect this. This changes everything. It's not about church attendance or being nice. It's not about my career or personal achievements. I don't know what to think. I believed it was true, but I never fathomed that God was *that* real and active today. This means he really did it. Jesus was actually here as God and went to the cross. How can there be so many religions when this is true? My concept of reality is crumbling!"

"Greg, calm down. You're getting yourself all wound up," Ruth said.

"I'm not going to calm down. Calm down? Do you understand what I am telling you? Do you realize what this means?" I exclaimed, still wiping tears from my eyes.

"I think so. I'm new to this, also. I grew up in church, but it was all about church."

"I need to do a lot of thinking, Ruth. The implications are profound and astounding. I'm going back into the office to think. I am overwhelmed."

"Okay. We'll talk more tomorrow. I love you."

"I love you too. Don't tell anyone about this conversation! Not a word about this yet. I really want to start telling people what has happened to me, but I want to gather some more information first. I need a little more time."

"Okay."

Chapter Seventeen

The Implications of The Cure

I felt relieved as I sat down in our home office. Ruth and I had a lot more to talk about, but I was glad she didn't think I was crazy. I slouched in the chair and kicked my feet up on the desk. I gathered myself together and began thinking through the implications. I wanted to stick to simple facts and build from there.

God seemed like an obvious place to start, since it was all about him. I began writing a list on a pad of paper.

GOD

Jesus Christ is God. Jesus is alive. He heard me.

I stopped there and pondered the implications of this. How could God hear me when there are over six billion people on the earth? How did he know I was sincere when I cried out to him that night? How could he know the intentions of my heart behind the words?

Then I wrote:

God is omniscient (knows everything) *and omnipresent* (is everywhere at all times).

At first thought this seemed obvious, since he is God, but the more I thought about it the more profound it became. What does this say about my concept of reality? I concluded:

I know nothing about the reality of my existence when God hears me and knows my heart.

I was blown away.

HEAVEN

Heaven is real. I am going there.

I wrote with a grin. The thought of death was always troubling to me, especially when I hugged my children and watched them lie asleep. I had wondered how my intense love for them could only have meaning and origination from evolved matter. If they tragically died then the object of my love would cease to exist and become meaningless decaying chemicals. How does a child that inhabits the heart and soul only represent evolved matter?

As a result, I was always afraid of death, but not anymore! The certainty of eternal life by the presence of God living within me eliminated many worries and fears. I was ecstatic that my family and I were more than evolved organic soup headed for the great recycling bin. Now I understood why death felt so wrong. Death isn't the end but the beginning. Death went from being a cold and meaningless recycling of matter to entering eternity with God. I never dreamed of such a radical reality change and paradigm shift! A wave of joy rushed over me. I felt free. I had real hope, a certainty of good things to come.

HELL

Hell is real. I had been headed there.

My hand was shaking a bit as I penned this one. If I was now saved, then I wasn't saved in the past. I remembered that Jesus talked about hell more than heaven. A torrent of terror and chills ran up my spine. I realized for the first time that I had been on the path to hell my entire life. All of my accomplishments, good times, and success in the world would have meant nothing. This freaked me out, but I knew it was true. God came to earth to save us from our sins, which would separate us from God forever without Jesus. The proximity and reality of hell haunted me. I burst into tears and thanked Jesus that he had saved me. I was overwhelmed with gratitude. I wiped away the tears on my T-shirt and kept writing.

MIRACLES

I am a living miracle.

I had been rewired at the cellular level. I was a real present day act-of-God miracle. I was walking and living proof that Jesus Christ is God and alive. He was right there in the room when I prayed that night. Suddenly, I believed all of the miracles in the Bible. If God can rewire a human being and know my heart, then he can do whatever he wants, like walk on water, part the Red Sea, or heal the blind. If Jesus was resurrected and I am counting on him to resurrect me, then why would I doubt any miracle in the Bible at all?

THE BIBLE

The Bible is the Word of God.

If God can hear what I say and know my heart, then he is aware of and involved in the tiniest details. Since the Bible is the revelation of God and his plan for salvation, then it must be exactly the way he wants it. A God of intricate details would certainly preserve the Scriptures. I had already discovered that copying errors, intentional changes, deletions, and additions over the centuries did not change the doctrine or main message of the Bible. The preservation and accuracy of the Scriptures was remarkable. God knew ahead of time that through the centuries the original manuscripts would undergo superficial changes, yet in his divine will and sovereignty he maintained via human instruments the core message and specific ideas he wanted to preserve and for us to know. The Scriptures still contain the key to eternal life.

Using an analogy based on my medical school knowledge, I considered the fact that our bodies and personages are made from DNA, which is a blueprint for life based on a five-letter code. The letters for DNA form a code that contains information and instructions for life. I knew from biology that my DNA accumulates small errors over time, but most of them are not significant. I am still alive. The information that uniquely encodes my body still works and has been preserved. The accumulated small "errors/changes" don't negate that I exist, anymore than those in Bible might make it not the Word of God. If God can know my heart, then he can put a paperback into existence that is his Word. If he changed the nature of my existence, why would I question his ability to make and preserve a book?

THE GREAT DECEPTION

My life was a lie.

A tear rolled down my cheek as I sat and stared at what I had just written. I began to realize that all of my major concepts of reality and purpose had been wrong. The paradigm of life that the world taught me and witnessed to me in every facet of life was a deception and lie. I felt as if I had awakened from a dream that had lasted thirty-six years. One by one I wrote down the contrasts between the old and new realities.

No God	God within me
No hope	Eternal life
God uninvolved	God hears me and knows my heart
Evolved from "cosmic soup"	Created by God
Life on earth is normal	Life on earth is fallen because of sin
I am inherently good	I am inherently sinful
I reached the pinnacle of success	I was headed to hell
I had everything in life	I had nothing without Jesus
All about me and my will	All about God and his will
I am a good person, healthy, alive & well	I am a sinner, spiritually dead
Unaccountable	Accountable
Self-sufficiency, Self-worth, Self-trust	I need God
I know everything	I know nothing

Tears streamed down my face. How could I have been so deceived? My entire life had been a lie. The world told me to strive for The American Dream and I had reached the pinnacle of success, but The American Dream had become a nightmare. I had to stop writing and thinking about this one for a while.

MY FAMILY AND FRIENDS
My children, parents, and friends are not saved!

Panic and dismay raced through my body like lightning. The reality of God, heaven, and hell jolted me out of the chair. I stood up in a panic. "Oh no, they don't have the Holy Spirit. They are still living in the dream. They have no idea!" I shrieked out loud. I suddenly felt an urgency to tell them and everyone I knew.

I put the pad of paper down on the desk and raced into the bedroom to talk to Ruth about the kids, but she was sleeping. I was overwhelmed by the reality of Christianity. It wasn't a *religion* I had decided to accept and follow, but the reality of my existence. I couldn't understand why I had not heard about it for most of my life. Did I somehow miss it? I wondered. Maybe I had been tuned out. I didn't think so, but I wanted to find out before I started telling people what had happened to me.

I decided to wait one week and closely examine everything around me in Cary, North Carolina. I lay down on my pillow and devised a plan to look everywhere for evidence of Jesus. I would listen to people's conversations, drive around the city, watch the news, look in stores, and watch what people were doing. I was going to look for evidence in everyday life that Jesus Christ was alive, personal, and impacting society. If people are saved and have God living within them, then they should be talking about it. This would be the most important thing in life. Certainly I would find people discussing this, wouldn't I? Was there something other than churches on Sunday proclaiming the truth? Was there Evidence of The Cure?

Chapter Eighteen

The Evidence of The Cure

It was Christmas season. For the first time in my life I realized that the word "Christ" was in the word Christmas. Jesus Christ had been lost even in the name of the holiday that celebrates his birth. Now that I knew what Christmas was really about, I realized it was the perfect occasion to look for evidence of the reality of Christianity. Since Christmas celebrates the birth of Jesus, it would surely be the most likely time to find people talking about him and how the Holy Spirit lives within them—right? Such a mind-blowing reality of God couldn't possibly live under the radar, especially at Christmas. I expected to find evidence of Jesus everywhere. *I live in the "Bible Belt,"* I thought. *What better situation could I ask for to conduct my research?*

I decided to pretend that I knew nothing. I wanted to see if the world around me would lead me to the truth, especially at Christmas time, if I was specifically looking for it in everyday life. Would I conclude that Jesus is the Savior of the world by observing the environment during the Christmas season?

CHRISTMAS DECORATIONS AND LIGHTS

I waited till it was dark and decided to take a drive. I grabbed my keys off the kitchen counter. "Honey, where are you going?" Ruth asked.

"I'm going to take a short drive. I'll be right back." I got into my car and headed out into the neighborhood. It was freezing! I could see every breath as I shivered and panted in the car. Everyone had their lights and decorations up by now. The timing was perfect.

I drove down the main drag of the neighborhood. It was lit up with lights. Blue, red, and green trees twinkled. White reindeer grazed in the yards. Santa, Frosty the Snowman, and Rudolph were smiling and waving, but Jesus, or anything that represented him, was nowhere to be found. I kept driving and covered the whole neighborhood but didn't see even a manger scene. I tried the neighborhood across the street but found the same thing. I kept driving and driving. My heart began to sink into my stomach. A tear rolled down my cheek as I recalled my own Christmas experiences.

I was taught, as a small child, to have faith in an imaginary jolly man, but not the living God who created me and was all around me. I had sent letters to the North Pole but never prayed to God, who actually heard my words and knew my heart. I trusted in Santa Claus to provide me what I desired but never asked my heavenly Father, who was only a breath away. It crushed me to know he was there all along while I didn't have a clue. For me, Christmas had been about the gifts, food, parties, lights, family, and songs, but not about the reality of Jesus.

I kept on driving but couldn't find a lighted cross, Jesus' name in lights, or a manger scene anywhere. "An outside observer would have no idea this holiday is supposed to be about Jesus," I said aloud to myself.

THE LOCAL DEPARTMENT STORE

In frustration I pulled into our local department store, which has everything. It was a madhouse! I approached the front doors and found Santa outside collecting money. Inside people were pushing, shoving, bickering, and fighting. Long faces, frustrated frowns, and impatient tempers abounded. I made my way through the chaos to the Christmas section. Angels, snowflakes, tinsel, lights, toy soldiers, and wrapping paper surrounded me. I searched the tree decorations, lights, and yard paraphernalia and found hardly anything biblical that I recognized except angels. I couldn't find a Bible, a manger scene, or anything with the name Jesus on it anywhere in the store. There was nothing about salvation or the Holy Spirit, either. It was as if people were oblivious to the reality of God. What good is Christmas if I don't have the Christ? In a way I felt vindicated, because I had never heard about Jesus or the need for salvation at Christmas time for over thirty years. Christmas was always a joyous time of presents, family, and friends. Now all those happy memories were tainted by a lifetime of deception. I trudged through the store, scowling at the lavish, meaningless displays, and shuddered at the false hopes.

RESTAURANTS

The next day I staked out a few restaurants at lunch and dinner. The Christmas rush had people spilling out the doors waiting to be seated. I eavesdropped on conversations, but Jesus was not on their minds. I paid attention to the tables being served but saw no prayer. A few places had Christmas trees and lights but nothing about God. I did the same things on Sunday, thinking Jesus would be fresh on people's minds. Nothing was different.

Everyone was going about their business like our existence in this world was normal. I began to wonder if anybody knew the truth. I realized in watching everyone that this is how I had lived my entire life. I had been clueless and self-absorbed to the point of blindness. God had been all around me and able to hear my words and know my heart, but I never uttered one word to him. I saw the old me in everyone around me, and it scared me to the bone.

I gave up, got in my car, and headed home. "Lord, if you can hear me and everyone else, then why aren't people talking to you? Why aren't people even talking *about* you? If people need to be saved, then why are they acting as if life on earth is perfectly normal?" I asked.

I had not started talking to Jesus yet on a personal level. I rhetorically asked him these questions to remind myself he was there, because everything I was observing was trying to convince me he wasn't.

THE OFFICE

The next morning at the office I was delighted to see The Bible Woman reading her Bible when I arrived. She didn't know I had been saved yet. I approached her as she was reading. "Tammy, why isn't anyone talking about God, even at Christmas?" I asked.

"What do you mean?" she replied, looking both startled and surprised at my question.

"Well, let's just say the Bible is true and people need to be saved. If salvation is a real event in a person's life when God then lives inside that person, wouldn't that be something worth talking about? Wouldn't that be the most incredible truth ever?" I stopped, searched her face to see if she was following me, and then continued, "I have been observing people and looking for evidence of that reality, but I can't find it anywhere. Why? How can I believe it's true when nobody is talking about it?"

She paused and got a very deep look on her face. "Many people don't know the truth and don't want to, even if they go to church. People want the idea of God and Jesus but not the reality and accountability of him," she said.

"But if it's really true then it's all good news. Heaven, eternal life, salvation, God within you, hope, peace, and meaning. There is nothing bad about it. I don't get it." I replied in exasperation.

Just then, the nurses interrupted our conversation with the morning schedule. The rest of the week I watched and listened to the patients. No Bibles, no prayer before surgery, and no talk about Jesus. No one seemed excited that God was there or concerned that people needed to be saved if they did know he was real.

I was seeing everything from a completely new perspective. I kept reminding myself that God hears each and every person in an incomprehensible way. I was astonished by the silence of our culture. The silence made me begin to question my own salvation. *Am I the crazy one?* I wondered. *I have been saved. God now lives within me. I have been changed and made spiritually alive. God hears me and knows my heart*! I reassured myself.

TELEVISION

At this point I almost didn't want to look any further, but I felt compelled to keep going. I turned on the television and scanned through some shows that were centered on families. There were no signs of God or Jesus except in cuss words. No one prayed, mentioned God, or included him in their daily lives. God was clearly portrayed as irrelevant in everyday family life. I recalled the past and realized many of the family shows I had watched for years were silently inscribing the same message on my mind by leaving God out. Now that Jesus lived within me, silence was no longer neutrality. I realized that this silence was also denial.

I was coming to grips with a new reality that shook me to the core of my existence. The contrast and great abyss between the world around me that didn't acknowledge Jesus and the truth of him being so close, being alive within me, hearing me, and knowing my heart was devastating. I began to feel that I was living in a "bizzaro" land. The joy of my own salvation was being sucked away by the new ability to see The Great Deception all around me.

I had to talk to someone, but I didn't want it to be anyone who might not understand. I felt that they would think I was crazy and report me to the medical board. I had to admit, these thoughts and insights would seem like a schizophrenic delusion to most people.

"I've got it!" I exclaimed exuberantly. "I'll tell Tammy. I can trust her. She's always talking about Jesus and reading her Bible." I had already briefly asked her about the lack of Jesus in people's lives and conversations anyway. I couldn't wait to get work the next day. I planned to tell Tammy I was saved and ask her more about the lack of The Evidence for The Cure.

Chapter Nineteen

The Bible Woman

The morning schedule of patients finished early. It was well before lunch time. I knew it was time to talk to Tammy, The Bible Woman. I realized I couldn't just tell her I was saved. I had to swallow my pride and also confess to her I had been mistaken. Would she gloat? Somehow I didn't think so, but what would she do?

I had rehearsed a number of times what I would say to her. Admitting I was wrong was not something I was accustomed to. I had a strange feeling I was about to get good at it. My palms were sweaty, and a tight feeling developed in my chest as I walked towards her desk. *You can do this*, I told myself.

I walked into the laboratory unnoticed. She was sitting at her desk reading the Bible, to no surprise. I came up behind her and hesitated. Part of me wanted to bolt while another part wanted to talk to her about God and why I couldn't find any Evidence for The Cure.

"Tammy?"She turned in her chair and peered at me with a curious look over the top of her sixties style cat-eye reading glasses, as if sensing the change in me.

"Hey, Dr. Viehman. What's up?"

"Uh, can we talk privately in my office?" I said, sounding as nervous as I felt.

"Sure. Let's go." We went and sat down in two chairs across from each other. My office was at the end of the building. Two of the walls were completely glass. It was located right by the parking lot so everyone walking by could see inside. I got up before we started talking and closed the blinds.

"Is everything okay?" she asked.

"Yeah. Don't worry. I just don't want anyone to see us talking. It's private."

"What is it?" she asked. She could tell by my voice that I was jittery.

"Tammy, I need to tell you what has happened to me. As you know, I started reading the Bible to prove that Christians were hypocrites. I didn't know anything about God and didn't want to. I grew up in a culture that made God unimportant and unknowable in every facet of life. Over the past month I have studied everything I can find about Jesus, his claim to be God, and the resurrection. I have given The Investigation every ounce of effort in me. To my surprise, the deeper I went the more believable the story became. What started off as a religious fairy tale quickly became a search for absolute truth in a world that says truth is relative or unknowable. I was shocked that the Bible seemed to explain the origin and cause for many problems in my life.

"After a lot of consternation and careful investigation, I finally reached a point where I decided I could intellectually believe in Christianity and go to church. That was a big step for me, since I was not a church kind of guy who likes to dress up on Sunday and act all nice and moral. But what did I have to lose? I was ready to try to be a better person, learn from the sermons, and acknowledge God at holidays and meals. I thought that's all there was to it.

"A few nights later, however, I became convicted of my sin and all of the wretched aspects of my life and personality. I cried out to Jesus and begged for change and forgiveness. I went to bed thinking I had just gotten sappy and religious. The next morning, Tammy, I woke up an entirely different person in every way. I can't even describe it in words. My thoughts, motives, priorities, anger, frustration, and many other things were either gone or changed. I didn't know what had happened to me and tried to diagnose myself, thinking I had a disease or hormonal imbalance, but nothing made sense. I went back to the Bible, and realized everything could be explained by salvation from Jesus. I had been saved and didn't even know it for a week. I had no idea when you are saved that God dwells within you! I was blown away."

"Wow, Dr. Viehman! That's awesome. I am so happy for you. My Bible study group has been praying for you. God is so good!"

"You guys have been praying for me? I don't even know these people and yet they cared enough to pray for me? That's amazing. Tammy, I was wrong. I was so wrong about God, the Bible, and almost everything in life. I am sorry for mocking you and making jokes in the lab. I am starting over in every aspect of my life. Please forgive me."

"I forgive you. I can't tell you how happy I am that the Lord saved you. When you have been forgiven it's a lot easier to forgive others."

"Thanks, Tammy."

"What did Ruth say? Did you tell anyone else yet?"

"Ruth knows. She was saved six months before I was after joining a Bible study. She is ecstatic but a little skeptical that the changes in me will last."

"They will last, all right, Dr. Viehman. You have the power of God living in you now. You won't be perfect, though. You'll still make a lot of mistakes and sin, but you'll never be the same. You seem a lot calmer and more relaxed."

"I feel as if I've been drugged, but in a good way. I was so high strung and irritable all the time that the peace I feel now is incredible. It's as if God popped the balloon and let out all of the bad air and tension that were built up inside."

"Have you been going to church?" she asked.

"Yes. I feel comfortable at a church right down the road from our house. I am a little uncomfortable during the music part, though."

"Why?"

"A lot of people are raising their hands and closing their eyes. Isn't that going overboard?"

"Do you watch sports, Dr. Viehman?"

"Yeah, but what does that have to do with anything?" I replied inquisitively.

"If your team scores a touchdown do you jump up and down and wave your hands in the air?"

"Yes," I said sheepishly. I knew where she was going with this now.

"Then why would it be strange to praise the God that made you and saved you by lifting your hands to him?"

"You have a point. I guess I'm not sure why it bothers me." She sensed I was uncomfortable and changed the topic.

"Does anyone else know you have been saved? Did you tell anyone else?"

"No. Not yet. I waited a week to see if I had somehow missed Jesus in everyday life. I went around and checked out Cary for signs of Jesus in people's lives. I went to restaurants, the mall, shopping centers, and all over town."

"What did you find?"

"Nothing. Silence. Tammy, if God is so close that he can hear what I say and know my heart, then why is nobody proclaiming it? Go out there and observe for yourself. See if you can find any signs of God in people's lives. This isn't something that should be kept secret or personal, since it's the essence of our existence. It's not religion. It's reality."

"God has been shut out of our culture, Dr. Viehman. There's a lot of religion out there but little relationship. People want the idea of God but not the reality and accountability of him. People will say 'I believe in God,' but that doesn't mean they are saved or have a relationship with God. You're right. We should be talking about him all the time. How can people believe Jesus is real if they don't see him in our lives?"

"Tammy, you are one of the few people I have met who lives it out in the open. I was watching you to see if God was real, but I never would have told you. I think deep down inside I wanted God to be knowable, but I was afraid of what the truth would mean for my life. A few people tried to tell me about Jesus in the past, but I wouldn't listen. If what they were telling me was true, then my entire paradigm of life was wrong. It made me, my childhood, my family, and my way of life a deception and a lie. How many people can swallow that, Tammy?

"I look back on my life and the silence haunts me. I lived separated from God since I was born. Years of relationships, school, and experiences were all lived without one utterance to God. It's strange and sad to realize he was right there all along. The silence is frightening. The reality of hell and the need for salvation are real. I feel as if I've awakened from a dream. When I was 'dreaming' everything seemed normal, but now that I am 'awake' it's a nightmare. I feel like Keanu Reeves in the movie *The Matrix*. Have you seen it?"

"No."

"It's a science fiction movie, but it closely parallels what I have experienced. In the movie a man named Neo awakens from a false reality. He discovers that his entire life has been a deception and a lie. I feel exactly the same way. Salvation, eternal life, and the heaven aspect of Christianity are exciting, but The Implications to my past are devastating."

"You need to start telling people, Dr. Viehman."

"Okay. Can you go get Dacia for me?"

"Sure." She hugged me and left the office. Dacia was the head nurse and a good friend. I had no idea what she believed, but I wanted to tell her next. As Dacia listened, she lit up with a huge smile. When I finished, she hugged me and told me she was a Christian.

"That is incredible, Dr. Viehman. I am so excited for you!"

I was so relieved. She didn't think I was crazy! She knew all about salvation and the Holy Spirit. *Whew!*

I began to enjoy giving my testimony, since it was so incredible and unbelievable. It was refreshing and energizing to tell people how I was saved. I had a strong intuition that this was something I was supposed to do. I also had a feeling there was more to the Christian life than telling people about Jesus and just waiting to redeem a ticket to heaven, but I didn't know what it was. *Is there more?* I wondered. Little did I know, God was about to answer my question and reveal to me a mind-blowing truth. He was about to unveil The Relationship.

Chapter Twenty

The Relationship

The next day after work, when I was finishing up in the office, Dacia, the head nurse, came in carrying a present.

"Dr. Viehman, I have something for you." She handed me a wrapped Christmas gift about the size of a small book. I ripped off the wrapping paper and found a suede covered notebook filled with blank pages.

"What is it, Dacia?"

"It's a prayer journal. Record your prayers and the date you make them. Then go back and check them off when God answers. This will also help you have a list to pray from."

"What do you mean, God answers prayers? How does he do that?" I asked.

She closed the door and sat down. "Dr. Viehman, God is your Father. He loves you, lives inside of you now, and wants a relationship with you. He is interested in the tiniest details of your life."

"How can that be possible? I have always lived without him. I have had millions of tiny details I never included him in. How can he work in my life? I thought that once you are saved then you're on your own until you die. Maybe if a big crisis arises then God will intervene, but not in the everyday details. If God is personal, then people should be talking about it. In all the years I have lived I didn't hear about this one time, even when a few people tried to tell me about God. What you are saying sounds crazy!"

"It's unbelievable, I agree, but it's true. He wants to be the Lord of your life and guide you in everything."

"Wow. That's actually pretty awesome, that I could have that kind of personal interaction with Jesus! I know he hears me, since he certainly did the night I was saved. I assumed the communication lines were mainly open for things like tragedies and being saved."

"No. He wants to be involved in all aspects of your life. He will be, if you let him," she said.

Bewildered, I asked, "How? What do I do?"

"Just start talking to him. Talk to him about everything. Ask him what to do. Most importantly, pray that he guides your life and decisions. Start doing that and watch what happens. Read your Bible all of the time. The Bible is the Word of God. That is God talking to you. Your prayers are you talking to him. It's just like you and me talking now. Relationship is a word exchange."

"How can God talk to me through the Bible?" I asked.

"God has revealed himself to man through his Word. You learn about who God is and what he is like from his Word, the Bible. The verses will speak to your heart. They will point out issues in your life. The stories of people's lives directly pertain to us. Their mistakes and victories are meant to instruct us. As you read the Bible, the Holy Spirit within you will show you things and how they apply to your life. Don't forget when you are reading that the Holy Spirit lives within you."

"This sounds too good to be true. It's exciting and bizarre at the same time. I feel as if I'm in a science fiction movie. An entire lifetime has shown me that God is unknowable or nonexistent in every facet of life, and now you are telling me he will guide every detail of my personal life?! If this is true, then the fact is that people are ignoring him in unbelievable proportions. Do you realize the implications of what you are telling me? I believe you, but you have got to understand where I am coming from."

"It takes time, Dr. Viehman. I know this is a lot to swallow. Just pray, surrender your life, read the Bible, and pay attention. God is supernaturally natural."

"What does that mean, Dacia?"

"The people you meet, the circumstances you find yourself in, and the thoughts and feelings in your heart—you'll find that he is in the midst of all of them, if you pay attention and follow his lead."

"Okay. I am so grateful that he saved me that I will do whatever he says. I want to know him because of what he has done for me. I wasn't even looking for God in my life."

"Do you realize, Dr. Viehman, that all of the circumstances leading up to your salvation were God seeking you? Christianity is God pursuing man. God is the initiator in The Relationship. It's incredible what efforts he will take to save someone."

I was dumbfounded and silent. I quickly thought about the events leading up to my salvation: The Ski Trip, Marco Island, The Bible Woman, The Patient, the book by Josh McDowell that Ruth had placed by the nightstand, and The Next-Door Neighbor who invited me to church. I was blown away.

"Whoa! I didn't actually find God through my intellectual study. He came and rescued me! He put all of the pieces together and brought the right people into my life at the right time. This is truly an amazing and mind-blowing concept for me to ponder. I need to think about this. Thanks for the journal. I have to get home. It's late."

"Good night, Dr. Viehman."

I got into the car and started the drive home. I kept thinking about what she told me. It seemed strange to just strike up a conversation with God, even though I was certain he heard me. My heart, however, felt compelled and drawn to him.

PRAYER

"Jesus, I know you hear me. I don't understand everything yet, but thank you for saving me. I want to know you and let you guide my life. Make me the person you want me to be. I'll do whatever you say to the best of my ability. I can't believe you were there from the very beginning and I never talked to you. The world told me I couldn't know you and acted as though you didn't exist. Why was no one talking to you or about you where I grew up? Why were you shut out of the schools? Since you are the true God, then why are there so many religions? I have so many questions. How do I hear from you? How do I know what you want me to do? I don't know where to start."

I drove the rest of the way home in silence. My mind kept dwelling on one thing. *My kids, parents, and friends are not saved. They are still living clueless just like I had all my life. I have to reach them. I have to tell everyone I know what has happened to me*, I thought.

I suddenly understood why The Ski Trip kooks approached me that year. I had to admit, they were right. My heart was immensely burdened and afraid for people who did not know Jesus. I could still taste hell—the hell I could have gone to. It was rattling my soul and compelling me to tell others who were not saved. I wasn't sure, but I sensed that was what God wanted me to do. Dacia had told me to pay attention to my heart and thoughts. Was The Relationship starting already?

That night after everyone went to bed, I went into the office. This became my place to pray, read the Bible, and seek after the will of God. I began to talk with God about anything and everything. It felt strange at first, as if I was talking to myself, but the awkward feeling quickly faded. I needed to make up for lost time, since I was many years behind in The Relationship and eager to get started. *What an amazing opportunity that God wants to interact with me!*

"Lord, Dacia told me you want to work in my life. I am here. I want to get started. What do I need to do?" As I said this prayer I felt a strong nudge to pick up the Bible. I thought maybe I was imagining it so I ignored it. I tried to keep praying but couldn't concentrate. The only thing in my heart and mind was the Bible. *Hmm. Dacia said God will speak to me through the Bible, since it's his Word. Maybe I need to start reading*, I thought. I wasn't sure where to start. I decided to open it towards the back, where I knew the New Testament was.

THE WORD OF GOD

"Teacher, which is the greatest commandment in the Law?"
Jesus replied: " 'Love the Lord your God with all your heart and with all your soul and with all your mind.' This is the first and greatest commandment." (Matthew 22:36-38 NIV)

Huh. That's funny. What are the chances of turning to this verse? I wondered. *What does Jesus mean, though? What does loving God look like in practice?* In the margins of the Bible were references to other Bible verses related to this verse, and I looked them up. The first one answered the question and got my attention.

"He who has My commandments and keeps them, it is he who loves Me. And he who loves Me will be loved by My Father, and I will love him and manifest Myself to him."
Judas (not Iscariot) said to Him, "Lord, how is it that You will manifest Yourself to us, and not to the world?"
Jesus answered and said to him, "If anyone loves Me, he will keep My word; and My Father will love him, and We will come to him and make Our home with him." (John 14:21-23 NKJV)

Wow! What does it mean that Jesus will manifest himself to me, and make his home with me? What an intriguing promise from God. I have got to find out what this means.

"Okay, loving God equals obeying his Word," I muttered to myself. *If loving God is the great commandment, then I have to know what his Word is, i.e. know the Bible, in order to obey it and love God. How can I love him if I don't know what his Word says?* I reasoned. At that moment I purposed in my heart to read and study the Bible all the time. In addition to prayer, this seemed to be essential to loving God in a relationship.

I began reading the Bible every free moment I had. I couldn't seem to get enough of it. I was learning at an exponential rate. Every time I picked it up I learned something new. It was strange, because I could sense the Holy Spirit revealing things to me. When I read, the words spoke to my heart. They guided my life, pointed out areas I needed to change, and began to reverse a lot of lies I had learned. Before I was saved the words didn't have the impact they did now. I truly craved it like food.

That same week I met a man at church nicknamed Bible Bill. He offered to take me through the Bible in a year. We started with the Old Testament. I could email him or call him if I had any questions, and we met once or twice a month for lunch to discuss what we had read. I remembered what Dacia said and realized that the Lord had put Bill in my life to help me learn the Bible. It felt really cool that God would do that for me.

In one of our first meetings Bible Bill asked me, "Why do you eat every day?"

"Because I'm hungry," I replied.

"What happens if you don't eat?" he continued.

"I would starve."

"What happens when you starve? Think, Greg, you're a doctor."

"You become weak, lethargic, sick, vitamin deficient, and waste away."

"Exactly! The Bible is your spiritual food. If you don't eat then you won't grow up. Remember, Jesus said that when you are saved you are born again. Can a baby walk, talk, feed, or defend himself? Does a baby even know he is a baby? Can a baby interact with his father like an adult?"

"No, of course not." I said.

"Then make sure you eat a balanced diet of the Word of God." He showed me a Bible verse.

Like newborn babes, long for the pure milk of the word, that by it you may grow in respect to salvation, if you have tasted the kindness of the Lord. (1 Peter 2:2-3 New American Standard Bible)

He continued. "Each book of the Bible has certain spiritual nutrition, vitamins, and minerals. The whole book together is a balanced diet. Leaving out portions of the Bible in your yearly reading leaves out nutrition. Many Christians are malnourished, and consequently many churches are malnourished because they don't methodically teach and read through the entire Word of God.

Remember, sin is like a disease. It damages us. What is the other effect of nutrition with respect to disease? It helps us to heal, repairs damage to our spirit, and overcomes the debilitating effect of sin."

WORSHIP

"Bill, I like going to church, but I prefer the teaching over the music part of the service. Why do they spend thirty minutes singing before the pastor teaches?"

"Worship prepares your heart to hear the Word of God. In worship you give worth to God and get your worth from God because he loves you. Man was created to worship God. If you don't worship him then you will worship something, even if you don't realize it."

"Like what?" I asked.

"How about yourself?"

"Ouch, Bill, that hurts. You're right, though. I definitely worshipped myself. I gave worth to myself and received it from myself in almost everything: accomplishments, career, looks, etc."

"Worship God, Greg. You were created to do this. It seems foreign and uncomfortable to you because you grew up worshipping yourself and things around you. Idolatry is when you worship something other than God, something that you can see."

"How do I worship God? What do I do?"

"Remember what I said. First, give him worth. Praise him for saving you. Thank him for dying for you. Recognize him as your Father, God, and Creator. When you worship the Lord you are surrendering your heart and life to him in faith, trust, and gratitude. It's a time of giving yourself to God and recognizing your need for him in your life.

"Second, get your worth from God. Praise him that he loves you. You have already witnessed how many things he aligned just to save you. Respond to him in gratitude and relish the fact that you are a child of the eternal God. Music can help you focus on him, and good worship songs have lyrics that kindle the principles that I have just taught you."

"That sounds so uncomfortable to me."

"Just start listening to praise and worship songs in the morning if you can. Think about who he is and what he has done for you. Listen to the words. Let God first give to you and fill you up, then give back to him out of what he's given you. Think about how it makes you feel when your son gives you a gift from the allowance you have given to him."

"Okay. I'll give it a shot."

FATHER AND SON

"Bill? One more thing, now that you mention it. Dacia, the head nurse at the office, told me that God is my Father and wants a relationship. How can I have a relationship with someone I can't see? I understand that prayer is me talking to God and the Bible is God's Word speaking to me, but what does he really want?"

"You are a father with two boys, right?"

"Yes," I replied.

"What do you want the most from them? What do you enjoy?"

"I want to spend time with them and enjoy each other's company. I want them to listen to me and love me back. I like hanging out together and playing with them. I really enjoy it when they hug me and jump up in my lap." He just stared at me and then raised his eyebrows. Just as I realized he was waiting for a light to go on, it did. I suddenly realized that God wants the same things from me that I want from my kids.

"Wow. That's pretty deep, Bill. It seems so obvious now that I think about it that way."

"You can't understand God apart from relationships. Remember, he doesn't want pious religious ceremonies or people, but relationships. It's not about rituals, reciting certain words, wearing certain clothes, or going to a building once a week. Imagine if all week long your kids ignored you and didn't talk to you, even though you were right there. Then suddenly on Sunday they dress up, parade through the house, and talk *about* you but not *to* you. What would you think?"

"That's crazy."

"God is no different. The principles of relationship are the same. Be yourself. Be honest. Be real. Start your day with him. That's the pattern Jesus gave us."

"Okay."

MORNING DEVOTIONS

Every morning before work, I started praying, listening to worship music, and reading the Bible. Bible Bill and Dacia had said these were the three pillars of a relationship with God. I kept remembering something Bill told me. It stuck with me. "The Word grows you up, worship fills you up, and prayer aligns you up with the will of God. You need growth, fulfillment, and guidance."

I kept at it every day and quickly began to feel and notice something happening. I felt refreshed, empowered, satisfied, and at peace even more than when I was first saved. Just when I thought it couldn't get any better, it did. The music began to grip me, prayer began to move me, and reading the words of Jesus started to enlighten and change me. I was a new and energized person after early morning meetings with him. It felt as if I was going to a recharging station. It felt right. I always left satisfied in an unexplainable way.

I could feel my awareness of his presence slowly growing, and it enraptured my heart. As I began to learn who God was, how much he loved me, and what he has done for me, I wanted to spend time with him and serve him. I wasn't obligated but dedicated. I literally couldn't wait to get up and spend time with Jesus. *I can't believe I get to spend time with God and he listens to me! This is really awesome!* I thought. I surrendered each day to Jesus and vowed to do whatever he wanted me to. I was so grateful not to feel empty and alone anymore.

One day I slept in by accident and had to go without morning devotions. The difference was noticeable right away. I was irritable, more impulsive, and less peaceful. It scared me, since I felt like the old me. I quickly learned that many aspects of my old self were still there, but somehow spending time with Jesus in prayer, worship, and reading the Bible kept the old man at bay. I didn't understand how this worked, but I knew it was true enough to never miss devotions again. I made each day of my life like driving a car. The key was to get up each day and let Jesus take the wheel.

A CHANGING HEART

Each day I tried to live out The Relationship by paying close attention to my heart, conscience, and circumstances. I lived day by day looking for God working in my life and expected him to. One of the first things I noticed was a change in heart towards things God wanted me to remove from my life. I had a subscription to a guy's magazine, for example, filled with pictures of girls and articles about sex, sports, and life in the fast lane. I canceled the subscription. I had no desire to look at that stuff anymore. I didn't *have to* give it up, but strangely, I *wanted to*.

I was initially concerned that being a Christian would make me a boring geek who "wasn't allowed" to do anything fun. I was amazed to discover this was not the case at all. The things that needed to go had already lost their appeal. In many cases, like with the magazine, I couldn't wait to get rid of them. God also revealed to me how I had been trying to fill my empty heart with *things* instead of him. Now that I had what my heart truly craved and was designed for, The Relationship with God, I didn't need those other things anymore.

The opposite was true for things that God wanted to introduce into my life. The things he wanted me to do, which I would have never done in the past, became appealing and interesting. On Friday nights I started attending a home fellowship with other Christians. We met together, talked, ate desert, and studied the Bible. Just a few months earlier I wouldn't have been caught dead at such an event. Now I loved it and looked forward to it.

DIVINE APPOINTMENTS

Dacia's prayer journal quickly saw some action from all of the praying I was doing. I prayed that I would find Christian friends I could relate to and almost immediately met a radiologist at church. Ruth already knew his wife from the gym. We became great friends and he helped me tremendously.

I prayed for an opportunity to tell someone about Jesus, and that day a woman broke down in the office. She was a nervous wreck and had come with her mother. I told her about Jesus and how to be saved. She went home and was saved that night. I was thrilled when she told me the next week. As I looked back, meeting Bible Bill was no mistake, either. It was as if God was bringing people to me—and he was! I just had to tell the story when they showed up, or find out why they were coming into my life.

I knew these were not coincidences. There were too many direct and unmistakable answers. I was amazed at how God could place me where he wanted me at the right moments. Dacia was right. I began to see how prayers were being answered and how my thoughts and circumstances were being shaped and guided by Jesus. I inherently knew that even my conversation with Dacia was a lesson from God on The Relationship. I learned that another way God communicates is through other believers.

FOLLOWING DOORS AND THE VOICE OF GOD

At times, however, I felt that I wasn't "hearing" anything. I asked Bible Bill about this.

"Bill, I don't feel that I'm hearing from God at times. How do I know how to make decisions? How do I know what he wants me to do?"

"First, see if what you are about to do lines up with the Bible. If you feel that you should do something but it's clear in the Bible that it's wrong, then don't do it. God has already answered many questions in his Word. That's why we need to know what it says. Sometimes he wants you to 'dig' in the Bible to find the answer when you feel he's not answering. He's really saying 'Greg, I have already told you, so go find it.' If you can't find it, then ask me or a pastor and we will point you to what the Bible says."

"Okay, but what about daily decisions in life? Taking a new job or making an important decision, for example."

"Start by analyzing what you are going to do. First, make sure it's not sin or headed towards sin. Does it line up with the Bible? Is it selfish or for other people? What is your heart telling you? Then look for 'open and closed doors.' Think of trying a bunch of door knobs and seeing if they open. If you are praying, surrendered to God's will for your life, and honestly trying to do what he is telling you, then he will open doors and close them to guide you."

"What do you mean?" I asked, still not getting it.

"Take steps in faith in the direction you feel led and see what happens. Let's say you are interviewing for new jobs. You won't get the interviews for jobs you are not supposed to have. In your gut you might have a sense that something is wrong or just isn't right. When the right job comes along, however, that is God's will for your life and things will go your way. He will confirm it with a peace and serenity in your spirit."

By trial and error I learned to follow "open and closed doors." If I started heading in the wrong direction then the doors started closing. When I was on the right path, however, all the doors started opening. There were two friends, for example, to whom I wanted to give my testimony. Every time I tried, though, something got in the way and prevented our meeting. I had an inner sense that the Holy Spirit was saying "no," but I didn't know why. I quickly learned that I don't always get a reason. In other cases, a chance to share what had happened to me fell right into my lap.

One day I felt that God told me to go to Israel. I was reading a magazine that featured a church trip to the Holy Land and was startled by a soft, quiet voice in my mind that said, "Greg, go to Israel." I ignored it once, but then I heard it again. "Greg, go to Israel. Go!" That's all I heard, but something in my spirit told me it was the Lord. I called Bible Bill and told him what had happened. I asked him if God directly speaks to us like that. He pointed out many examples in the Old Testament where people heard directly from God speaking to them. He said that God does talk directly, but hearing a voice is not the most common way he communicates with us. It was an amazing feeling to realize I had heard his voice. The Relationship became much more personal from that moment on. *He said my name!* I kept thinking to myself. This really lit my fire.

Bill told me to start taking steps in faith to go on the Israel trip and see if the doors opened. I did and found they were all open in an amazing way. I had enough vacation. There were no conflicts in my schedule. My wife Ruth said it was okay. I had the money to go. There was still space on the trip. My partners at work approved. Most of all, I wanted to go. My heart wanted to see Israel, and I had a deep peace about the decision to go. I went on the trip and it was life changing.

FOLLOWING THE PEACE

I learned that I didn't have to do anything each day except follow the clues. I kept paying attention and let my heart guide me. I learned that if I was ignoring something Jesus wanted me to do, then it began to bother my heart and mind. It reminded me of a friend urging me to do something. "Come on, do it! Don't be afraid." I could feel something inside of me compelling me to act. It was the Holy Spirit. When I finally accomplished what God wanted, the peace and serenity returned. My friend Jesus stopped prodding me.

At other times I received a warning or "check" in my spirit that something was wrong with a situation. This always proved to be accurate. It was like a warning signal telling me to be careful and pay attention. I learned to follow the peace. I began to look, watch, and wait, but I never knew when, how, or why. The Relationship was exciting! I woke up each day not knowing what God was going to do with me. The next day was one of those moments.

Chapter Twenty-One

The Kids

It was five-thirty and I had had a long day at work. It had been crazy and I didn't have much time to think about Jesus and The Relationship. I got into the car and started talking to the Lord.

"Whew! What a day, Lord. We were busy, weren't we? We are headed home."

I was babbling about anything to God, since I had never talked to him before. It felt good to do so and reminded me that he was really there in a world of silence. All day long I kept thinking about who I was going to tell next. I realized that God had given me an awesome story to tell.

"Lord Jesus? Who's next?" Immediately after I said this, Brendan and Cameron, our two sons, came to mind. They were five and six, old enough for me to start explaining Jesus and salvation to them. A little fear gripped my heart, since I didn't know how I was going to tell them or what to say. I also sensed personal pride not wanting to admit to five- and six-year-olds that I had been wrong and needed their forgiveness. The urge became stronger as I got closer to home. I tried to think about other things, but my mind kept returning to the kids.

"Okay, Lord. I am going to tell the boys about you." Dread and fear came over me, since I realized that if Jesus hadn't saved me then I would have continued to raise them to ignore God just like I had done. The reality and necessity for salvation gripped my heart. I was determined to make sure that they didn't grow up as I had.

I arrived home, had dinner, and told Ruth I was going to talk to the kids.

"Ruth, I'm going to tell the boys that we have been saved and that Jesus is God and real. My heart is burdened and sick over the fact I had been leading our entire family in the wrong direction. They would have grown up like I did, ignoring God and not being saved!"

"Okay, but how are you going to tell them?"

"I don't exactly know. I am going to be honest and keep it simple. Kids are smarter and more observant than we realize. I think they will get it. I feel the Lord is telling me to reach out to them. We are going in an entirely new direction in this family, and the boys need to know about it. I just have to trust that God will bless my honesty."

She agreed and got everyone together in the living room.

"Hey, guys. Dad wants to talk to you," Ruth said. They were playing with Matchbox cars on the steps leading upstairs. Miniature cars were flying through the banisters and tumbling down the steps.

"Okay, Mom," they said with a little trepidation. This usually meant they were in trouble and about to get a lecture from Dad. They brought a few of the cars with them. I was nervous and my heart was pounding in my chest. The boys sat on the big blue leather sofa next to each other with their feet dangling over. Ruth and I sat together on the ottoman directly in front of them. We were all nervous!

"Hey, guys. I need to talk to you. You know how our neighbors have been ignoring us?" The boys were still fidgeting with the cars by making them drive up and down their legs and on the sofa arm rests.

"Well, I got mad and started reading the Bible."

"Why, Dad?" Brendan interrupted.

"Because they say they are Christians, and I wanted to prove they were not acting like they should."

"What's a Christian, Dad?" Cameron interjected. He continued, "I heard one of the kids down the street tell another one that she was not a 'real' Christian. What does that mean?" he added. I could tell I was beginning to get their interest.

"A Christian is someone who believes that Jesus is God. They ask him to forgive them for all of the bad stuff they have done and then God does." I stopped there, because I knew if I mentioned the Holy Spirit I would get another "why" question I wasn't ready to explain yet.

"Do you believe in God?" Brendan asked as he drove a Matchbox across his stomach.

"I didn't really before, but I do now. He is real, guys. That's what I want to talk to you about."

As soon as I said this, both of them put their cars down and gave me their full attention. This surprised me, but I kept going. "I started reading the Bible because I was angry at our neighbors, but I ended up believing in Jesus."

"Is that what you were doing all of the time? You weren't playing with us like you normally do," Brendan said.

"Yes. I was reading and studying the Bible and books about it."

"What did you learn?" Brendan asked.

"That God is real. He has changed me already. I am sorry I didn't teach you guys about him, but I didn't know any better. From now on we are going to start praying, reading the Bible, and going to church."

"How do you know he is real?" Cameron asked.

"Look around, guys. Where do you think everything came from? You, me, Mom, the dog, the trees, and the entire world. Even though we can't see him, we can see his workmanship all around us. It's obvious there is a God who made everything. I also know he is real from the Bible. The Bible is a book that contains hundreds of stories of people who talked with God and had relationships with him. In the Bible God explains who he is and how we can know him. He actually came in person to the earth two thousand years ago as Jesus. Men who lived with Jesus for three years recorded what happened, and it's all in the Bible. I cried out to God a few weeks ago. I asked him to forgive me for all of the bad things I have done. He heard what I said. God is that close and real. He heard your daddy."

"Then why haven't we talked to him before?" Brendan asked.

"Because we were wrong. We didn't know any better. I grew up never talking to him and rarely hearing anyone else doing it, either. Mommy went to church, but it was only about church. She was never taught how to be saved."

"What does 'saved' mean, Dad?" Cameron asked.

"When a person asks Jesus to forgive him, God forgives him and kind of erases any record of his bad stuff. God lives inside a person when he is saved."

"God lives inside you, Dad?" Brendan asked.

"Yes, son, and inside Mommy, too."

"Wow. That's really cool. What does it feel like?"

"Before all this, I always felt alone, frustrated, and unhappy inside. I was angry and yelled at you guys over stupid things. I was wrong. I am sorry." A few tears were welling up in my eyes and my voice was wavering. "Now I feel different and much better. I don't feel alone or on edge anymore. I feel peaceful."

"You were yelling at us a lot, Dad," Cameron said.

"I know. I was wrong. I am sorry. Do you guys forgive me?" Their little heads both shook up and down.

"We are going to start learning about God and talking to him every day from now on."

"How come I haven't heard anyone else talk to him if he's real?" Brendan asked.

"I'm not sure why people don't talk to him more. Daddy is still trying to figure things out. We are not going to ignore him anymore."

"Okay, Dad. Can we go play now?"

"Yes. Go on." They immediately resumed their car and tractor sounds.

Ruth just listened and nodded. She was dumbfounded to hear these words come out of my mouth. She didn't say much the rest of the night, but I could tell she was happy.

I immediately felt better after our conversation. It was like releasing a pressure valve by beginning to make changes, admitting I was wrong, apologizing, and starting to lead the family in the right direction.

After Ruth went to bed I went into the office. I turned out the lights and got down on my knees. "Jesus, I did it. I told them. Please help me to know what to do next. I know Brendan and Cameron need you. Thank you for saving me while they are still young enough to listen to me. I am so grateful, Lord." Tears began to pour out of my eyes as my heart wrenched from the pain of being a bad father since they were born. "I would have led them to hell, Lord. I would have led them to hell! Oh, my goodness, I would have made them like I was!" I sobbed. "Thank you, God. Thank you. Please save them. Please, please save them. Don't let them grow up without you like I did. Please forgive me and help me. I am yours. Whatever you want from me. You have me."

The words flowed as a torrent of tears and sobs overwhelmed me. It was like the night I was saved, but even stronger in my heart. I was coming to grips with one of the potentially biggest mistakes of my life. I would have raised my family in a false reality that everything was okay without God in our lives. They would have thought we had it made when we actually had nothing at all without Jesus and his salvation. I was mortified and couldn't stop thinking of ways to change everything in life.

My heart then began to turn to the rest of the people at The Office. It was time to tell everyone I was saved. Telling the people at the office should be a snap, right? They were friends, they had seen the changes in me, and they would be happy to know why, wouldn't they?

Chapter Twenty-Two

The Office

The next morning during the drive to the office, I felt a strong nudge to tell the nurses the entire story. I kept having images in my mind of telling them about Jesus and how I had been saved. I was new at following God, but I was certain this is what he wanted me to do. I felt an indescribable link to God through the Holy Spirit that helped synchronize me with his will. One of my partners was out of the country, and the office was a lot less hectic since were there fewer patients. It was the perfect time to have a meeting, especially if we finished early with our morning patients.

By ten-thirty in the morning all of the patients were treated and out of the office. Only Tammy, *The Bible Woman*, and Dacia, the head nurse, knew what I was planning. Dacia gave me a look like "See, God is in control, all the patients are gone." It seemed like a crazy coincidence since we were rarely done so early. I tried to ponder how God could do that. That would mean he knew in advance that I wanted to meet and he somehow arranged our schedule of patients. In order to plan a schedule so we were done extra early, he also had to know how big the patients' cancers would be and how long it would take for us to remove and fix them. My mind began to get dizzy trying to think this through. I had to just realize that God can do anything he wants since he is God.

THE NURSES

I gathered together the eight nurses working that day and brought them into one of the operating rooms. They had no idea why we were meeting. They came in chattering, but silence quickly fell upon the room as they sensed the serious and nervous expression on my face. They glanced at each other looking for someone who might know what was happening. A weight was on my heart and they could see it in my eyes. I had never called a nurses' meeting like this before as the only doctor present. In the past, meetings like this included the other doctors and usually announced that someone was no longer with the company. Eyes glanced at me and then darted away when we made eye contact. I surveyed the room to see who was there and who was absent. I had a good relationship with the nurses, but what I was about to tell them was going to be way out of character for me.

"Something incredible has happened in my life. It will affect everything. I never believed that there was an absolute knowable truth about God. I grew up without going to church or hearing any mention of God in the home, the schools, the media, my relationships, or the entire culture around me. The silence made him irrelevant and unknowable—until a few weeks ago. I want to tell you, he is a lot closer than you think."

As I was speaking, I noticed a few nurses squirming, making faces, and looking very uncomfortable. I paused and then continued.

"Jesus revealed himself to me in a way that I didn't know was possible. I wasn't looking for him and didn't want anything to do with religion, but God was coming after me! This is the most important event in my whole life, and it can be just as important for each and every one of you. My entire concept of life, its purpose, origin, meaning, and ultimate end, have been turned upside down. If you want to hear what has happened to me, then I will be holding a separate meeting in my office in about ten minutes."

Five of them bolted for the door as soon as I was done. Three wanted to meet with me. The five didn't want to know any more information. I was surprised that they wouldn't want to at least hear what had happened.

I met with the three nurses who did and told them the entire story, which took forty-five minutes. Their eyes were glued on me the entire time. I could tell they were amazed, confused, and even a little afraid. The absolute reality of God and the tangibility of him in salvation shocked them. I was telling them that I was a present day miracle of God and living proof that Jesus Christ is God and the answer to eternity, death, and sin. All of them had witnessed The Transformation at work over the past few weeks, and it boggled their minds. They knew me as well as my family and could see the changes in me.

At the end one of them said, "I grew up in church, but I will have to check with my mother about the 'born again' thing you mentioned. I am not sure about that."

I had explained to them that being saved *is* being born again and is another way of saying the same thing; it's a synonym for salvation. I showed them where Jesus himself said a person *must* be born again to go to heaven (John 3:7). I wondered, *Had one or more of them gone to church and learned about Jesus but never personally engaged him to forgive and save them*? I was shocked and perplexed at how this was possible, but I didn't say anything. I was alarmed that any church person would not understand what I was talking about. I had thought that Ruth's experience of growing up in church but not being saved or hearing about salvation was an anomaly, but it appeared that maybe it wasn't. *How can this be?* I wondered.

Over the next few months every one of the three I had met with were saved. Their lives and families were forever changed.

THE PHYSICIAN'S ASSISTANT

After I met with the nurses I talked with our physician's assistant, who was a wonderful man about thirty years older and a good friend. We met in the office. I went through the story again. He didn't say a word, and I had no idea what he was thinking or what his religious background was. At the end I said, "Paul, I just want you to know that Jesus is real and alive. He is not an old Bible story or an intellectual belief system of acting nice. If you personally call on him to save you and forgive you of your sins, then something actually happens to you. The Holy Spirit enters you. There is proof, Paul! Real proof! Something radical has to happen to our state of existence in order to go to heaven. This is not simply my version of Christianity but the reality of our existence. He hears what we say! Ponder the implications of that one fact."

He sat there in the chair with an uncomfortable look on his face. Finally he said, "You know I grew up going to church and went through all of the motions. I served at the church as a boy and listened to hundreds of sermons. In all of those years I have never heard what you have just told me. I was never taught that I needed to be saved by repenting and asking Jesus to save me. They put me through an official religious ceremony called confirmation, but I was taught what to say and do. I believed it, but it was more like a rite of passage. We were expected to do this. We were taught this is what you do to officially become a believer. It was like joining a club. If you sign up, agree with the bylaws, take a few classes, and sign on the dotted line, then you are 'in.' " He paused, took a deep breath, and then continued.

"I have never done what you have. I have not had a personal relationship with God. I knew of 'the Father, the Son, and the Holy Spirit,' but I had no idea the Holy Spirit lives inside of you when you are saved. We also didn't read the Bible nor were we taught we needed to. I attended religion classes over the years that included things from the Bible, but I didn't read and study it myself. We were taught that we are saved by what we do, not solely by what Jesus did."

Now I was the silent one. I was shocked, stunned, and confused beyond description. As he was talking I kept thinking to myself, *How can this be? How can he not even know the basic doctrine of salvation? Why wouldn't they have taught him biblical salvation? What good is any form of Christian religion if people don't get saved?* When he finished I realized something I never expected. It sent shock waves through my soul. *Oh, my goodness! Christian religion has prevented this man from knowing God.* The fear and reality of hell combined with the need to be saved wrenched my heart.

"Paul, just go home and pray to the Lord. Call on him and repent. It's not too late. You can start a relationship with God now. Go get a Bible and start reading. Everything I know comes right from the Bible. This is real. Please pray tonight for Jesus to save you."

He thanked me, got up, and left. That same night he was saved and began The Relationship with God, also. His life was never the same again.

It was time to start the afternoon schedule. At the end of the day I stayed in the office pondering everything that had happened. I sat back in the chair with my feet up and looked at all the walls. They were filled with awards, honors, degrees, and accomplishments in life. I suddenly felt sick inside as I realized this was a personal wall of fame. Bible Bill was right. *I have been worshipping myself and all my accomplishments.* I was horrified, but I knew it was true. Over the next thirty minutes I took all of them down and put them in the closet.

When I was done, I sat back in the chair and stared at the blank walls. I was starting over in many areas of my life, and it felt good. Over the next few weeks, I filled the walls with drawings and artwork that the boys made in school. I sat there for a while and thought about everything that happened that day. I was afraid and confused, because I didn't understand how salvation was either being missed or not taught. Something was wrong. I had talked to two groups of people and realized there was a deception about salvation, especially in churched people. It seemed that people who had never heard about Jesus had an easier time than religious people.

I felt moved to pray. "Lord, what is going on? Why don't people know what I am talking about? Why am I freaking people out? Why isn't everyone excited and overjoyed like Tammy and Dacia? I don't understand this."

I knew something was really wrong. I expected that since the Christian message was true then everyone supposedly "believing" in Jesus would be saved. Eternal life and the complete forgiveness of sins are incredible gifts that I assumed everyone would want and had already obtained. I was about to discover this wasn't the case at all. This new information was just the tip of the iceberg. I wanted to talk to someone else about this, but I wasn't sure who to ask.

I've got it. I'll call The Patient, *the one who asked me if I had accepted Jesus as Savior a few days before I did. I can thank him for his comments, let him know I am saved, and ask him some questions about salvation.* I immediately felt better. I had a new plan of action!

Chapter Twenty-Three

The Patient

THE PRINTED SCHEDULE

"Dacia, I need you to pull some old printed schedules from the file," I said to the head nurse. I gave her the dates of the exact week I needed. Our office kept all of the old printed schedules on file that were used in the clinic each day. Important information was handwritten on them, like which room the patient was in and who the nurse was. The Patient I was looking for had been an "add-on" patient. I couldn't remember his name, but I knew he had been seen on a Thursday morning three weeks ago and he had been treated in room four. I specifically recalled his name being handwritten on the schedule in blue ink, the standard process since he was added at the last moment.

"No problem, Dr. Viehman. I'll bring them to your desk." She brought me a folder with the schedules for that week. I excitedly rifled through them and found the schedule for the day I was looking for. My eyes immediately looked for the name written in blue ink, but it wasn't there. I checked the rest of the patients and found one for every room except room four. In other words, every room number was written by a patient's name except number four. It was obvious his name was missing. *His name should be here! This is weird. I must have the wrong day*, I thought. I quickly checked the rest of the week, but his name still wasn't there. None of the schedules were missing, either. I was perplexed. *I know it was that week,* I thought.

"Dacia. Please bring me the schedules for the week before and the week after."

"Okay. What are you up to?"

"I am looking for a particular patient. His name was written on the schedule and he was treated in room four. I am certain he was here that week, but maybe I made a mistake. Let me check the other weeks. He must be in there."

"Here you go. Have fun," she said.

I first checked both Thursdays but couldn't find him. There wasn't anyone's name written onto the schedule as an add-on surgery for room four anywhere. His name was gone!

"Dacia, look at this," I said pointing to the schedule for the day I knew he was in the office. "I have patients for all the other rooms, but no one for room four. That's the room he was in. His name was written on the schedule since he was added on at the last moment. I saw his name that day written in blue ink. I can see it in my mind. By looking at the names of the other patients from that day, I know it's the right day. I specifically remember the other patients I treated the same morning I saw this guy! I even checked the weeks before and after. He's not there. Every other day has a patient in room four on the regular printed part of the schedule. This is the only day we can't account for who was in room number four. How can his name disappear?!"

"That's crazy, Dr. Viehman. Why are you so anxious to find this guy? Are you sure about this?"

"I'm sure I'm sure." I said with exasperation creeping into my voice.

"Well, check the database. We also log each and every patient into the database schedule. You should know. You designed it. His personal photo will be in his notes and operative reports. Maybe we forgot to write his name on the schedule and you just think you saw it there. Check it out. He has to be in the database. Then you can confirm it's the right guy by his picture."

"That's right! Why didn't I think of that?" I wheeled my chair around and turned on my computer.

THE MEDICAL RECORDS DATABASE

I opened the database and clicked on the list of patients for that Thursday. The database list, however, didn't provide the info about which doctor the patient saw or what room they were in. I printed out the relevant patient list and checked all of the male patients. It was only a list of about twenty names. I opened each record and was able to view the photo and know which doctor treated them, but I didn't find him. I got down to the last name and felt my stomach sinking. I double clicked on the photo tab and held my breath, watching intently as the photo came into view. "It's not him! He's not there!" I yelled aloud in the lab. "This is ridiculous!"

There was also another search feature of the database that I realized I could use based on the medical info. I knew the type of tumor, the date of the procedure, and the location of the cancer. He had a basal cell carcinoma on his left temple. I entered in the search criteria for that particular Thursday, but nothing matched. I next searched "left forehead and scalp" in case the location was entered wrong, but still no results. I then applied the same searches for a two-week period before and after the date he was treated. A few cases matched these results, but none of them were The Patient. His database record was gone at multiple levels. "I can't believe this!" I shouted in frustration.

THE SCHEDULING SYSTEM RECORDS

I raced up to the front desk. "Please pull every chart of every patient seen on this particular week. I want you to use the scheduling system records to do this," I said to one of our assistants. "Please also print me a patient list from the Thursday of that week. A man was added to my schedule and I need to find him."

"No problem, Dr. Viehman. When we add patients we have to enter them into the scheduling system. His name might have gotten handwritten on the paper schedule, since we usually print them the day before, but he would have been registered, as well. Here is the list now. I'll print this out for you and get you the charts by the end of the day."

Our office had two separate and independent systems, one for scheduling and another for medical records (the database). Every patient was entered into both systems. When The Patient checked in he would have been added to the scheduling systems records. His name was handwritten that day since he was added after the schedule for the day had been printed. The computer scheduling system, however, should still have had his name on the list.

I grabbed the schedule and raced back into the lab. I compared the list of names she gave me from the scheduling system with the original printed paper schedule and the database schedule. If somehow he was erased from the printed schedule and the medical records database, then the schedule she gave me from the scheduling system should have an extra name. They all matched exactly. There should have been an extra name on the list she printed me, but there wasn't! A wave of anger and frustration raced over me. Tension and pressure built up inside like the old me—before I was saved. I was incensed at the absurdity of this.

"Dr. Viehman, what's the matter?" a nurse asked me. "You don't look good. Your first patient is ready."

"Nothing is wrong! I'll explain it later. Let's go."

"Uh, okay, Dr. Viehman, if you say so," She stuttered. She gave me a look like she knew something wasn't right but couldn't figure out what it was.

The rest of the morning I kept checking and re-checking the schedules thinking I must have missed his name, but I knew I hadn't. He wasn't in the database, on the original printed schedule, or even in the scheduling system. How could his name be removed from all three?

Lunch time finally arrived. I called the programmer who wrote the software for me. There was one more area I wanted to search, but the software needed to be revised to do it. I wanted to scan all of the patient's personal identification photos to look for the missing man.

"Barry, I need a favor. I'll pay you for this. I need you to build me a search engine that searches all of the personal photos by any criteria I want: sex, date of visit, tumor type, doctor, etc. I need to be able to scan the photos to look for someone who came into the office."

"Sure, no problem. Give me a couple of days," he replied.

"Thanks, Barry."

THE MEDICAL CHARTS

By the end of the day the charts were piled up at the microscope, where I sat and kept my computer. Several of the nurses came into the lab and one asked me, "What are you doing with those?"

"Do you remember the guy in room number four? The one who asked me if I had accepted Jesus as my Savior, and then I ran out of the room? He was a bit strange and stared at the ceiling the whole time while lying back in the chair. I think you had him, Cindy." The other nurses looked as if they had no idea what I was talking about.

"Oh, yeah. He was an 'add-on' to the schedule. I told a few people how he freaked you out. I thought he was really strange. He didn't say hardly anything and then suddenly cornered you about Jesus out of nowhere. How could I forget?"

"I am so glad you remember him! I was beginning to think he didn't exist. It's a long story, but that patient asked me if I had accepted Jesus, and since then that is exactly what I have done. I have become a Christian. I was saved several weeks ago, and now I want to find that man. I want to thank him, tell him I am saved, and ask him a few questions."

"Saved from what, Dr. Viehman?" another nurse asked. She was part of the group who had decided not to hear my testimony. I realized I had the perfect opportunity to tell her.

"From hell and separation from God is what I was saved from. I never thought I would believe it, but Jesus is real and alive. I cried out to him and he saved me. I didn't even know it until a week later. It's a long story and I will share it with you whenever you like." I cut my reply short because I could tell by the looks on their faces that they were wigged out and didn't want me to continue. They were not expecting the answer I gave them. Faces contorted, eyebrows scrunched, eye contact ceased, and motions to leave ensued.

I flashed back to The Ski Trip and the Marco Island incidents. I remembered how I felt when people told me about Jesus. I surmised the nurses now were experiencing the same kind of tension, pressure, fear, and uncomfortable vibes that I had felt back then. Talking about Jesus and salvation invokes these responses, but I didn't know how or why. *There must be something that subconsciously causes this reaction.* It was strange to be on the other side this time. I felt the need to ease the tension.

"I understand this sounds crazy. I too was freaked out before when people would talk about Jesus to me. I have been there and understand. I can only tell you it's true."

"Yeah. Okay, well..." Searching for words, a nurse asked, "Why don't you just pull the original printed schedule from that day? Why the charts?"

My frustration at not finding the patient erupted. "Because his name isn't on the schedule anymore! He is gone from the database and even the scheduling system. There is no record that man was ever here. I am not crazy; other nurses remember seeing him, too. I am pulling the physical charts from that day and checking them, even though there isn't an extra name on the scheduling program list, just to be certain.

"Look. Here is the actual printed schedule from the day he was here. See? There is no patient assigned to room four. He was in room four! Numbers are written next to all of the patients' names, but not for room four. I've checked every day that week and even the week before and the week after. His name is nowhere to be found! I know this was the right day. His name was written right here in blue ink. I remember seeing it. So do others."

A look of horror filled their faces. One of them began to turn white as she stared at me and then at the paper. "Oh, my God! Oh, my God!" she yelled and ran away into the nurses' work room.

"Ahh, ahh, let us know what you find," another said. She couldn't look at me. She fumbled with the papers in her hand as she tried to escape the implications. Then they all took off like a bomb was about to explode.

Things changed from that moment forward. Several nurses were uncomfortable around me and avoided eye contact. Everyone heard about what had happened, but some didn't want to know. They didn't want to talk about it or hear me say anything. In the depths of my heart I knew why and empathized. The Patient and my Transformation were obviously causing cracks in their concept of reality that frightened them, and justifiably so. After all, a man who had visited our office and had surgery, who was seen and touched by multiple people, had disappeared from all of our records in multiple locations.

I stayed late that night and went through the stack of charts. I eliminated the charts of the female patients and checked each and every male chart. I knew The Patient worked for a church. In my mind I could still see the writing on the schedule. I checked all of the charts, but not one patient worked for a church. I had to conclude that his chart was gone, too! After that I went home but didn't tell Ruth. I wanted to wait for the database search results.

THE MEDICAL RECORDS DATABASE SEARCH ENGINE

The next day the programmer called and said the special search engine was ready and the system was updated. Before I got started, I quickly reviewed what types of records would have been created in The Patient's electronic record the day he was here for surgery. Every new surgical patient has two separate electronic notes created in the system, one for the evaluation and another for the surgery operative report. I realized that even if one of them was accidentally deleted then the patient's personal picture would still be in the database. Patient notes almost never were accidentally deleted. The chance of two parallel records being deleted for the same patient was highly unlikely and had never happened before. The computer automatically generated the date of visit, so it couldn't be a matter of the wrong date being entered by a nurse.

Finally, lunch time arrived and I fired up the program. I started by searching the day I knew he was in the office. The computer screen filled up with head and shoulders photographs of every patient seen that day. If a photograph was somehow not taken that day, then the screen showed a black area above the patient's name. I checked every photo and he wasn't there. I examined each physical chart for every patient who did not have a picture, but none of them was him, either. Next I checked every day that week and the weeks before and after, but he still wasn't there. All records of his visit were gone!

THE LABORATORY RECORDS

"I can't believe he's not there!" I said aloud in the lab. Tammy was working at her desk and came over.

"What are you talking about?" she asked.

"That guy who asked me if I was saved. I can't find any record of his being a patient here. His name is even gone from the schedule. It was a handwritten add-on the day of surgery. He's gone from the original schedule, the database, and the scheduling program, Tammy. That's two separate systems. This is nuts!"

"Did you check the laboratory records? If he had surgery then we would have logged his name, location of the tumor, and type of tumor in our log book."

"No," I said with hesitancy, since I had forgotten to do this. I was embarrassed. My eyes then shifted to the surgery log book sitting right across from me on the table. I made a beeline to it and grabbed it like it was gold. I flipped through the pages in a frenzy until I reached the day he was in the office. I compared this list with the schedules I had. His name was gone! There was no record that he had surgery that day. For that whole week, there wasn't anyone I treated with that type of cancer in that location who had all of the cancer removed during their first stage. I checked the other weeks, just to be certain, but still couldn't find him.

"Tammy! Look, he's not there. See, I told you. I am not crazy, Tammy, honest. He was really here! Hey, wait a minute," I said as something occurred to me. "Tammy, the surgery patients are given sequential numbers when their cancer tissue comes through the lab."

"I know that. I log in their names, Dr. Viehman," she replied with a sarcastic, but kidding tone.

"If he was here that day, then his name would have gotten a number, right?" I continued.

"Yes, of course."

"The other patients treated that day got numbers before and after him. The log book has continued to be sequentially filled with the appropriate numbers in numerical order corresponding to other patients' surgical cases since the day he was here."

"Yes, go on."

"Well, if his name is now missing, why are all of the numbers still in sequence with no empty spaces or missing numbers? It's impossible to remove his name from the list and not leave a gap or throw off the numbers for all of the other patients. Do you understand what I am saying?!"

"Yes. If I gave him case number 100, for example, then the next patients would have been 101, 102, etc. If later you removed his name, then there would be a missing space in the log book. If you removed all of the other names and rewrote the log book, the case numbers would be off by one or a number would be missing."

"Exactly! How can that be? This is absolutely ludicrous! I feel as if I am losing my mind."

"Maybe you're not supposed to find him," she said with a smirk.

I was stunned. "What does that mean? Don't give me anymore crazy one-liners that leave me thinking for weeks, like the one about the Holy Spirit."

"Maybe he was a messenger," she said, smiling.

"What are you saying?"

"You are not going to find him, Dr. Viehman," she said and walked away.

"What do you mean? What do you mean?"

She glanced back, smiled knowingly, but didn't answer. I knew what she was inferring. This "man" was an angel sent by God to personally confront me with the Gospel message of salvation. I had read in the New Testament about angels being used by God as messengers, but for some reason I didn't think they were still being used today, not for me, anyway. The reality of having possibly encountered an angel was very intriguing, but I wanted to make sure I had checked everything thoroughly.

I feverishly spent another three to four hours over the next several days searching and re-checking everything. There was nothing left to check. I was exhausted and frustrated. I couldn't find him and gave up.

"Can you take this stack of charts back to medical records?" I asked a nurse. She was the one who had run out of the lab saying, "Oh, my God."

"Dr. Viehman?" she said hesitantly. I knew that she knew why the charts were there. I could sense she was afraid to ask me a question. Trepidation was in her voice. Her pupils were open wide. "What did you find out?" she asked with a deer-in-the-headlights look of expectancy.

I paused and looked her dead in the eyes and said, "He's gone. He doesn't exist." Her face turned white. She paused with the charts in her hand and stared at me for a few seconds. The implications were sinking in.

"Oh, my! Oh, my goodness!" she said again as she bolted out of the lab.

I looked over at Tammy, watching this from the other side of the room. She had a big grin on her face. My idea of reality had already been shattered when I discovered God was living within me and I didn't know it, but now even the pieces of my new reality were falling apart. How could The Patient's paper chart, electronic medical records, laboratory records, photographs, and all records of his visit to the office disappear? How could his name written in blue ink be gone from the same printed schedule I saw that day? The answer and implications were obvious, but I didn't want to face them. God is in absolute control of every detail, and there is a lot more going on than what I can see in this physical world.

I thought about everything, and I was amazed. Did God love me that much that he would send an angel to me to reinforce my need for salvation? The answer, I had to admit, was *yes*.

Chapter Twenty-Four

The Inoculation to The Cure

THE BEST FRIEND

That night when I got home from work, I decided to call my best friend who lived in Washington, D.C. We grew up together since grade school and had remained good friends. He was Jewish but his wife, from what I had heard, was a Christian. I was excited to tell them what had happened to me. I assumed that this could be the opportunity his wife was looking for to share the story of Jesus with him. I was expecting a positive response, since Christianity was a Jewish story from start to finish. Between me and his wife, I was sure he would believe that Jesus is the Savior.

I dialed his number. My heart was pounding in my chest.

"Hello, Phil?"

"Yeah, Greg, what's up?"

"Something incredible has happened to me. I have been saved by Jesus. Phil, it's so awesome. God is really there. You can know for certain right now that you will live forever. Even better, it's entirely a Jewish story!"

"What?! What are you talking about? Where did this come from? Have you flipped your lid?"

"No. Let me tell you the entire story." I told him everything. He was silent and didn't say anything until the end.

"Greg, that's great. I'm glad you have found something that makes you happy."

"No, no, Phil. Don't you understand what I have told you? *You* need to be saved. This isn't a religion I decided to intellectually accept, but the reality of our existence. The God who created you and me is the LORD God of Israel. He is the same God. He came as a man to earth and died so we could be saved from our sins. You know that both you and I are sinners. Come on, Phil, don't make me start listing examples."

"Greg, talk to Alyssa. She grew up going to church and went to a Christian school. Tell her. I don't understand it all." I could hear him hand the phone to his wife.

"Greg? What's up?"

"Alyssa, I was saved by Jesus. I am a Christian now. I have the Holy Spirit in me. It's all true. Jesus was really here and did it. He's alive and hears everything we say. It's incredible. Help me convince Phil to be saved."

"What do you mean, saved? The Holy Spirit is in you?! What does that mean? Look, Greg, Phil believes in God and so do I. What's the big deal?"

"Alyssa, a person has to be born again to go to heaven. Jesus himself said this. Read it for yourself in John chapter three. Didn't they teach you that in church or school?"

"No, they didn't. What does born again mean? Why are you bothering Phil with this and making him feel as if something is wrong?" Her voice changed and she said disbelievingly, "You, of all people, have become religious?"

"No. It's not religion at all. Christianity is a change in the nature of your existence, not intellectual acceptance of moral doctrine. God lives within you when you are saved." I said this with increasing urgency. I didn't understand why she was fighting me on this.

"That sounds crazy, Greg. Here's Phil back."

"Phil, I am not crazy. You are my best friend. You know me. I am the least likely person to become a Christian. Why would I call you up unless this was real? You have got to believe me!"

"I have to think about this, Greg. You've surprised me. It's not something I expected from you."

I felt deflated. "Yeah, I understand that. Okay. I'll call you next week. See ya."

"Okay. Talk to you later."

I hung up the phone in shock and disbelief. I thought everyone would want to know that God is real and eternal life is possible. *What in the world is going on? She should know what I am talking about. She doesn't even know what salvation is. How can this be? Why wouldn't she care about her husband needing to be saved? This is the third person I have encountered who is unfamiliar with the most important aspect of Christianity, salvation. She seems to think that they are okay because they believe God exists. If I didn't know better, I would think some forms of current Christian religion seem to be inoculating people from receiving the real cure.*

From that point on I began to pray for Phil and his family to be saved. My prayers were eventually answered, but not in the way I was expecting. Phil was diagnosed six years later with terminal cancer. When death looked him dead in the eye, he finally saw the need for salvation, the forgiveness of sins, and eternal life. He and his wife were both saved during his battle with cancer. He is in heaven now with the Lord. That answered prayer is in my journal. And when I think about it I am amazed. God used cancer to change Phil's heart. Something bad resulted in a miracle. God works in strange ways.

CHURCH PEOPLE

After I hung up the phone with Phil, I felt a panic inside to find someone else who knew the truth. I decided to talk to another friend who grew up in church. I arranged a meeting with him the next day. We talked in his office.

"Jim, I need to talk to you," I said with urgency.

"Okay. Sit down. What's on your mind?" I sat down in a black leather chair across the desk from him. I was leaning forward with my arms on my knees. He sat back in a large leather chair.

"I have been saved by Jesus. I have the Holy Spirit within me. The Lord radically changed me when I was saved. Overnight he changed my personality, my emotions, and the motives of my heart. I am freaked out because no one seems to know what I am talking about, except two of my co-workers."

I watched him very closely as I told him the entire story. The further I went, the more uncomfortable he became. He was squirming, fidgeting, and avoiding eye contact with me. Whatever I was saying was bothering him immensely. *I can't believe this is happening again*, I thought.

"Greg, that's quite a story. You and I believe the same things, just in a different way."

"What do you mean, a different way?"

"I believe that Jesus died for my sins. I believe in God. I think you are using different terms than others do."

"Different terms? I am using the terms that Jesus used. If he is God and the Savior, why would I use any other terms than his?"

"Not everyone interprets them the same way. I am glad for you that you have found God. I have heard the Holy Spirit mentioned in church, but I don't exactly understand what you are talking about. We have lines from the Bible read to us in church. I was baptized as a baby. My family has always done it this way," he said while he kept repositioning himself in the chair.

I pressed on. "I don't think so. There is no 'interpretation' here. What is there to interpret? The Bible is clear. Unless a person has the Holy Spirit within him, then he is not saved. You receive salvation from God when you repent of your sins and cry out to him for forgiveness and change. It doesn't have anything to do with going to church or being baptized."

"My church and denomination don't believe that."

"Where in the world are you getting what you believe?"

"We are taught what to believe by the church," he said with a hint of uncertainty.

"Do you read the Bible?" I asked. His eyes widened.

"Not really."

"Why not?"

"Why? The Bible was written by men. You can't take everything in the Bible seriously. It's important, but don't go too far with it."

I had personally covered these same questions in my original investigation and had more than satisfactorily answered them in my mind. I knew, however, that this wasn't the time to go through all of that. "Jim, I need to go. I'm sorry I bothered you. Thanks for your time."

I felt it was better to leave than to get into an argument. His answers took me by surprise. I could tell he was very uncomfortable with me and irritated by what I had told him. I didn't understand, but I surmised he had been taught things that were not biblical. Rather than admit he could be wrong, which would have dire implications for his salvation, he naturally resisted what I was telling him, even though I was using the words of Jesus. *Why would he have been taught such things? Another person inoculated from the cure by church! How can this be possible?* I mentally lamented. My mind was racing with thoughts.

I feel as if insanity is setting in. Jesus is real and alive! I have his eternal life living inside of me by virtue of the Holy Spirit. I am headed to heaven, and free from the fear of death and the destructive meaninglessness of evolution. God is my Father who created me and loves me. If the truth I have found is so incredibly awesome and full of hope in a hopeless world, why aren't people being taught to receive the cure? What good is visiting the doctor's office every week talking and singing about the cure if you don't take it into your body? This is akin to telling patients, "Take the cure," and having them say, "We have taken it," while it clearly remains unused and in their hands.

"This is ludicrous!" I said aloud on the ride home. I needed to talk to the pastor of the church I was attending. I called the church office and asked if he could come over for a short meeting. He graciously agreed to meet me at the house the next night.

Maybe I am the one with a problem. I thought to myself. I didn't think so, but I was a brand-new Christian. I did not tell Ruth or anyone else what was happening. I needed to gather more information.

I sensed what I needed to do, so I prayed. "Lord Jesus. God, please help me to understand what is happening. Why don't people believe me or understand what I am telling them. Am I wrong? What is this about, Lord?"

THE PASTOR IN THE OFFICE

The next day at the office I eagerly anticipated the end of the day when Pastor Rodney would be coming over. Ironically, one of the afternoon surgical patients just happened to be a pastor of a nearby church. He was there for surgery on his forehead. After the first stage of surgery was completed, I had some spare time and struck up a conversation with him.

"Pastor, I was just saved a few weeks ago. I set out to prove Christians were hypocrites. I started reading the Bible to find hard evidence of their hypocrisy. I didn't know anything about the Bible and wasn't the least bit interested in God. However, I quickly became interested in Jesus' claim to be God and set out on a mission to see if it was true. I ended up being saved and initially didn't even realize I was saved or that there was such a thing as salvation. The Lord radically changed me overnight. My personality, motives, and self-centered ways were all changed. I thought I was sick with a disease! I didn't understand that the Holy Spirit was within me." I stopped talking suddenly when I saw consternation on the face of the pastor. His eyes got really wide. He stared at me in surprise and, more startling to me, it seemed with a slight look of fear.

I continued uneasily. "I have a question, though. I have been giving a lot of people my testimony, but most people don't understand what has happened to me even if they grew up in church. They don't understand that God lives inside you from the moment you are saved.

Christianity isn't church attendance and following moral doctrines, but a living relationship with God that emanates from within our own existence. Why is this? It's so clear in the Bible, at least to me. Pastor, if people attending church regularly are frequently unsaved, then church is useless. Hell is real. Why isn't this taken seriously?"

There was a long pause. He just stared at me. He looked over at his wife with a nervous expression, but she didn't say anything. I knew something was really wrong. I could feel it and sense it. A cold silence fell upon the room.

"We focus on the love of God. God is a God of love. He loves us." I waited for him to say something more, but he didn't! He left me with just that. I was at a loss for words, because even though his statements were true, I knew something was drastically wrong with what he was really trying to say.

"Pastor, what are you really saying?"

"We don't teach about condemnation and hell. A God of love wouldn't send anyone to hell. There are fundamentalist Christians out there causing a lot of problems and anxiety in the world. Jesus loves us. He doesn't condemn us."

"Excuse me, pastor, but salvation and eternal life are the fundamentals of Christianity. If I don't stick to the words of Jesus and these concepts, which are clearly presented in the Bible, what am I doing? The fundamentals are everything. I also see a God of love who stepped down from heaven, became a man, and went to the cross, where he was beaten and crucified to save us. The penalty for sin is death, eternal death. God loves us so much that he sent his only son to die in our place. I see God's love on the cross, but he came to save us from eternal separation from him. If there isn't a hell, why did he have to come at all? What are we being saved from?

"Yes, God is a God of love, but he is also perfectly righteous. He has to punish sin. God's love wants to save sinners, but also demands that sin be dealt with. That's why Jesus did it all on the cross. God punished sin and at the same time provided a way to save sinners all by himself. True love doesn't overlook sin. Which parent loves their children? The one who disciplines them or the one who lets them do whatever they want?"

"Not everyone believes what you believe, Dr. Viehman. I think you'll find life a lot easier if you calm down and let everyone decide for themselves what the truth is."

"Pastor, I am sorry for bringing this up. But I can't do that. I know what has happened to me, and it's not a matter of interpretation or simply choosing to view Christianity in a different way. I am compelled by my heart to tell everyone about Jesus and how to be saved."

We didn't talk about God for the rest of his office stay. My heart was in my stomach. I felt sick and depressed. In my passion to offer eternal life, I had instead offended, irritated, and unsettled yet another person—and a pastor at that!

THE PASTOR OF THE CHURCH

"Ruth, I'm home from work. Where are you?"

"I'm upstairs. Be right down." She came down while I was unpacking the knapsack I carry to work.

"Pastor Rodney from Calvary is coming over tonight. I forgot to tell you."

"Okay. What for?"

"I've been telling a lot of people what has happened to me, being saved and all. Ruth, it's the weirdest thing. Almost nobody believes me or understands what I am talking about."

"Greg, you can't expect people to just believe. Think about where you were one year ago. Would you have listened?"

"You're right, I agree, but the people I have been telling go to church. They say they are Christians. I'm telling people who should know about salvation. It's the entire point of Christianity, for crying out loud. I feel as if I'm living in a bad dream. Am I the crazy one? How can church people not know about being saved and the Holy Spirit living within you? It's an awesome thing, not something to deny or hide from. Ruth, I can tell by the way people behave when they listen to me that they are freaked out, don't know what I am describing, and don't want to hear it."

"Wow. Well, I can tell you, I grew up going to church and never heard about salvation, either. The Bible was read and Sunday school Jesus stories were taught, but we were never led to salvation. It was all about church and church activities, but not Jesus. I never read the Bible and wasn't told I needed to. My sister Becky, now that I look back, was saved one night when she went to a different youth group in high school. She came back and went wild telling people about Jesus. She was handing out salvation flyers and everything."

She paused and then continued, "I recently started going to a Bible study, and learned that most of the women in the study had not read the Bible for themselves. They were talking a lot, but when I asked them if they had read it, they said no. I decided I was going to, however."

"This is one of the craziest things I have ever discovered. It doesn't make any sense. It's ridiculous. How did things get this way? Why?"

"I don't know," she said thoughtfully.

"I hope Pastor Rodney does, because I am ready to check myself into the insane asylum. I can't believe that people going to church their whole lives have not even heard about how to obtain what God gave his life for. I never went to church, Ruth. What in the world are they doing in these churches if people are not being brought to a place of repentance and salvation that leads to a personal relationship with Jesus?"

"It's sad but true. I lived it. Let me know what the pastor says. I'll watch the kids upstairs for you."

"Okay."

It was finally seven o'clock. The doorbell rang. I let the pastor in, and we went downstairs to the basement. I had already met with him at the church a week ago and given him my testimony.

I had two brown leather couches across from each other in front of the gas fireplace. He sat back in one nice and relaxed while I sat forward in the other, leaning on my knees in anticipation.

"Rodney, thanks for coming over. I need to talk to you about something that just came up."

"What's up? You look flustered."

"I've been telling people about how I have been saved. I have told them about being born again with the Holy Spirit living within me. I have explained the incredible reality of God that exists within me and all around me, but they don't get it. Rodney, these people I have talked to are church people. One of them was even a pastor! They act weird, get uncomfortable, and don't want to hear what I have to say. I expected them to be rejoicing that I was saved. Isn't that the reason Jesus came? To save people? Why in the world is the salvation message avoided and misunderstood? I feel as if I'm doing something wrong. Am I the problem?"

He busted out laughing hysterically. "Greg, you are a trip, my brother. Oh, my goodness." And he couldn't help but continue chuckling, "Where do I begin with you?" he said between giggles.

I was getting annoyed. Why wasn't the pastor being serious? "Rodney, what's so funny?"

"You! You are funny, Greg. You don't even realize what you are doing! Your testimony is powerful and unmistakably proves that Jesus is real and alive. What God did to you is so profound that people are forced to deal with the reality of God and Christianity. You have to understand that there are a lot of people out there playing church on Sunday.

Man is inherently religious, Greg, because we are created by God. But people don't want to admit they are created, because this makes them accountable. They want to quiet their religious conscience without having to answer to a God who lives inside of them and knows their every thought. Churches have arisen that give people what they want and tell them what they want to hear. Many churches have become Sunday social gatherings where people can feel religious and ease their consciences in order to avoid accountability and changed lives. False doctrine, manmade traditions, and rituals have largely replaced a personal relationship with Jesus Christ to the point that the beautiful message of the Gospel of salvation has been lost."

"But, Rodney, that means they are not saved."

"Yes, it does, but they are blind to it. They are comfortable where they are because they have religious leaders wearing official clothing telling them they are okay. When someone like you comes along, you rip the veil from their hearts and expose the charade they are living. You force them to confront the fact that God created them, and he is so close that he hears what they say and knows their hearts. Your testimony proves there is a reality to salvation. I was laughing because the Lord was using you to reach them and you didn't even know it."

He began to chuckle again, and then stated forcefully, "Of course you freaked them out, Greg! It's worse than talking to an unbeliever, because at least that person doesn't think they already have Jesus, at least not the Holy Spirit living within them. When you tell people your story they will know in their hearts that they don't have what you have. Don't forget that the Holy Spirit will be convicting their hearts with the truth. The strange faces, squirming, and irritation means they were under conviction. It's funny, because God sent you, who never went to church, to reach people who grew up in church and you didn't know it. It's not funny that they are lost. Please don't misunderstand my laughter. We need to pray for these people. Just keep praying for them. You can't convince them. You have done your job; let God do his. I think it is a good time for us to pray."

We prayed for the people I had talked to, and then we talked for a while. He explained how even some of the seminaries that teach pastors have abandoned biblical salvation and the reality of Jesus. Evidently, quite a few of them even deny the miracles of Jesus and the Bible.

"Pastor Rodney, if the entire message of Christianity hinges upon the resurrection of Jesus, how can a seminary deny the miracles? The resurrection is the greatest miracle of all. Doesn't denying the miracles of Jesus indirectly deny the resurrection?"

"Yes, it does, my brother."

"Why would they do that?"

"That's a good question. Don't forget, Greg, that the enemy is real. There's a lot more going on here than seminaries and men deciding to deny biblical salvation and the miracles of Jesus." He opened his Bible and read me a verse.

And even if our gospel is veiled, it is veiled to those who are perishing. The god of this age has blinded the minds of unbelievers, so that they cannot see the light of the gospel of the glory of Christ, who is the image of God. (2 Corinthians 4:3-4 NIV)

"A lot of people think they are saved, but they are deceived," he continued. "Jesus warns us about this several times." He showed me another verse.

"Not everyone who says to me, 'Lord, Lord,' will enter the kingdom of heaven, but only he who does the will of my Father who is in heaven. Many will say to me on that day, 'Lord, Lord, did we not prophesy in your name, and in your name drive out demons and perform many miracles?' Then I will tell them plainly, 'I never knew you. Away from me, you evildoers!' " (Matthew 7:21-23 NIV)

"Do you hear what Jesus is saying? 'I never knew you' means there was no relationship. Greg, these people are religious and think they know Jesus, but they don't. It's one of the scariest verses in the Bible."

"That's frightening, Rodney. I want to reach these people!"

We discussed The Great Deception at length. He also explained that there are many excellent Bible teaching churches whose members are following God in daily personal relationships. Even though there is a Great Deception, there is still a plethora of churches, missionaries, and servants around the world demonstrating God's love and power to save. He encouraged me to talk with more people from church. "Ask them how they came to Christ. You will learn a lot from people's testimonies," he said as he was leaving. "You will learn who is really saved."

"Thanks, Rodney. See you Sunday."

I was in shock from the past few days. I had always sensed there was something wrong with the world, but this topped it all. I took Rodney's advice and began to talk with people after service. Many of them had a "story." I talked with as many people as I could find to discover what was happening to cause the great deception in many churches. I met some fascinating people. Their testimonies and the answers are in the sequel to this book.

As I now look back on my life, it is apparent to me that God was all around me even in a culture that has tried to shut him out. I ignored the obvious and suppressed the truth when I heard it because I was self-absorbed and didn't want to be accountable. In my dedication to do things my way, I got what I wanted but ended up utterly miserable, empty, and depressed. Now that I let Jesus guide my life, however, I have only just begun to live. A relationship with Jesus is the most wonderful, awesome, fulfilling, and exciting way to live—even more than I could have imagined. It is the sole reason we exist and goes far beyond salvation itself. God is my Father, Lord, Creator, Shepherd, Light, Best Friend, Passion, and Everlasting Strength.

Do you know Jesus Christ as your personal Savior? Do you have the courage to engage the most important question of your life that will affect eternity? Your reading this book could be one of the ways God is trying to reach you.

If you consider yourself a Christian, have you really repented of your sins and trusted Jesus alone to save you? Are you certain the Holy Spirit is living within you? Does your church teach the entire Bible as God's Word? Does it focus on a personal relationship with Jesus? Do you have a daily personal relationship with him? Is he guiding the details of your life? Do you *really* know him? Does He really know you?

"The word is near you; it is in your mouth and in your heart," that is, the word of faith we are proclaiming: That if you confess with your mouth, "Jesus is Lord," and believe in your heart that God raised him from the dead, you will be saved. For it is with your heart that you believe and are justified, and it is with your mouth that you confess and are saved.

"Everyone who calls on the name of the Lord will be saved."
(Romans 10:8-10, 13 NIV)

"I am the resurrection and the life. He who believes in me will live,
even though he dies; and whoever lives and believes in me will
never die. Do you believe this?" (John 11:25-26 NIV)

End Notes

Chapter Three: The Investigation - Phase I

1. Norman L. Geisler, *Baker Encyclopedia of Christian Apologetics*, (Grand Rapids, MI: Baker Books, 1999), 4-8,46-48.

2. A. N. Sherwin-White, *Roman Society and Roman Law in the New Testament*, (Grand Rapids, MI: Baker Book House, 1978), 166-171, 189.

3. Sir William M. Ramsay, *The Bearing of Recent Discovery on the Trustworthiness of the New Testament*, (London: Hodder & Stoughton, 1915).

4. Sir William M. Ramsay, *St. Paul the Traveler and the Roman Citizen*, (London: Hodder & Stoughton, 1903), 383-390.

5. Merrill F. Unger, *Archaeology and the New Testament,* (Grand Rapids, MI: Zondervan Publishing House,1962).

6. Colin J. Hemer. *The Book of Acts in the Setting of Hellenistic History*, (Wiona Lake, Ind: Eisenbrauns, 1990).

7. Ramsay, *The Bearing of Recent Discovery on the Trustworthiness of the New Testament*, pg 222.

Chapter Four: The Investigation - Phase II

8. Josh McDowell, *The New Evidence That Demands a Verdict* (Nashville, TN:Thomas Nelson, 1999).

9. Frank Morison, *Who Moved the Stone?* (Grand Rapids, MI: Zondervan, 1958).

10. Geisler, *Baker Encyclopedia of Christian Apologetics.*

11. Simon Greenleaf, *The Testimony of the Evangelists*, (Grand Rapids, MI: Kregel Classics, 1995).

12. McDowell, *The New Evidence That Demands a Verdict*, pg. 258-63.

13. William D. Edwards, MD et al, "On the Physical Death of Jesus Christ," JAMA 1986; 255:1455-1463.

14. McDowell, *The New Evidence That Demands a Verdict*, pg. 225-31.

15. Ibid, pg. 243-48.

16. Josephus, *Antiquities of the Jews*, IV.xiii.

17. John A.T. Robinson, *The Human Face of God,* (Philadelphia, PA:Westminister, 1973), page 131.

18. McDowell, *The New Evidence That Demands a Verdict*, pg 243.

19. Ibid, pg. 262-72.

20. Ibid, pg. 239-240, 248.

21. Ibid, pg. 250.

22. Ibid, pg. 250-1.

23. Ibid, pg. 272-279.

24. Ibid, pg. 252-253.

25. Josh McDowell, *More Than a Carpenter,* (Wheaton, IL: Tyndale House, 1977), pg. 60-71.

26. Ibid.

27. Ibid.

28. Ibid.

Chapter Five: The Investigation - Phase III

29. McDowell, *The New Evidence That Demands a Verdict*, pg. 197-201

30. Ibid, pg. 164, 193-194.

31. Ibid, pg. 193-194.

32. Ibid.

33. Peter W. Stoner and Robert C. Newman, *Science Speaks* (Chicago, IL: Moody Press, 1976), pg. 106-112.

Chapter Six: The Investigation - Phase IV

34. McDowell, *The New Evidence That Demands a Verdict*, pg. 32-45.

35. Ibid, pg. 33-44.

36. Ibid, pg. 38.

37. Ibid, pg. 33-44.

38. Geisler, *Baker Encyclopedia of Christian Apologetics*, pg. 532-533.

39. F. F. Bruce, *The New Testament Documents: Are They Reliable?* (Downers Grove, IL: Inter Varsity Press, 1964), pg. 16,33.

40. McDowell, *The New Evidence That Demands a Verdict*, pg. 45-53.

41. John W. Montgomery, "Evangelicals and Archaeology," *Christianity Today*. August 16, 1968, pg. 29.

42. Norman Geisler and Thomas Howe, *When Critics Ask: A Popular Handbook on Bible Difficulties*, (Grand Rapids, MI: Baker Books, 1992).

43. Greenleaf, *The Testimony of the Evangelists,* (Grand Rapids: Baker, 1984), vii.

44. McDowell, *The New Evidence That Demands a Verdict*, pg. 53-54.

45. Ibid, pg. 25-26.

46. William Kirk Hobart, *The Medical Language of St. Luke* (Dublin, Ireland: Baker Book House, 1954)

47. John chapter 9

48. John 12:9-11

49. Acts chapter 4

50. Walter A. Elwell, *Evangelical Dictionary of Biblical Theology,* (Grand Rapids, MI: Baker Books 1996), pg. 582-584.

51. McDowell, *The New Evidence That Demands a Verdict*, pg. 53-68.

52. John McRay, *Archaeology and The New Testament,* (Grand Rapids, MI: Baker Academic 1991).

53. Unger, *Archaeology and the New Testament.*

54. McDowell, *The New Evidence That Demands a Verdict*, pg. 61.

55. Ibid, pg. 61-66.

56. Ibid.

57. Ibid, pg. 67-68.

58. Ibid, pg. 53-54.

59. Ibid, pg. 53-54.

60. Ibid, pg. 58.

61. Ibid, pg. 55.

62. Ibid, pg. 55-56.

63. Ibid, pg. 58.

64. Ibid, pg. 58-59.

65. Ibid, pg. 36, 38.

66. Ibid, pg. 42.

67. Lee Strobel, *The Case for Christ,* (Grand Rapids, MI: Zondervan, 1998).

68. Ibid, pg. 14.

Chapter Twelve: The Disease of Sin

69. Billy Graham, *The Holy Spirit*, (Nashville, TN: W Publishing Group, 1988).

Chapter Fourteen: The Cure for Sin

70. Ibid.

71. Ibid.

About the Author

Dr. Viehman was born and raised in Wilmington, Delaware. He graduated magna cum laude from the University of Delaware. Dr. Viehman attended medical school at Jefferson Medical College in Philadelphia, Pennsylvania and graduated number one in his class. He completed an Internship in Internal Medicine at the Hospital of the University of Pennsylvania in Philadelphia, and a dermatology residency at Duke University Medical Center, where he was chief resident. Dr. Viehman completed his fellowship in skin cancer surgery also at Duke. Dr. Viehman cofounded the Cary Skin Center in Cary, North Carolina, and worked there 1998–2008. He is now in solo private practice at Sea Coast Skin Surgery in Wilmington, North Carolina.

Dr. Viehman has lectured nationally on dermatologic surgery and authored several published scientific research articles. He has multiple interests, including, running, Cross Fit training, missionary work for orphans in Ukraine with New Life Ministries, and collecting rare Bibles. Dr. Viehman's family includes his wife Ruth, two sons Brendan and Cameron, a daughter Hannah, and a border collie named Pepper.

Be sure to check out Dr. Viehman's website for additional information, companion study guide, updates on his next book, speaking and book signing engagements, ordering personalized signed copies and contact info: www.goddiagnosis.com.

If you feel this book may help some people you know, please order 10 copies to distribute and consider using the book in a small group bible study. Info on a companion bible study guide can be found at the author's website. And of course we would appreciate your review on Amazon.

THE ABUNDANT LIFE
A STUDY GUIDE

"I have come that they may have life, and that they may have it more abundantly." –
John 10:10

A 10 week Bible study designed to help Christians enjoy an abundant and fruitful relationship with God. You can have victory over sin and actually know the God who created and saved you and live a life of joy and abundance.

You can purchase 'The Abundant Life' at these digital locations:

www.everlastingstrength.org

E verlasting Strength seeks to demonstrate the love of Jesus Christ by evangelism, biblical teaching, and charitable giving so that people may know God in a growing, personal, and saving relationship that increasingly glorifies Him with their lives. Visit Everlasting Strength to sign up for Dr. Viehman's blog, view his testimony and select speaking engagements, and interact with other biblical resources to grow in the Lord and be on fire for the Gospel! The Lord and His Word are awesome and something to be excited about!

www.everlastingstrength.org